ES. B30

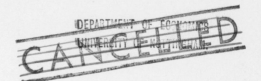

UNEQUAL PARTNERS

VOLUME ONE

The Theoretical Framework

UNEQUAL PARTNERS

PARTNERS

VOLUME ONE
The Theoretical Framework

BY

THOMAS BALOGH

OXFORD
BASIL BLACKWELL
1963

© *Basil Blackwell*, 1963

PRINTED IN GREAT BRITAIN
BY A. T. BROOME AND SON, 18 ST. CLEMENT'S, OXFORD
AND BOUND BY THE KEMP HALL BINDERY, OXFORD

To three true international civil servants

GUNNAR MYRDAL
RAOUL PREBISCH
B. R. SEN

who tried, against great odds, to create

partnership in equality

'Of course, I know that it was pure philanthropy which flooded India with English-made goods, and surely, if slowly, killed out every indigenous industry—pure philanthropy which, to facilitate this, repealed the import duties and flung away three crores a year of revenue which the rich paid, and to balance this wicked sacrifice raised the Salt Tax, which the poor pay; . . . Free Trade, fair play between nations, how I hate the sham! What fair play in trade can there be between impoverished India and the bloated capitalist England? As well talk of a fair fight between an infant and a strong man—a rabbit and a boa-constrictor. No doubt it is all in accordance with high economic science, but, my friends, remember this—this, too, is starving your brethren.'

(LALA MURLIDHAR to the 1891 Session
of the Indian National Congress.)

CONTENTS

    VERSUS DYNAMIC MODELS

13 What is Elasticity?   177
14 Exchange Rates and National Income   191
15 Static Models and Current Problems   200
16 Surrealism in International Economic Policy   208
    Postscript   215

SECTION SIX: INTERNATIONAL INVESTMENT

17 Post-War Foreign Investment Policy   216
18 The New Plan for an International Investment Board   ...   230
19 Domestic versus Foreign Investment   233
    Postscript   247

    References   249
    Index   250

PREFACE

I

THE essays in this volume span thirty years. Perhaps their best description might be: ' This is where I came in.' Once more the old slogans and fallacies to which I addressed myself in the early 1930's have come to the fore. The obvious lessons of those years of deflation which created Hitler, and led to the Second World War, have been forgotten. Financial journalists can be found suggesting that Hitler's rise from ridicule and contempt to power—from September, 1930, to January, 1933—was prompted by *inflation*. These same people are hard at work unwittingly to weaken the growth and enfeeble the cohesion of the countries outside the Soviet orbit, beset as they are in any case by deficiencies inherent in a system of decentralized decision-making. Those who think themselves most uniquely dedicated to fight Communism seem to do the work for it most effectively.

The new challenge to our system does not originate in demonic tribalism, the basis of Nazism. It is a systematic—if often dogmatically misguided—application of deliberate planning methods to further economic growth. Its superiority in the past decade has not been based on the excellence or imagination of individual decisions. It has been due to the facility with which a collectivist system can internalise external, and externalise internal economies in production. It has been due, that is, to the immense structural advantage of coordinated investment, in which every single decision supports every other in the sense of yielding superior external economies to one another. Thus a steady, high level of investment can be maintained securely in the certain knowledge that it will not prove abortive merely for the reason that others will not follow suit. Mistakes can easily be rectified or absorbed by the rest. It has been based, in the second place, on the inevitable underestimate in individual (even corporate) income disposition of the advantages of a higher savings rate, which is not entirely due to (but is, of course, very much enhanced by) the first cause. In a planned economy more rational decisions can be made, taking full account of the indirect benefits of sustained, all-round maintenance of high investment on the rate of growth of national income, and eventually on the standard of life and social security.

It has been no less due to the capacity to concentrate technical research for whole industries, indeed for the whole economy, in a web of research institutes, thus making full use of talent and avoiding

duplication of effort. The results of this research can be communicated
to the production units without inhibition. The success of the
American agricultural research in increasing productivity shows the
potency of such collective endeavour. In contrast, technical research
in individualist economies has, in the main, been carried on by private
firms, in search of profit. This inevitably wastes effort and can only
yield benefit to the initiator as long as its secret is kept (or safeguarded
by patents) from the rest of the producers. This necessarily slows down
economic progress.

Should these inherent *structural* shortcomings of the decentralised
economies be aggravated by unnecessary *functional* defects, the outcome
is bound to be disastrous to them in their relation, both to centrally
planned economies, and to the poor non-committed areas of the world.

Among these functional defects, much the most important is the
palpable incapacity to deal with the problem of rising prices without
at the same time causing unemployment and slowing down growth.
Internationally, this creates (and is aggravated by) pressure by strong
and dynamic economies on their less privileged, unequal, trading
partners, as it imparts a deflationary bias to any international monetary
system based on fixed exchange parities. Effort in the former to keep
prices down through monetary means results in balance of payments
surplus and exerts a positive deflationary pressure in the latter, and
especially in primary producing areas, among the poorest in the world.
The consequences to these areas of the U.S. policy before the 1929
crash, and again in 1948 and 1953, as well as 1957 and 1959–60, contains
a warning. The German economy at the head of the Common Market
seems to be playing an analogous role now.

If this tendency is coincidental with a failure of international liquid
means or reserves to grow *pari passu* with trade, and if Central Banks or
Governments attempt, or expect to hold a reserve which is in some
rather rigid relation to the volume of trade, the rate of growth of the
unplanned economies will be further menaced. This handicap of the
non-Soviet world could only be removed if the dilemma between
growth and stability were resolved internally, and if, at the same time,
international balance were established through the acceptance of
sensible rules of international economic behaviour, together with
institutional arrangements to create a sufficiency of liquid reserves.

It is hardly a matter of coincidence that recessions in large areas of
the non-Soviet orbit have, as the post-war period went on, deepened
and lengthened, so that the recovery from setbacks has become more
sluggish and incomplete. It is, in my opinion, a direct result of
decontrol and reliance on monetary policy, combined with a fear of
inflation and of unbalanced budgets, both of which are unreasoned and

sociologically determined. Technically, no doubt, the remedies, budget deficit through tax reduction, public works, creation of liquidity, and international grants, are well known. The question is whether they are socio-politically feasible.

This apprehension about the insufficiency of the performance of the non-planned economies is not incompatible with the view that they rely for their functioning on a misdirection and waste of resources, a misdirection which Professor Galbraith has aptly termed ' social unbalance '. The waste of resources, implied in the creation of conspicuous wants in order to reap profit by satisfying them, does not mean that a faster rate of growth and an expansion of resources are not needed for other purposes, including the assurance of enjoyable leisure.

Moreover, Professor Galbraith, by limiting himself to the problem of rich communities, to the exclusion of the international setting, has failed to perceive the far greater problems created by this misdirection of resources in poorer communities. In these, conspicuous consumption is not merely a source of psychological malaise—however important, morally and politically, that may prove in the end to the rich communities—but also the main, and increasingly resented, reason for the degrading poverty. The spending of their income by the rich on imported consumers' goods, and the use of their saving to provide mainly luxury housing or land speculation, contributes to the frustration of hopes for cumulative growth and a more even distribution of the ownership of land. The consequential stagnation is rendered graver by the incapacity of the price-mechanism to give effect to comparative real social advantages in an economic framework which contains an appreciable primitive subsistence sector. Efforts to start industrial growth would be doomed even if the predominance and profitability of mercantile monopoly and the absence of entrepreneurial ability did not rule them out. The organisation of the banking system favouring international trade seals the fate of the dependent territory. It remains condemned to primitive primary production until conscious planning disrupts the web of stagnation in which it is held. Here again, economies without central planning and conscious direction are at a grievous disadvantage.

In republishing these essays I hope to contribute to the recognition of these technical defects of the non-Soviet economies in general, and of a Britain dominated by a dilettante Civil Service in particular. They can be overcome. Indeed, from the point of view of sheer technical functioning of the economic system, they could in my opinion, be overcome without fundamental changes in private ownership, though the process of decision-making would have to become consciously coordinated. But I doubt whether the moral or psychological handicaps could be overcome without extending public ownership and, at the same time, radically strengthening the accountability of management.

Unfortunately, economic literature in general, dislikes and shirks acute political controversy. In no field is this more true than that of international economic relations. Economists from fully developed, opulent societies are faced with embarrassment in having to explain the reasons for growing inequality and unrelieved misery. The flight into abstraction, into the mathematical precision of simple systems which have only an accidental relationship with the real world, becomes attractive. Mathematical or geometric elegance (however primitive if judged as mathematics or geometry) seem an accepted ground for judging the excellence of the product (and, presumably, the political safety of the author).

The theory of international trade, as it has evolved over the ages, and as it is still practised, has contributed to inequality and instability, rather than to enlightened policies stimulating a balanced growth of the communities based on decentralised decision making. By assuming factors, which are variable and inter-dependent, to be constant and autonomous, it has failed to give assured guidance to economic policy. Its existence in a twilight of mathematical elegance which has little, if any, relation to reality, is a constant source of muddle and confused advice, as authors, irresistibly impelled to intervene in great debates, put forward propositions derived from models whose construction and functioning are in sharp conflict with relationships in real life.

II

The proof of the pudding is in the eating. The proof of theory is in historical applied economics. On this test I do not have to be bashful about my cooking. By far the most serious lapse in judgment of which I was guilty, was the fear that the United States might not be able to maintain full employment and would, in consequence, denude the world of liquid resources and thrust it into a deflationary spiral. Like the persistent dollar shortage, this short-term problem was solved, inasmuch as it was solved, by politics, by the cold war and it sconsequences on the U.S. internal balance, as well as on her international relations. These could not have been anticipated during the war. No one could assume then that the U.S. would spend, year in, year out, over $40 billion on arms and put a further $6–7 billion at the disposal of the rest of the world. Hardly anybody expected a population explosion. And the toleration of budget deficits and the retention of redistributive taxation (to the extent it was retained—mainly as a result of the cold war) was helped along by our criticism of orthodoxy. All these strengthened the forces of expansion.

Even so, the U.S. was plunged into four recessions, in 1949, 1953, 1957 and 1960–1, by the mistaken desire to control her economic destiny almost entirely by indirect, monetary means. And the fact should not be unexpected that the severity of the recessions has steadily increased: the effectiveness of monetary control depends on entrepreneurs and trade unions being convinced that it would be carried to the point where expansion is effectively stopped and unemployment of all productive resources ensues. As modern democratic governments must intervene once unemployment *has* materialised, for its persistence would lose them the chance of re-election, and as this intervention is anticipated, the severity of the recession, sufficient to convince both sides of industry that the Government means business, necessarily increases, while rising prices make the disadvantages of deflation appear rather less. Thus the increasing amplitude of recessions is not accidental, and bears out my fears. Should world tension abate, and agreement be reached on disarmament, the problem of underemployment might become acute, as I feared after the war, for socio-political reasons, though it could, of course, easily be dealt with by pragmatic policy.

In other respects, even such qualifications seem unnecessary. My case against the Bretton Woods agreement and the post-war solution of German reparations has been fully borne out. So has my consistent and completely vain criticism directed against the policies pursued by a British Civil Service, quite unfit to give advice on economic policy. The unrequited drift towards convertibility, the insensate policy of dismantling the Sterling Area, and the refusal to give a lead in a constructive economic organisation of the Commonwealth and Western Europe (in contrast to mere negative liberalisation of trade)[1] has had precisely the effects I predicted—the decline of British power and influence. The dominance of the British Executive, irrespective of party, by dilettantes as eager to get rid of controls as they were (possibly subconsciously) to subordinate the economic fate of the country to the interests of high finance, has brought its retribution in terms of failure and debility. Most ' unorthodox ' concepts, so hotly contested at the time, such as the dollar shortage, the importance of high investment and dynamism for, and the impact of unequal technical progress on, the balance of payments, the need for discriminating trade and exchange controls to enable an optimal development of national income and trade, have come to be recognised and accepted. Although I am not flattered when the learned scholars who now put these conclusions forward—mostly far more elegantly, if less realistically, than I ever was able to do—publicly do not recognise the original authorship, what

[1] Cf. especially *The Dollar Crisis*, Blackwell, Oxford, 1949.

B

matters really is that the ideas so violently combatted should have found their way into the citadels of respectability. I hope they will take up the case for a well-staffed international central bank and investment fund. If these essays contribute to the final explosion of ' theories ' based on exploring relations between nameless countries 'A and B ' and comparing two ' equilibrium positions ' whose interaction on one another is disregarded; if these essays lead to a faint recognition of the complexity of the problem and some shadow of hesitancy about mathematical gimmicks, I shall be quite satisfied.

I, in my turn, am grateful and happy to acknowledge my personal intellectual debts, which I owe in such profusion, in the first place to my pupil, colleague and friend Paul Streeten. Three of the essays are direct products of our collaboration, but most other papers benefited much by his patience and ingenuity in interpreting my intuitive doubts in a coherent and consistent language. I owe an immense debt to O. T. (Foxy) Falk, whose intellectual courage is only equalled by his originality; to Dr. Coombs' sagacity and unique combination of technical, practical and theoretical capacity, and to Pete Garland with whom I have worked over long years; and the late Sir Hubert Henderson, whose support at a critical juncture was of inestimable value, and who fought valiantly against the same attitudes and policies as I did, even if from the opposite political approach. Professor Richard Kahn has been a great help (as in the case of so many other works) in stimulating and criticising my efforts. I owe much to Sir Donald MacDougall, who was as formidable an opponent in many of the earlier disputes, as he has come to be an ally in more recent ones; and to Gunnar Myrdal and Raoul Prebisch, to whom together with B. R. Sen, this volume is dedicated. I want to thank Professor Kenneth Galbraith with whom I share many doubts about conventional wisdom, Professor Pasquale Saraceno who has succeeded in combining a firm grasp of practical problems with analytical finesse, and Professors François Perroux and Jean Weiller who gave me opportunity to benefit by discussing their own work on similar lines. And I must thank Mr. Michael Posner for his patience and help in editing these essays and stimulating my efforts to get the work finished. Without him these volumes would never have appeared. I owe thanks to the editors of the Journals and Papers for kind permission to publish these essays. Finally, I should like to express my gratitude to my colleagues at Balliol and the University of Oxford, who gave me sabbatical leave, and to the Rockefeller Foundation which twice supported my research since giving me the first chance as one of their Fellows in 1928–30.

Oxford and Cambridge (Mass.)

June–August, 1960.

THEORETICAL INTRODUCTION

The Theoretical Implications of a Realistic Approach to International Economic Relations

I. DYNAMIC ECONOMIES AND STATIC ECONOMICS

THE history of economic thought in the century and a half between Smith and Keynes is strange, indeed pathetic. The period represented a stormy break with the state of primeval stagnation of poverty. New, unexpected, technical horizons were opened, first by individual genius working systematically, and later by systematic research achieving the work of genius. Observing this violent revolution for over a hundred years, economic theory could offer no more than an explanation of price and income relations in a strictly static state.

Capital accumulation changed the face of the earth, girding it with railways, steamships and airplanes. Vast new industries were created. Vast new metropolises arose. Vast varieties of new goods and services were thrust on people. Multitudes (especially women) were set on new demands and vied with one another in increasing mass-extravagance. Economics concentrated on explaining consumers' preference and justifying the allocation of an unchanging set of resources (whatever meaning could be attached to that phrase), on the basis of the unchanging taste of representative individuals living in a state of blissful introspection and social harmony, unrelated to the consumption or taste of anyone else, untouched by the screaming blandishments of would-be sellers, and uncontaminated by social conflict.

Despite (or perhaps because of) the vigour of its expansion, the world economy was beset with a new kind of problem of unemployment and consequent destitution, misery, uncertainty and waste, in increasingly stark contrast to the potential abundance proffered by the profusion of productive capacity. This represented a complete contrast to the underemployment of primitive agriculture, which still prevails among the majority of mankind; that underemployment is caused by the insufficiency of productive capital equipment, and not by the disturbance of markets. Economic theory was, for a century, completely hoaxed by an utterly meaningless 'proof', Say's 'Law', according to which supply could not outrun demand. Unemployment could then be treated as a 'residual' problem, due solely to 'frictions' resisting the ideally smooth functioning of the economic system. These frictions, it was insisted, were mainly, if not entirely, due to rash or thoughtless efforts to protect special interests, or obtain undue gains. The system was said to revenge such infractions of its logic in the form of losses, and a less than full utilisation of available resources. Yet the very periodicity of the fluctuations flouted that ponderous explanation. Economic theory nevertheless used the doctrine of the inexorability of the working of the economic system to derive and ' prove ' the existence of complete harmony of interest between all classes, in the sense that intervention would leave them all worse off. On the other hand it was—somewhat illogically—asserted that such intervention was in any case futile: the system had an innate tendency to improve the fate of all and reduce the inequality between them. The euthanasia of the rentier was as certain as the increase in wages.

In particular the optimistic theory held strongly (if rather illegitimately—for, as we have seen, it was grafted on a completely *static* model, with given resources and no growth) that technical progress *anywhere* would benefit *all*. Behind this view was the tacit—and indefensible—assumption that the location of such advances would be random. The probability of its occurrence anywhere would be similar. Progress would just happen without any systematic geographic, social or economic bias. Moreover, the effect of such improvement would spread directly—by cheapening products—and indirectly—by stimulating production of other goods. Thus an increase of overall productivity and income in one place would increase them everywhere.

The historical evidence, on the contrary, pointed unmistakably to the need for, and the success of, State intervention—the so-called welfare state—for securing an amelioration of the fate of the non-privileged in domestic economic affairs.

The pristine simplicity of perfect competition, for which universal and unconditional validity was claimed, seemed to fit less and less the contemporary scene. Atomistic producers striving independently, regardless of one another, to supply an identical, and standard commodity to a market of alert experts in possession of all the facts, seemed to be increasingly confined to agriculture. It should be noted that even in the case of such an unimportant part of the economy as, e.g., the market of turnips or carrots, the downward slope of the demand curve and its independence from the supply curve can only be postulated by disregarding the history of the market and consequently the pattern of anticipations. Once these are admitted, the simplicity of timeless equilibrium vanishes even in this case. With the coming of the 20th century an agricultural revolution took place in the highly industrialised countries, which shattered the picture of increasing costs, even in this field. It had certainly little to do with the picture of vast corporations, increasingly aware and linked with one another, carefully calculating the consequences to themselves of any action they might take, selling what were (or pretended to be) ever new or improved articles. The view that entrepreneurs act mechanically, irresistibly impelled by all-pervasive market forces, was less and less easy to square with the spread of evidently conscious management of output, of the consumers, their demands and the prices they were charged. The dismissal of monopoly as an aberration, because it was contrary to principles on which the theory of determinate static balance depended, seemed less and less permissible, however damaging its admission would be to the 'proud and scientific' structure of pure economic theory. Yet because the general abandonment of the assumption of perfect competition would obviously have 'very destructive consequences for economic theory', as the 'basis on which economic laws can be constructed is shorn away' one proceeded *as if* the assumption were valid. The consequences on the applicability of these 'laws' were not considered.

The model of static equilibrium seemed to be constructed not so much because it was able to contribute to the explanation of reality, but because it was easy to handle diagrammatically or mathematically. Consequently, functional interrelationships seemed to be assumed, not because they fitted best to elucidate reality, but because they yielded satisfying answers. The tendency to dismiss without empirical evidence complications as 'perverse', became more and more disturbing. Economists appeared to use definitional identities as significant equations, and to assume that certain relationships were sufficiently stable to be legitimately regarded as constants. Stability, symmetry and reversibility of relationships were assumed, and it was thought permissible to postulate their independence, so that their interaction could be made to yield a unique and determinate position of balance.

From data which consisted of sets of observations of points established at different times, there is thus derived a really wonderful array of curves going through each of these observed points and each resembling the other in their mathematical, or at least their diagrammatic, simplicity.[1] Each of this family of curves depicted formal

---

[1] And assuming quite illegitimately that these observations are part and parcel of an *equilibrium*, when in fact no equilibrium, in a comparative static sense, can possibly be assumed at any one point of time. A typical instance of this type of fallacy is represented by 'estimates' of the gains from freer trade with Europe (e.g. contributions to *The Free Trade Proposals*, edited by G. D. N. Worswick, Blackwell, 1960). The disregard of employment, investment, i.e. growth effects, renders such 'estimates' exceedingly dangerous for the uninitiated who are deceived by the apparent determinateness of the answer and are only warned at the end, in a short sentence, of the flimsiness of the construct. The overwhelming, dynamic aspects of the problem, the impact of policy on change of the rate of growth of resources, remain disregarded.

timelessly-enduring reversible relationships between two or more factors of production, as in ' production possibility ' curves, between prices and quantities, and between firms and their products. These relationships were unlike anything ever experienced, for the observations were made at different points of time, and no one knew (because large-scale changes happened all the time) whether or not these inter-relationships would in reality persist or change. They could not be ' proven ', but (this last being their inestimable advantage) *they could not be disproven either*. Their meaningfulness, as so many abstract paintings, was restricted to the mind of the author. No predictive value could be attached to them.

The reasoning, of course, implied that the *two relationships which determined equilibrium*, e.g. supply and demand for some commodity, *were given independently* of one another. Hence a second new equilibrium position could be postulated and derived from the ' elasticity ' of ' schedules ' which were timeless. This procedure was obviously illegitimate. If the existence of a schedule was inferred by the comparison of two historical observations it merely implied a *description* of the change and not its *explanation*. It was implicit theorising in the worst sense, and might be seriously misleading if used predictively. If, on the other hand, the schedule was not derived from the historically observable change, but inferred from hypothetical considerations based on the original equilibrium, neither the direction nor the magnitude of the shift could be predicted. Yet, such is the strength of the convention, that doubts of the legitimacy of such schedule-mongering would be dismissed as ridiculous, as a proof of hopeless ignorance.

The treatment of change in this setting ought also to have given rise to doubt. It seemed essential for ' scientific ' generality to be able to analyse the effects of change without having to investigate the special problems resulting from the historical setting. Nor was it possible to admit that, in reality, the reaction to change, to shocks, might itself turn into an autonomous factor of change, of a force which could not be dismissed as ' secondary ' in importance.

A simple contrivance was used. Two ' long-run equilibrium states ' were compared, in each of which all necessary adjustments *had already* been made and perfect balance achieved. The long run was itself defined as ' a sort of timeless long run throughout which nothing new happens except the full mutual adjustment to each other of the primary factors existing at the beginning of the long-run period.'[1] Between the two states it is assumed that there is only one difference. Only one

---

[1] Viner, ' Cost Curves and Supply Curves ', reprinted in *Readings in Price Theory*, p. 205. Neither the meaning nor the operational usefulness of this concept were ever analysed.

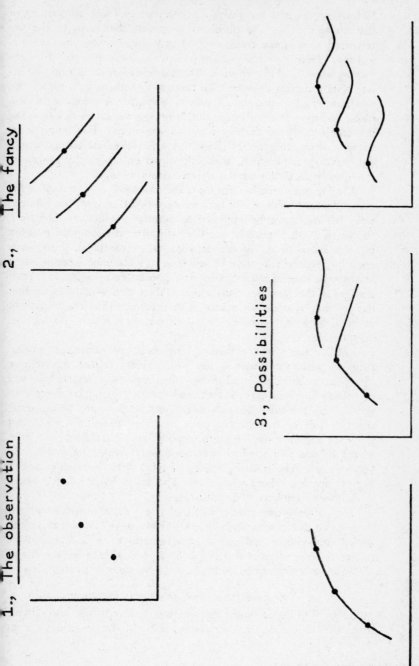

factor changes, and the analysis is confined to the consequences of that change. Thus the problems to which change gives rise are restricted to a single factor only; the problem to be analysed was isolated. Hence simple mathematics or two-dimensional diagrammatic analysis could be applied. The use of this method yielded startling results in many fields and was taken as a touchstone for the scientific character of economics. A sort of semantic autointoxication took place, and the pseudo-mathematical language was taken as a proof of the admissibility of these speculative constructs. For infinitesimal changes of an unimportant factor, i.e. a factor whose change would only have an infinitesimal, negligible impact on others, this procedure is evidently justified, even though trivial and boring.

The use of this method for more ambitious purposes, to explain the consequences of choice, not between carrots and turnips, but between ways of life, must be regarded as plainly illegitimate. Short-run shocks, if at all important, are likely to affect the long-run position through cross-effects. Moreover, changes are continual, adjustments are imperfect and take time. These time lags and imperfections might assume the role of autonomous new impacts (even without further changes in the basic position) which in their turn would further alter the position of eventual balance to be reached. Thus the concept of eventual ' long-run equilibrium ' itself becomes, if not meaningless, inapplicable.

Finally, there was a further unresolved problem—the relation between what were termed the basic, ' real ' factors determining ' long-run equilibrium ' and the so-called monetary factors, ' the veil of money ', which intruded themselves with particular force into short-term problems. This complication was overcome by assuming that short-term disturbances of a monetary character would not influence and alter the long-term equilibrium. That would be determined by real forces which were assumed ' stable ' or at any rate ' stationary '. The quantity theory of money thus was supposed to explain absolute short-run prices. The more basic relative prices would obey completely different rules.

The self-balancing character of the system was completed with the assumption that it automatically tended towards full employment (and at full employment real income was assumed to be independent of monetary demand), and that it was highly sensitive in its response to all ' relative ' price changes and also to movements of interest rates.

II. THE ANOMALY OF INTERNATIONAL ECONOMICS

In no field of economic enquiry was this approach less suitable than that of international economic relations. In no field were its predictions and policy advice so patently and consistently proven disappointing and misleading, if not fallacious. Yet in no field were its adherents more rigid, more obstinate and more dogmatic.

It is, I am sure, very difficult, even for the few surviving disputants immediately involved, to recall the completeness of the intellectual dominance of the Free Trade School around 1930. Even the doubts and qualifications voiced by Wicksell or Sidgwick had disappeared. List had been completely obliterated. If Say's Law, that greatest of scientific hoaxes, was the *pons asinorum* of ' pure ' economists, belief in the *objective* superiority of free trade as a policy was the test of his ' soundness '. There was a complete dissociation between academic theory and political practice; the 'scholars' (Schueller and Manoilescu[1] were the exceptions) regarded the ' protectionists ' as the exponents of minority privileged interests out to capture favours to the detriment of the community. Now there was often ample justification in the *leading* countries for this view.[2] But its application to international economic relations *generally* was completely unjustified.

The reasons for this are not difficult to state.

(1) *The problem of distribution*

In the domestic social relations of democratic countries, the problems of distribution raised by the uncontrolled forces of the market became less important. Within the powerful and the industrialised countries (at the great universities of which economic analysis developed) differences in living standards, if possibly still glaring, certainly were no longer increasing. In any case, grinding poverty has been eliminated. At the same time, the state has become increasingly powerful, and its administration has been perfected so as to make it capable of successful intervention in case of need. A measure of social and economic integration has been achieved.

Thus it can be argued with some plausibility (even if quite wrongly in principle) that distributional questions can be left out of account when looking at the problem of ' efficiency ', of 'maximising' output, irrespective of its distribution (if any meaning can be attached to this distinction). The solution of distributional questions, it is said, is better left to automatic play of countervailing political forces. In the

---

[1] M. Manoilescu, *The Theory of Protection and International Trade* (1931); R. Schueller, *Schutzzoll und Freihandel* (1905).

[2] Though with increasing opulence, the moral case against redistributing income in favour of some less efficient sectors of the community, menaced by foreign competition, rapidly disappears. The only case that remains is the duty to aid poorer areas abroad. This could be done, and much more efficiently, by means other than free trade.

same way the problems arising from the non-existence of perfect markets lost their urgency with increasing welfare, continued prosperity, and the immense strengthening of the trade unions, whose defence of the less privileged became increasingly successful. Finally, and perhaps most important from an analytic point of view, there was domestically, within the framework of a growing and increasingly integrated community with strong welfare services and redistributive taxation, some justification for concentrating analysis on *small-scale* adjustment, rather than *large choices* between ways of life and ways of livelihood. Thus the neglect of the further consequences or cross-effects and repercussions of policy measures can be defended without falling violently foul of the facts of life.[1]

None of this is applicable to international economic relations. Supranational intervention cannot, on the analogy of deliberate government policy, be assumed to mitigate, if necessary, the possible rigours of the working of the unfettered economic forces, or hold a balance between them. Thus the welfare aspect of policy assumes a decisive importance: ' world income ' in the sense of the output of all participating countries valued at current prices loses all meaning if its distribution is disregarded.

(2) *Equity and efficiency*

The equation of efficiency and non-intervention was, in its turn, achieved by demonstrating that money prices were, ' as a rule ', strictly proportional to real social cost. The doctrine of Comparative Cost had been originally expressed by the classical economist in terms of socially necessary expenditure of labour. Under the impact of the use of the latter concept by Marx for demonstrating the exploitation of workers by the propertied class, the explanation of value by labour was abandoned. ' Real cost ' was redefined as ' all subjective costs directly associated with production '.[2] This procedure, however, involved treating land rent and interest as subjective costs associated with disutility. This was so obviously implausible that the need was increasingly felt of reformulating the theory of international trade in

---

[1] The word ' secondary ' was used to suggest that all but the immediate effects of change could be disregarded. This became absurd once large scale changes, or large scale factors, became the object of enquiry, and when the ' constants ' of the analysis were themselves affected by the change.

[2] Cf. J. Viner, *Studies in the Theory of International Trade*, New York, 1937. If Professor Viner successfully destroyed Professor Haberler's formulation, Professor Haberler's assault on Professor Viner's as not ' remotely representative of the real world' is cogent—if surprising—in view of his own sublime disregard of reality. (*A Study of International Trade Theory*. Princeton University Special Papers No. 1, 1955, p. 13.)

terms of opportunity costs,[1] which would avoid the political or value judgments, implied so implausibly in the 'real cost' approach. Unemployment continued to be dismissed as frictional. The advantages and economies of large scale production were equally put aside as ' incompatible with perfect competition ', the ' usual assumptions of the general equilibrium theory '.[2]

There was no question of investigating whether these assumptions, ' usual ' as they were, were also legitimate in dealing with the problem of international trade. It was argued (and the textbook writers duly agreed) that deviations from the ideal of a perfectly competing world —the existence of ' monopoly ', of gains from large-scale production, or from the establishment of ' infant ' industries—were exceptional (and—by implication—negligible). Their exploitation would in any case demand knowledge, detachment and skill which would be beyond the ordinary human, and particularly beyond the ordinary politician. Thus non-intervention (or rather intervention to enforce the absolute rule of the unbridled free market forces) was claimed to be, with due modesty, if not an absolute optimum, at least the best *possible*, 'welfare position ' for the ' world '.

No doubt, countries could 'exploit' monopolistic selling or buying positions by a judicious mixture of tariffs or other ' artificial ' regulations or barriers. But here again appeal was made to doubts about the existence of the wisdom necessary to utilise such advantages (and the immorality of ' exploitation ' was hinted at). The impression was given that the impairment of ' world ' income would somehow wreak general havoc—without showing that (apart from the infant industries case) improvements in the terms of trade, due to protection, might occur in backward and poor countries, and would then be justified morally and politically. And finally, of course, the concept of ' world income ' was still not defined in an adequate way.

If historical evidence pointed at the solution of the most urgent domestic social problems through the rise of the welfare state; and this suggested that its absence was at least a powerful contributory cause of the deterioration in the position of the poorer areas of the world, relative to that of the more privileged. If then, Marxist writers did their best in the face of reality, to deny the former and prove growing misery of the masses, Western economists were in the same awkward position with respect to international economic affairs, where their special pleadings, claiming increasing harmony, had a rather paradoxical

[1] Especially Prof. Haberler, *The Theory of International Trade*, London, 1936. This diagrammatical treatment implicitly assumed fixed factor supply and disregarded disutility.
[2] Haberler, *A Survey*, op. cit. p. 12.

similarity to those of their Marxist counterparts behind the iron curtain.[1] Reference to population trends was quite insufficient as an explanation of the growing discrepancy in living standards, as in highly developed countries an acceleration of the growth in numbers, far from retarding, seems to have invigorated economic activity.

(3) Unequal Partnership

The disregard of problems connected with the international distribution of income, and the effectiveness of the price system to express relative social advantages, was even less forgivable because it became increasingly clear that:

(a) differences in the stage of technical and economic development are closely related to national boundaries;

(b) the units affected by, and acting on, international economic relations, are not, indeed, small productive units competing atomistically, but national units in a most important sense competing oligopolistically, unable to disregard the policy of each other;

(c) these national units—these trading partners—are, to use the expression which serves as the title of this book, *unequal, in the sense that there is no similarity in the probability of their initiating new development*;

(d) even within these national entities, the productive units are undergoing a violently discrepant development: in industrialised countries, large scale units are predominant and prices are ' administered '. In the rest of the world primitive agriculture and handicraft remain predominant with some enclaves of modern enterprise.

In analysing problems pertaining to international economic relations the details of the particular situation, the character of the countries concerned, the historical context, the general monetary position, cannot legitimately be disregarded. They form the essential basis for any prediction of probabilities.

' Theory ' elegantly eliminated these difficulties. A ' standard case involving two countries and two commodities '[2] was evolved with given resources, on the basis of which the analysis proceeded. One of the ' countries ' was taken to be very small in contrast to the other ' representing ' the rest of the world. By thus treating countries as though they were individuals in atomistic and perfect competition, or

---

[1] This resemblance was especially marked in the sycophantic defenders of the merits of the international market economy against the powerful criticism of Professor Myrdal and Dr. Prebisch.

[2] Professor Haberler, *A Survey*, op. cit., p. 16.

rather conducting the analysis in terms of producers and consumers acting in perfect markets (dismissing when convenient the macro-economic unit) the problem of their respective magnitude became irrelevant. This necessitated the assumption that there were no economies of scale—for otherwise the problem of monopoly would have had to be introduced. The quest for determinate answers and an ingrained habit of thought, prevented the realisation of the obvious, of the illegitimacy of using this model to study concrete problems. To assume atomistic relationships *within countries* may not be very sensible because of the rise of giant firms, but it is not such nonsense as it is to assume it in relation to the trade *between nations*. Nor is there, in the international field, any reason to assume that the rise to predominance of any single unit will be mitigated or counterbalanced automatically. No coalition of the threatened smaller units will necessarily follow, as in politics. Moreover, the limits set to the growth of firms do not apply with the same force to nations: the diseconomy of size does not affect the multiplication of giant firms within one country.

The consequences of the assumption of perfect competition and given resources are momentous. A one-sided domination of a powerful country over the less fortunate partners is excluded from the purview of the analysis. The destruction of the large and prosperous Indian cotton industry by Britain without any compensatory long run advantage to India simply cannot be explained in these terms: it is altogether different from an event, such as the end of the silk-industry in Coventry. In the latter case there *was* compensatory expansion. In the former there was not. Indeed, the opening up of the Indian inland market by railways, far from spreading prosperity, spread ruin.

A completely new approach was obviously needed and was equally obviously impossible on the basis of ' traditional ' foreign trade theory.[1]

It remained for Professor Ohlin to select this particularly shaky foundation to build a further argument for ' freedom ' by ' establishing ' the presumption not merely that non-intervention would yield the best *possible* results, but also that it would promote equality, even

---

[1] It is one of the charms of economics that this limitation, implicit in the assumptions of the ' standard model ' has been explicitly recognised by Professor Haberler (ibid., p. 27) as soon as it worked against his own policy bias. Professors Samuelson and Stolper demonstrated ('Protection and Real Wages,' *Review of Economic Studies*, 1941), that under the ' standard ' assumptions of traditional theory, the relatively scarce factor of production will suffer *absolutely* under free trade. This demonstration was dismissed by Professor Haberler because it was based on ' unrealistic ' assumptions. A few pages earlier (ibid., p. 14), the device of analysing a model based on two unspecified countries with two commodities and a fixed supply of factors indifferent as to their employment, was characterised as ' facilitating presentation '.

if mass-production reduced costs. *Differing endowments* of countries with productive factors, with not merely land, labour and capital but climate, social institutions, in fact with all factors influencing the ease of production, become in this view the main *reason* for trade. Thus countries are forced to specialise in that type of production which demands much of the abundant factor, in which it has therefore a comparative advantage. As production expands, however, costs are driven up and comparative and absolute advantage diminishes. The rewards of the relatively abundant factor rise, compared with the rewards to the relatively scarce factors. Thus specialisation not only increases the income of all but narrows the divergence between factor rewards in *all* countries.

Here, then, was a powerful 'scientific' demonstration of the likelihood of complete harmony of interests between the rich and the poor, in a field in which, until recently,[1] no system of direct income redistribution seemed possible, and in which inequality was demonstrably growing.[2]

Yet there could be no doubt that the first result of trade is specialisation, that specialisation makes the existence of ' perfectly ' competing national units less likely, inasmuch as single countries become the oligopolistic suppliers of their produce. Trade, moreover, stimulates the growth of a productive resource, capital, which is ' specific ' and cannot be shifted from one use to another in the short run, and whose supply in the long run cannot be taken as ' given ' and independent of the short-run developments.[3] It was clear, moreover, that technical knowledge and entrepreneurial ability had a decisive impact both on the effectiveness of the use, and the accumulation, of capital. Moreover, manufacturing seemed the best, indeed the unique, way towards overcoming poverty.[4]

---

[1] Multilateral aid furnished through international agencies is the nearest approach to such deliberate redistribution. But its motives, like those of purely bilateral aid, are still to a large extent ' *raisons d'état* ' of the giver in the international competition generated by the cold war.

[2] Ironically enough, this theory reached its logical climax only after the Second World War in Professor Samuelson's essay (discussed in Section 5, No. 15) which proved ' rigorously ' that free trade would—in circumstances which the author seemed to hold not implausible—result in not merely narrowing, but completely eliminating, inequality in factor remuneration. As Professor Haberler (*Survey*, op. cit, p. 20) caustically remarked, this was done by ' *emptying* the theory of all *empirical content* ' (my italics) and reducing it to ' a useless tautological system '. In contrast, Professor Haberler's logically similar constructions and short-cuts are euphemistically termed by himself ' necessary simplifications ' or ' first approximations '.

[3] Attempts to ' prove ' that the size of countries does not matter (cf. below) fall into the same category of prevarication.

[4] The disingenuousness of liberal economists is nowhere as obvious as in their laboured examples of enrichment through agriculture.

Despite List's path-breaking study, and Carey's work in the U.S., neo-classical theory completely excluded the recognition of the basic importance of the ' infancy ' of *countries*, rather than merely of industries, however much lip-service was paid to this ' exception ' to the ' rule of non-intervention '. Yet there could be no doubt, that if ' falling marginal costs due to internal economies . . . were not reconcilable with free competition ',[1] it was the concept of ' free ' competition which had to be modified. But the neo-classical school declined to treat ' perfect ' competition in international economic relations as a 'useless tautological system'.[2] External economies, which could also lead to cumulative growth and inequality were similarly regarded as exceptional.[3] Moreover, their effect on technical knowledge or availability of capital (which was clearly one-sidedly favouring manufacturing centres) was thought to be symmetrically offset by diseconomies— such as air pollution!

(4) *Frozen production*

If a two country model constructed in this way evades several all-important problems, analysis in terms of two commodities obscures most others. The relationship between the two commodities *defines* rather than explains the mechanism of change. The results obtained are trivial. If it is further assumed that these commodities cannot be ' inferior ', i.e. perverse reactions to price movements are excluded, a large area of the impact of innovation on trade is also eliminated from the scope of analysis as the displacement of exports by innovation cannot be analysed in a two country model. Problems of trade, especially international trade in manufactures, can hardly be investigated in these terms: far from being identical, goods change all the time. Thus price comparisons mean very little.[4] It would, for this reason, be impossible to establish statistically, with any accuracy, whether the efficiency or the prices of a given country have risen relatively to another.

If the concept of ' goods ' stands for aggregates, for ' bales ' or baskets of products, index number problems of the utmost difficulty appear, as any significant, non-infinitesimal, changes (such as need to be analysed) will distort the original comparative cost position, and change the composition of the aggregate.

The consequences are momentous. The Marshallian reciprocal demand curves in foreign trade are shown up as *mixta composita*,

---

[1] Haberler, op. cit., p. 53.   [2] Ibid., p. 20.   [3] Cf. below.
[4] Attempts to derive ' schedules ' over years for such goods (e.g. cars) seem ridiculously out of place. The Volkswagen of 1960 is perhaps the only car which has not changed completely. And advertising really can ' change ' even an identical product by giving it a new ' image '.

which obscure in their simplicity the extremely complex problems which lie behind their ' shifts ' (which must be accompanied by, and are inseparable from, changes of shape). The concept of a ' shifted curve ' and its (ex-post) ' elasticity ' is even less legitimate.

The blissful picture of a simple static ' reallocation ' of ' given resources ' ' to minimise cost ' equally fades away. Both the *resources* and *tastes* change through the opening of trade. Thus the ' proof ' that free(r) trade ' maximises ' (whose?) income is invalidated from both directions at once.[1]

In other words, the path in time through which any adjustment has to pass, is no longer a matter of indifference, It will be influenced by monetary factors and will influence, and be influenced, by induced or autonomous changes in productive resources, in particular in capital. The assumption, therefore, that we are here confronted with a reversible relationship, and that, therefore, the comparison of final equilibrium situations could yield meaningful answers for predictive purposes, is fallacious. If the path from the original position can be different and if it were to yield different final equilibria, according to what happens as a reaction to the first autonomous impulse or change, then the comparative analysis of two given final equilibrium situations will not yield *generally* acceptable conclusions. Long-run *equilibrium* will, of course, in fact never be established, because the whole system will undergo continual changes, and adjustments to the first disturbance are not permitted to work themselves out.

(5) *The monetary problem*

The vital importance of the path of readjustment would be immediately demonstrated by an analysis of the overall monetary situation in which the process of ' adjustment ' takes place. Traditional theory therefore neatly side-stepped this vital problem by *implicitly* assuming the automatic maintenance of full employment and laying down set rules under which the monetary system is supposed to function, the old ' Hume Law '—hardly less objectionable than Say's—of assuming unalterable and quantitively set sequences for the mechanics of the monetary balance. Macro-economic entities, Governments and their policy, were made to vanish from the analysis as by a wave of the wand. There were no financial centres imposing their will or economic

---

[1] Prof. Samuelson's ' rigorous ' proof of the gains from trade are restricted to a model based on free competition; the opening of trade produces a once-for-all reaction and the change is not one-sidedly imposed on the weaker partners. Thus the *emergence* of repeated losses is *a priori* excluded from purview. Nevertheless, he could only show that *some* trade is better than none, and not that free trade produces an optimal solution. (' Gains from International Trade ', reprinted in *Readings in the Theory of International Trade*).

rhythm, nor a periphery of weak countries to be dominated.[1] Country 'A', gaining gold, would experience a rise, country ' B ', losing gold, a fall, in its price level, strictly proportional to the impulse and just sufficient to bring about balance. The system, one presumes, would remain in some ' neutral ' ' equilibrium ', somewhere in between.

In reality if ' country ' 'A' were, say, the U.S.A. of 1948, with more than half of the world's money income, and if ' country ' ' B ' were represented by a number of countries with scant gold reserves and precarious balance of payments positions, a gold gain by the U.S. will hardly make any difference to the latter, given the quantitative relationship between domestic and foreign savings and investments, if the American economy is not in any case in an expansionary phase. But country (ies) 'B' will be forced immediately to deflate, and the whole system might be pushed into a deflationary spiral. Without specifying what the situation is in each country, and how the transfer is expected to affect spending power and willingness to spend, the application of a comparative static analysis yields obvious nonsense. The locus of the change and its character become of paramount importance.

Once this was realized, the conventional approach modified the traditional formulation by adding *explicitly* the ' assumption ' that full employment is maintained throughout by some *machina ex deo*. This was what one might call the neo-Keynesian ' solution '. Thus real income would be still, as in the classical system, determined by the long-run availability of resources. The original protest of Keynes was emasculated. Yet in modern circumstances this assumption was even less defensible in international than in domestic relations. For the inequality of the trading partners, the unequal distribution of wealth, of international resources, and the divergence in the rate of growth, necessarily introduce further complications not present in the analysis of closed systems.

III. TOWARDS A REALISTIC APPROACH

The modifications, or qualifications, of the traditional theory to which the essays collected in this volume might claim to have contributed, can be grouped under several subheadings.

1. *The concept of welfare* underlying the neo-classical case was shown to be so seriously defective in principle, and based on assumptions which were so unrealistic as to rob the analysis of all practical value. In any but trivial problems, the importance of this failure seemed enhanced by the fact that the working of the price system is biased against the welfare of smaller, poorer and less developed countries.

---

[1] Prof. Weiller's contributions to this problem were as fundamental as Professor Perroux's.

C

2. The neo-classical formulation of the theory of international economic relations in terms of two countries and two (in some cases four) commodities was analysed and shown to lead to a complete disregard of the direct casual relationships to foreign trade of *unemployment and underemployment* and of its consequences. This neglect, resulting from illicit assumptions, was demonstrated to be the more serious as the effects of recurrent crises and unemployment are severely aggravated by

3. the biased unevenness of the changes in *factor endowment*, especially the accumulation of capital, directly connected with, and enhanced by, foreign trade, which would militate against the weaker or less dynamic countries. The increased profits in the rich areas would lead —partly through capital accumulation—to a continual change in comparative costs and force repeated readjustments on the weak. Thus the gain from trade is offset (and might be more than offset) by losses due to the consequential changes.[1] The assumption of ' given resources ' which underlies the traditional theory of international trade is meaningless in a dynamic context, and even if some meaning could be attached to it, it would be illicit in explaining the most important aspects of historical development and consequently for policy recommendations.

4. As a second aspect of the same methodological problem, the historical neglect by the traditional theory of *decreasing costs* was also shown to be inexcusable. Far from being the rare exception, economies of scale were shown to embrace a widening field—not excluding even a considerable part of agriculture. Once the importance of increasing returns is admitted, and their nature is analysed, they will be seen to be largely irreversible. In other words the historically observable relationship between output and capital is unique, and a reciprocal one connected with the conjunction of capital accumulation and technical progress. On the one hand, *in the poor areas* the difficulties and imperfections of effective decision making, the lack of entrepreneurial ability and of capital, vitiate the assumption that potential fields of investment opened up by trade will automatically be exploited.[2] The ' exceptional ' case of infant industries expands into infant countries

[1] Through the loss of undepreciated capital assets and the cost of human adjustment.
[2] Steel industry in India certainly possessed comparative advantage. Yet in the absence of steel-using industry it was not established (and once established it was not expanded commensurately to its advantages). Cf. ' The concept of a dollar shortage ' reprinted in Section I, No. 1. Mr. Kaldor pointed to the importance of the neglect of the implications of capital accumulation in a different context (' Increasing returns '. *Oxford Economic Papers*, vol. 13, p. 2, Feb. 1961). The importance of the monetary factor as a determinant of accumulation has still to be recognised.

and regions, and discriminatory policies become essential to any sane conception of maximum economic progress. On the other hand, in the rich, progressive areas, there loom the (so-called pecuniary) external economies, windfall profits which would be reaped by nearly all if growth were to accelerate. In a fast growing economy the risk of mis-investment falls, and an increasing number benefit from the intensifica-tion of activity. An acceleration of accumulation would vitiate con-clusions arrived at on the basis of unchanging factor endowment. In my opinion, this factor will play a decisive role in the vital struggle for productive superiority between the two world systems—the planned and the decentralised economies.

5. Finally, still on the same point, and contrary to traditional views, the pattern and location of *technical progress* is not random. It is systematically skewed to the detriment of the poor and weak, as the fully industrialised economies reduce dependence on imported raw materials, a process which itself is asymmetrical and likely to be irreversible.[1] Thus the lack of symmetry in the process of develop-ment is further accentuated. Contrary to conventional assumptions, the effects of progress are not evenly spread. They are one-sided and result in a repeated, though irregular, displacement of those products in which the poorer and weaker countries have relative advantage; this recurrent displacement is additional to that which results from the fast accumulation of capital in the rich countries, with which it is in close relationship.

6. Thus these essays denied that economic relations between countries could be analysed on the basis of a perfectly competitive model, dismissing from the analysis macro-economic entities which are in oligopolistic relations to one another; the short-term monetary policies determining money incomes and investment become a decisive determinant of long-range development and competitive power. Variations in employment and accompanying changes in income come to dominate the reciprocal demand of countries for each other's pro-ducts. Thus the size of countries and their monetary reserves must be considered, and the relation of foreign trade to national income. Nor can these factors be dismissed as short term, frictional deviations from a ' norm '. Inasmuch as employment and income determine the rate of accumulation, the ' real ' or long run equilibrium is inextricably influenced by these short term factors. The divorce of the ' monetary ' from the ' real ' analysis vitiates meaningful conclusions.

It was argued in these essays that the relations and reactions to one another of such oligopolistically competing units are not simple. They

---

[1] Dr. Prebisch contributed largely to the elucidation of this problem, as did Professor Myrdal and Dr. Singer.

do not follow irresistible and unchanging rules laid down by an invisible hand. They are in the nature of strategic relationships, subject to bluff and threat. General statements and mathematical formulae derived from traditional analysis are shown to be tautologies empty of empirical content. The possibility of the reaction over-shooting the limits of necessary readjustment, of readjustments leading to a renewal and possibly the perpetuation of unbalance, further limits the predictive properties of traditional static, or comparative static, neo-classical or simple Keynesian, analytic methods.

These conclusions have momentous consequences, both for historical analysis and policy, and on the theoretical-methodological plane, and I shall briefly summarise the most important ones.

(a) In the policy field, this analysis changes the appreciation of the nature of ' fundamental ' (or structural) disequilibrium in international economic relations and therefore the consequential policy require-ments.[1] These disequilibria can no longer be considered as the con-sequences of accidental, autonomous changes or of simple monetary excesses.[2] The effects of continuous and biased changes in com-parative costs, their impact on employment, all these subtler points of modern analysis, can no longer be assumed away. The disequilibria originate in the very pattern of technical progress.

Thus if technical progress is uneven, as it evidently is, and especially if wage-movements are not determined by productivity changes alone,[3] as they evidently are not, the recurrence of ' fundamental ' disequilibria in the balance of payments of the less dynamic partners is inevitable.[4] Suggestions that such disequilibria should be treated by monetary restriction, i.e. by measures primarily aimed at cutting investment are inevitably self-defeating: they will result in a further relative decline of growth of productivity and accentuated need for restriction. Devalu-ation or a policy of fluctuating exchanges in these circumstances would invite disaster, as it would have to be repetitive or continual. Such a process would create anticipatory destabilising speculation abroad and wage-demands at home. The traditional view of the needs of ' read-justment ' seems the opposite of the requirements. Only a weakening

[1] Cf. Vol. II. *Historical Reflections*. Dollar Shortage.

[2] E.g. Sir Roy Harrod's contemptuous dismissal of the dollar shortage as ' one of the most brazen pieces of collective effrontery ' while it was ' in fact no more than a young man going forward and living beyond his resources without leave '. (*Are these Hardships Necessary?*, 1947, p. 42.)

[3] But in periods of rapid change against the older types of products it is not even necessary to assume asymmetry of Trade Union behaviour, however justified it appears. [Cf. Productivity and Inflation. *O.E.P.* (loc. cit.)]

[4] This is evident in the case of manufacturing exporters. It has been the case also with weaker and poorer primary producers, mainly because of the technical revolution.

of Trade Unions or the speeding up of growth can provide an answer.[1] This means that discriminatory protection by the weak against the strong might well be one of the essential conditions of restoring balance. The formation of trading group or Common Markets to increase the scope for export trades of the poorer countries might be the only answer to inequality.[2]

(*b*) On the methodological plane, the conclusions of these essays have, I would claim, equally striking results. They deny the legitimacy of the comparative static analysis based on given, unchangeable, long-run schedules showing *reversible* reactions of two variables to one another, akin to the demand and supply schedules of turnips and carrots, which can be assumed to be given and independent of income and investment effects, i.e. independent of the path of adjustment which determines the position of an eventual equilibrium (which is never in fact reached as changes are continual, and inherent in a dynamic economic system). *We are here concerned with irreversible reactions, and not with movements on independently given demand and supply curves whose stability through time can be assumed, and adjustments represented as reversible movements along the curves.* They are unique, historically determined, phenomena.

(1) *Welfare and International Trade*[3]

I intend to deal at length with problems of so-called welfare economics and their relation to policy in a different context.[4] I can restrict myself to a short summary of those considerations which apply with special force to international economic relations.

These relations are characterised by differences, often startling, between the trading partners, in their historical background, their income and wealth; in their technical knowledge and skill; in the availability of entrepreneurial ability and administrative capacity; in

---

[1] This emphasises the limited value of statistical enquiry into whether the disequilibrium has been caused by 'pure' inflation or not. The 'prices' as we have already said do not show changes in quality or innovation. The traditional theory necessarily had to come to the conclusion that accelerated growth would result in increased deficit. Indeed this was acclaimed as the new 'dynamics'. Its conclusions were completely confounded before they got into print. The recent efforts to provide a statistical test of the interrelation between unemployment and wage-stability are in the main based on crude logical fallacies. Their success shows the blatant political bias of recent economic writing.

[2] Cf. Section 2, No. 4; and Vol. II, Section 7, No. 24. This is the overwhelming case in favour of a West African or Latin American Common Market.

[3] In this section I make use of the transcript of my first lecture at Delhi University of January 1955. In its main trend it closely resembles the argument of Professor Galbraith's *Affluent Society*, but it differs from it in its emphasis and in some significant policy conclusions. I should like to express my thanks to Professors Rao and Raj of Delhi University for stimulating discussions.

[4] *The Political Economy of Coexistence* to be published shortly by G. Weidenfeld and Nicholson, London, and Macmillan, New York.

fact in the stage of their social and economic development, of their occupational and politico-communal integration. In this they differ sharply from the domestic scene of highly developed, closely integrated democratic communities.

They are, perhaps, even more significantly characterised by the fact that the decisions on initiating trade (or even of liberalising it, and freeing it from direct controls) involve largely large-scale (grosso modo) changes having irreversible consequences. Moreover, there is no over-all sovereign machinery, as in domestic matters, to modify or mitigate the possibly stark and undesirable consequences of the free interplay of uncontrolled market forces. Thus a different degree of caution and reticence is needed than in advocating small-scale domestic changes.

The dangers have always been great that authors will make an abrupt, if often surreptitious, transition from modest model-building, justifiable within its limitations, to advocacy of policies on a large world canvas. Conclusions which might perhaps be not unjustified when it comes to a judgment on the choice between sausages, are used to pronounce on what, in effect, are decisions affecting the future of countries.

There was, until recently, no hesitation or questioning on the part of economists—and for that matter of politicians—about the relationship between production and welfare, or satisfaction, as an aim of social and economic organisation and policy. Explicitly or implicitly, increased production was taken as a certain proof of increasing welfare. This sounded common sense. On the basis of a few assumptions which appeared sensible, a proud and complicated structure was built up. This gave, or purported to give, a rounded theory of consumers' demand, and thus enabled the economist to give determinate answers to policy questions.

For this to be done, for economists to be able to choose between policies, it suffices to assume that *general* welfare' is somehow, but *uniquely*, related to something called ' *economic* welfare ', and further that ' economic welfare ' can be measured by valuing production on the basis of market prices. In other words the enjoyment or satisfaction obtained from consumption by individuals is taken as the final criterion of general welfare of the group, the country, and in international trade theory, of the world. And this enjoyment is measured by the summation of available goods and services at prices ruling at some given time.

But the money price system does not value certain things at all and only partially values others. It therefore produces a bias in favour of these things which are fully valued in money prices.[1] In particular

---

[1] On the restrictive concept of ' rational consumer ', cf. the essay on ' The concept of a dollar shortage ', Section 1, No. 1, p. 60.

(i) leisure and the conditions of work,
(ii) security, especially the sacrifices and miseries involved in adjustment to change, and to fluctuations experienced by the market economy,
(iii) equity of distribution

are left out of account. Thus increases in ' economic welfare ' measured in this way might be offset or even more than offset by the worsening of the conditions—in its widest sense of the word, i.e. including the social system, the degree of security—in which man in his capacity as producer supplies the goods and services for his satisfaction in his capacity as consumer. In addition there is the supreme complication due to the distribution of income, i.e. to the fact that the well-heeled consumer often contributes little or nothing to production, and the worker might get little of the increased consumption.

Moreover,

(iv) tastes are not given and become more dependent on the conspicuous consumption possibilities of others. If ' freedom of choice ' is imposed on a poor country by a rich,[1] its way to increased domestic capital investment might be barred (or made dependent on increased reliance on foreign capital). The change might be catastrophic even though ' real income ' ' increases ' in the short run.

Thus it is quite illegitimate to use the conventional measure of real income of individuals as a measuring rod on which to base fundamental policy making in contrast to small scale changes. It might be catastrophic in international economic relations.

The matter must not be pushed to extremes. Innovation and improvement of course have an important and genuine welfare aspect not connected with salesmanship and sales pressure. New products, the cheapening of durable consumer goods, and the opening of wholly new fields of consumption through hire purchase for wide strata of the population which were not able before even to think of obtaining such products, and the increase in real income this permitted, have been the great achievement of mass-production. But this would not have been possible if it had not been accompanied by increased equality in distribution. The quality of changes has to be judged from case to case, bearing in mind that their psychological impact is by no means uniform in various countries, and, in different stages of development, and that the social mechanism by which that impact is moulded, if not determined, is itself on trial.

In a Western society, the Judaic-Christian ethic demands that

---

[1] As it happened in the relation of the Eisenhower regime to countries dependent on U.S. aid.

income or welfare of groups should be judged exclusively in terms of the income or welfare of the individual making up the group. This obviously creates further difficulties in the way of appraisal of policy-making, because of the possible conflict between the change in the level of the group income and its distribution between its members. It was apparently not realised that when ' real income ' was measured by prices of a given period, these prices were dependent on, and the reflection of, the then existing distribution of income, from which they cannot be separated.

It was, however, the absence of any supra-national agency to redistribute income internationally, which made the traditional approach totally inapplicable to international economic problems. The assumption that equity could be secured through equalising taxation without tempering with efficiency was untrue. The maximisation of ' world income ' through an ' optimal allocation of resources ' irrespective of its distribution became meaningless because of the vast difference in income between partners and the unequal incidence of gain that could be secured from trade. Belated attempts to deal with this objection by assigning different weights to the welfare (i.e. income) of different members of the group (countries) still fail to deal with the problem of the large scale changes—due to international trade—in the social framework, and especially in social security, which are inseparable from changes in ' global ' income Thus general welfare in international economic relations cannot be equated with the conventional evaluation of economic welfare. The deliberate neglect by the traditional theory of these problems invalidates its conclusions.

Such trained observers as there were in the weaker countries, confronted with the direct barrier to development and equality which the traditional theory represented, suspected that economists from the opulent countries were out to rationalise a system which inevitably worked against the less developed and less privileged areas, and which buttressed those vested interests in the latter whose luxury consumption and failure to accumulate was most responsible for their stagnation and poverty.

(2) The Problem of Unemployment

The theoretical framework of the neo-classical theory of international trade (as indeed of general equilibrium theory) excluded unemployment or underemployment. There was an awkward super-imposition on this ' real ' framework (conducted mostly in terms of two countries and two commodities) of a ' monetary ' superstructure based on the quantity theory of money. But references to Say's law (and, subsequently, to the impossibility that unemployment should persist if the 'flexibility' of wages was restored) excluded, even on this plane, the contemplation of situations of less than full employment. Yet it is clear that persistent unemployment would reduce the marginal social cost of output towards zero, and thus invalidate for single countries the 'law' of comparative costs.[1,2] The first of the essays in time sequence (1931) develops and generalises the argument put forward by Keynes[3] in 1930–1 against the free trade case under conditions of less than full employment.[4] In this particular case unemployment was due to both cyclical and structural causes.

The Keynesian revolution led to a general acceptance of this argument; the free trade case was restated in terms of full employment being either consciously or 'automatically' maintained. There was in this view no need for protectionism to eliminate unemployment. The international propagation of depressions was to be met, and free trade and domestic full employment policies harmonised, by the provision of liquidity, some penalisation of creditors, and devaluation (or fluctuating exchanges), but without restricting the scope of trading by direct controls or discriminatory measures. The illusion that monetary measures such as devaluation or credit restriction were 'neutral' and that policies which promoted 'efficiency' through 'maximum international division of labour' also promoted maximum growth, was once more revived. Thus the neo-classical world was re-established with a verbal obeisance to the need for maintaining full employment.

These efforts were founded on a complete misapprehension in the simple Keynesian world of the character of the forces acting between nations of unequal strength and causing unemployment. Unequal technical progress acts through liberalisation of foreign trade and changes the distribution of incomes, the propensities to save and to invest, and thus the possibilities of increasing the supply of capital. It also affects the propensity to import, while the capacity to export is not unlimited and efforts to stimulate it might require a sharp worsening of the terms of trade.

Thus it is possible that measures of liberalisation, designed to permit indeed, to enforce, *present* monetary values to determine the magnitude, shape and pattern of *future* production and trade would not,

---

[1] Lord Beveridge (at that time under the influence of the ultra-liberal economists of L.S.E.) wrote a letter to *The Times*, showing complete ignorance of the problem. Cf. Vol. II. Section 1, No. 1.

[2] Inasmuch as unemployment would alter the rate of accumulation, and thus influence the change in comparative costs, it would further limit the applicability of the static analysis to real life.

[3] *New Statesman*, 4th April, 1931. Cf. Vol. II. Section 1, No. 1.

[4] Cf. Haberler, *Theory of International Trade*, London 1936, p. 259.

in the longer run, lead to an optimum national income. Indeed they might lead to a decline of income due partly to the fall in export prices, and partly to unemployment, due to the need for, and difficulties of, shifting from activities which had been rendered comparatively disadvantageous by the technical progress abroad. Liberalisation thus might well retard and distort the growth of the weaker partner. Thus mere reference to ' world ' income maximisation and to the ' cosmopolitan interest ' is meaningless. It is essential to know whether it is the weaker or the stronger of the unequal partners who is reaping the gain.

This interruption of growth and the consequential unemployment though *recurrent* in pattern, is ' *structural* ' in character. It is due partly to the impact of international trade on income distribution, and partly to the impact on trade, and through it, on the industry of the weaker partner, of divergent technical progress. A static view of the consequences of foreign trade as a once-for-all adjustment rules out of consideration the most important aspect of modern dynamism, the *recurrent* displacement of the industry and trade of the weaker partner,[1] mainly as a result of the combined effect of technical progress and capital accumulation. Thus the comparative advantage of countries constantly changes and these changes are initiated by the strong and rich, and imposed upon the weak and poor.

The possibility of recurrent obsolescence and unemployment without any compensating advantages will necessarily increase the riskiness of enterprise in the weak countries.[2] Thus the incentive to invest is reduced. This effect is distinct from, and additive to, the equally unfavourable deflationary pressure emanating from the greater flexibility of a more dynamic system. This last will arise through the non-price advantage of quick deliveries on the one hand, which can only be secured by under-employment in less dynamic economies, and the credit facilities, already mentioned, on the other. In addition, the dynamism of the rapidly advancing countries exerts pressure on their relative money wage level by freeing labour continuously. It is obvious historically that money wage rates do not, in modern conditions, necessarily rise proportionally with the rise in productivity. This means that the money cost per unit of output in a fast growing economy tends to rise less than in more sluggish countries.

My attitude to this phenomenon developed slowly, and I confused it for some time with *recurrent* unemployment due to the *cyclical*

---

[1] A striking example is the increase in comparative advantage of agriculture in highly developed areas.

[2] The rapid spread of knowledge would increase risk in the highly-developed—if the poor countries had the capital and entrepreneurial capacity to exploit that knowledge.

instability, and to the anti-inflationary policy of the dominant country of multinational systems, i.e. with unemployment induced by an instability, combined with the oligopolistic desire to increase or defend reserves. The recurrence of monetary disequilibrium due to the former phenomenon might give rise to serious further consequences through anticipating speculation.

The difference between the two lies in the short-term reversibility of the cyclical unemployment induced by restrictive monetary policy. In contrast, unemployment due to technical displacement is not easily reversible: resources must be created and new occupations made available. If, of course, the state of less than full employment should last any length of time, it will cause permanent changes in the structure of production and trade. But in the short run it would yield to a ' natural ' increase of world liquidity (increased gold production), and could, in principle, be dealt with by providing ' artificially ' for the creation of liquidity, e.g. through an International Central Bank and increasing world demand through an Investment Board. Recurrent wasteful specialisation by weaker partners, on the other hand, could only be tackled by organic measures equalising opportunity for growth. It represents the total loss of undepreciated and displaced capital resources, and not merely the temporary loss of the output of those resources.[1]

At this point the case for conscious planning of development, based on periodically recurrent but not necessarily cyclical unemployment in unplanned systems, merges with more subtle arguments against the working of the unfettered market mechanism.

(3) Accumulation, Technical Progress and International Trade

I

Traditional theory, and in particular also the traditional theory of international trade, has, as we have seen, been based on a strictly static model of the economy with given, fixed resources, including technical knowledge, and given tastes. There must have been in the minds of its authors a sort of idyllic picture of a placid (and most profitable) ' simple and static ' rearrangement, ' reallocation ' of ' given factors among industries to minimise costs '. So long as this ' reallocative ' process in fact takes place in rural simplicity—on both sides—this picture might not be altogether misleadingly distorted. One can

---

[1] This is a potent reason against plans which link the creation of liquidity irreversibly and fixedly to the channelling of aid (resources) to poor countries.

see Arcadian maidens turning from milking cows to spinning wool; 'capital' would not totally or fatally lose its value. An easy 're-arrangement' can take place and the benefits from the cheaper imports will not be offset by losses. The most painful consequence of these losses is the elimination of the entrepreneurial capacity[1] and the ability and willingness to undertake investment. So long as 'resources' are pictured as land and (mobile) labour potentially capable of adjusting themselves to alternative uses this picture might have been acceptable. The Jeffersonian agricultural U.S. was perhaps the last instance of this blissful state.

Nothing can be further from modern reality. The problem now consists of the reciprocal influences (including trade between generally speaking unequal partners) which determine the rate and direction of growth of members of an open system. Trade will co-determine growth and growth will co-determine trade. Capital accumulation which raises the productivity of land and labour; the advantages of large scale production; and technical progress; the all-pervasive importance of these three related factors make nonsense of the conventional approach.

By posing the problem in terms of a *once-for-all adaptation* of the productive structure to the opening of trade, or rather a comparison of 'real' income positions before and after trade, assuming that capital was maintained 'intact' and just 'reallocated', the question was neatly side-stepped by an *ignoratio elenchi*: it was never asked whether the capital needed to develop the new 'production possibility' favoured by the 'opening of trade' would be available and from where.[2] If there is a one-sided bias against manufactures in poorer areas—and the fact that increasing returns can be obtained through mass-production, and that the development of ancillary industries decreases cost, renders this highly probable—compensatory development becomes doubtful if not precarious.[3] Unless (as was the case in the U.S., Canada or the Pacific Dominions) land is relatively abundant and entrepreneurial ability available and willing to develop it, and subsequently industry, trade will favour feudal landowning elements unlikely to use their gains in a productive way. The distortion and stagnation thus engendered might be aggravated by the bias against

---

[1] As it happened in India in the XVIII and XIX Century.

[2] The case of the development of Malaya and of some African and South American areas where there was no industry and which developed by way of export of agricultural or mining products is, of course, irrelevant. The question in these countries is rather how to maximise future progress.

[3] Quite apart from the distortion of money costs relative to social real cost by (i) structural underemployment (ii) the divergence between income and marginal product in agriculture. Cf. below Section I. No. 2, esp. pp. 72–3.

industry of the feudal organisation itself, and of the international financial system.[1]

The problem which has to be analysed is not one of the quasi-static readjustment of two anonymous countries, but the interaction of a limited number of dynamically developing systems each with an independently determined rate of growth likely to differ from one another. The problem is thus not the ' reallocation ' of *given* resources —a meaningless term in this context—but the mutual interaction of trade and the growth of resources. In other words, the relevant problem is the adaptation or reaction of differing communities to continual change, and in particular the fate of the less advanced territories.[2]

Now there is little doubt that, if the question is viewed in this light, the answer is unlikely to support the optimism of the traditional pseudo-dynamic analysis.

II

The very concept of *given factor* endowment is not merely inapplicable to, but meaningless in, the historical context, as is that of trade in *identical commodities* over time in a dynamic system of continuous growth, growth being due to the combination of capital accumulation and technical progress. Trade between countries is inseparable from the determination of the growth of those countries.

The assumptions of *given* resources, of a limited number of goods, of a continuous maintenance of full employment, and of a balance in trade are therefore illegitimate. Resources are not ' given '. Not only does accumulation take place all the time, but trade has been, and necessarily will be, one of the main determinants of the growth of resources, especially the vital resource of capital and entrepreneurial ability and technical skill. Thus relative factor endowment and comparative cost levels continually and necessarily change and the very fact of trade is one of the inseparable codeterminants of this change. Consequently the eventual outcome, the precise character and shape of this so-called ' equilibrium[3] position reached *after readjustment* ', is analytically *inseparable from the path of the readjustment*. Thus it is also illegitimate to disregard the ' short-term ' factors, their interaction and impact on the national income and its distribution. What we know is the position which has been established after a change. Whether this was movement *on* a curve or a shift *of* a curve is not

[1] Cf. ' Economic Policy and the Price Mechanism '. *Economic Bulletin for Latin America*, March 1960, and 'A Note on the Monetary Controversy in Malaya '. *Malayan Economic Review*, Oct. 1959. ' Trade ' is not equivalent to ' aid '.

[2] Cf. ' The Dollar Crisis Revisited ', Section 4, No. 10.

[3] The definition of long-run ' equilibrium ' is itself nonsense in this context, because of the inseparability of growth and trade.

ascertainable: these schedules are figments of the imagination which might be helpful in certain cases where supply and demand are independent of one another, and income effects can be neglected. This is not the case with the macroeconomic problems of international trade: income effects cause a continuous shift of the ' curve ' if such a ' curve ' exists at all. What we can observe are points, and it is not merely empirically but also logically impossible to say whether these points belong to a ' family of curves ' in any meaningful sense of the word, or to a single curve; nor do we know what the shape of any of these is. Knowledge of the historical background is needed, for otherwise the cross-effects of changes cannot be gauged.

The concept of ' elasticity ' of demand for exports or imports ex-post is not merely an empty economic box, it is a dustbin in which the nature of the determinants of the reactions of a country's demand for other countries' goods becomes lost. If the ' elasticity ' of demand is derived from a comparison of the initial with the historically observable final position, the propositions derived from this comparison, i.e. from the comparison of the interaction of price changes on the change of the imports or exports, are trivial: what happened has happened. It is entirely illegitimate to assume that general propositions can be derived from it, as the eventual outcome depended on the historical path of adjustment. Thus propositions derived from static theory on the basis of historical comparisons are trivial. Demand and supply of exports and imports cannot be assumed to be independent from one another as they necessarily codetermine each other. The final position of ' equilibrium ' (which need, of course, never be reached in principle and will never be reached in fact) can therefore not be derived legitimately from a ' schedule ', the elasticity of which is assumed to be unchanged by the ' shift ' which is necessarily not infinitesimal and necessarily affects income. Thus the initial relationships change and their change cannot be predicted from the data included in ' schedules ' such as an ex-ante Marshallian reciprocal demand curve. If a large shift of demand or supply, i.e. a large change in the composition of the bale, occurs, the word ' elasticity ' in an ' ex-ante ' sense loses all meaning. In the field of such macroeconomic concepts as imports or exports (or labour) its derivation is logically impermissible, as the determinacy of the solution is ruptured by the (short term) impact on income and demand and (in the longer run) on factor endowment.

Since it is specific capital equipment that in the main determines the average productivity and national income, the concept of ' reallocating ' ' given resources ' also lose, its meaning (if it ever had any). A (large) portion of capital might undergo economic annihilation through the innovation and continuous process of the opening of trade.

Whether the consequential favourable increase of opportunities will yield sufficient additional income, savings and investment, is a question impossible to decide *a priori*. The path which the adjustment takes in the short run (including the monetary processes) becomes decisive in determining the character of the eventual ' final ' equilibrium.[1]

It is easy to demonstrate that in actual life a few years' economic progress far outweighs in quantitative importance any conceivable ' improvements ' as a result of ' better allocation ' of *given* resources. Now the opening or liberalisation of trade might lead to an ' underselling ' of the main industries of the weaker countries, so that a sharp net deflationary shock ensues. The gaining, stronger territory might in the process expand its own industries. Thus such destruction of capital might be caused in the poorer ones as might be irremediable. Trade between unequal partners is not likely to have symmetrical impact on their factor endowment (especially if the initial discrepancy is further heightened by biased technical growth.)

The opening of trade might render large parts of industry in the weaker country unemployed.[2] Capital is lost, and with it, very likely, the chance of replacing it. Rural nymphs can no longer be shifted because there is nowhere to go. The fact that agriculture or some other field ' benefit ' potentially need not provide full compensation. The new capital structure has yet to be created. Moreover, the opening of trade might, indeed is likely to, shift the distribution of income in underdeveloped countries against profits and savings in favour of landowners, of rent, and the conspicuous luxury of the few. Thus the capacity to invest (already severely handicapped by the difficulties caused by being an unequal partner) is further reduced, and with it the long run efficiency and capacity to compete in industry. While the ' total ' income of the ' world ' may well have increased, the poorer

[1] This type of analysis is of course not more absurd, or less justified, than attempts to ' prove ' the case for free(r) trade by diagrams showing ' production possibility ' and ' community indifference curves ' which remain unchanged despite the opening of trade and the passing of time. The recent rash of articles and manifestos favouring Britain's entry into the Common Market has been mainly based on the nonsense of implicitly assuming a symmetry of favourable and unfavourable effects on existing industries and predicting a ' net ' gain for the country as a result of the consequential increase in productivity due to the ' extension of the international division of labour '. There is no justification for this procedure.

[2] The unequal working of the gold standard even in pre-1914 days has come to be ignored. Britain lent on short-term and the poor countries had to carry the gold reserve on which they paid handsome rates of interest. When the point came and at the precise moment when they wanted the loan in order to use the reserve, tight money called the capital back and the peripheral country had to deflate even more sharply to readjust to the simultaneous credit restriction and fall in prices. Conversely the British benefited on both counts. They felt the cycle only in consequence of the flagging of their exports. Cf. Lord Beveridge, *Full Employment in a Free Society*, Part 1.

territory might well become impoverished and incapable of making use of the opportunities offered by trade. If increases in demand flow towards manufactures, while demand for primary produce increases only sluggishly, the distribution of gain will work even less advantageously to the poor.

The examples of Scotland, Ireland, India, Southern Italy, and of the post-1848 Hungary, spring to mind. It is the illegitimacy of the assumption that the destruction of capital will be more than offset by the creation of new capital as a result of the possibilities occasioned by trade which is the crux of the problem. The triumphant ' demonstration ' of the futility in England of Luddism was easy because England was the paramount economic power in the world in the early XIXth century. It was obvious that she would benefit by the rise of new industry in her own territory far more than she would suffer by the decay of old ones because the latter was caused by the former. In a poor area the destruction of capital is caused by the rise of industry in *other* countries.[1] The thoughtless application of such reasoning to India and other weak areas (including XX Century England) of the case of the XIXth Century England is wholly illegitimate and fallacious.

Thus trade is likely to foster the growth of resources of the dominant country, and its superiority. The weaker partner, on the contrary, is confirmed as the hewer of wood and carrier of water. But even there the outlook is unfavourable. The risk of markets suddenly weakening is difficult to overcome. The gains of more intensive international division of labour might be offset by the reduction, due to the new risks, of the rate of investment in poorer countries and thus of progress, and the change in the distribution of income. The relative advantage of production in the dominant countries is likely to change not once but continually; further losses might be caused in the poorer areas. No sooner had they adjusted themselves to a new situation and begun a new type of production, having been forced out of a previous line by the superior competitive power of the dominant area, than technical progress forces yet a further change. With increased capital accumulation and technical progress, moreover, natural advantages which have, from the beginning of economic thinking, been assumed to govern trade, are replaced in importance by capital accumulation and technical progress over an increasing field. New materials replace natural products; an agricultural revolution is taking place, reducing the cost of production by increasing productivity. The division of labour not only between industrial countries themselves, but also

---

[1] This does not necessarily mean that every technical progress necessarily harms poorer areas: it might induce the use of compensating economic activity. The point is that there is no logical necessity for doing so.

between industrial and primary producing areas, accordingly becomes subject to continuing change. This change is biased against the poor, the small, and the weak. Only endowment with natural resources in strong and continuing demand (e.g. oil—or uranium—which is itself menaced by the possibility of controlled thermo-nuclear production of energy) can offset this handicap. On the other hand, it is clear that the small and the weak cannot escape from their predicament by protecting themselves individually because it is their smallness which is one—important—cause of their poverty. Their poverty in its turn is self-aggravating.

Indeed, the likelihood of unequal partnership resulting in the disadvantage of the smaller and weaker countries is increased by the all-pervasive importance of *gains due to the scale of production*.

The optimistic conclusions of traditional theory seem based on the assumption of perfect competition, of increasing, or at most constant, costs. In the field of international trade in which difference in the stage of economic development and size might *a priori* have been expected to play a vital, if not decisive part, increasing returns were dismissed as an academic exception of no importance.[1] If we pause to reflect that even apart from the giant machines and the vast networks of public utilities, apart from communications, power and transport, apart from common services such as banking, even the human source of progress, education and research activity, necessarily depends on ever-increasing specialisation, impossible without a growth of the scale of activity, we can hardly fail to be surprised by this innocence. The problems of historical capitalism are rigidly excluded from purview by these assumptions. A model based on them is utterly useless as a tool to discover the causal connections and processes of economic development, all of which are essentially in connection with investment and invention.[2]

I have little to add at this point to the replies I wrote more than ten years ago to Professor Samuelson[3] and to Professor Haberler.[4] The pervasiveness of geographically uneven increasing returns vitiates the view that trade will equalise factor remuneration.[5] There are, as we have said before, *infant countries and regions*. The formation

---

[1] Increasing returns in the usual sense of the word, but including pecuniary economies.

[2] Cf. e.g. Viner, *International Trade and Economic Development*, Cf. my review reprinted in Section 5, No. 16.

[3] *Oxford Economic Papers*, 1950 'Static models and international economic problems', Reprinted, Section 5, No. 15.

[4] 'Welfare and Free Trade,' *Economic Journal*, 1950. Reprinted Section 1, No. 2.

[5] This includes the degree of uncertainty in the economy which is related to the scope of foreign trade. The larger this is, the greater the uncertainty and the possibility *in weaker countries* of being suddenly confronted with new threats. The advan-

D

of discriminating regional economic blocs might be the essential basis for the achievement, if not of equality, at least of equity, between countries—even if the richer countries are, as they should be, profuse in their help to the poorer.[1] This conclusion will, as we shall see presently, be very strongly reinforced by the results of our analysis of the pattern of technical progress. The apologia for keeping the monopoly of manufacturing and technical ability in the hands of its initiators fails miserably, not least because of its effects on the efficiency of the people thus condemned to backwardness in other fields.[2]

III

Beyond increasing returns in their usual sense, principally important to the development of single, and interaction of a restricted number of

tages of being able to call on foreign supplies in case of need does not offset the impact that his type of uncertainty has on the willingness and ability to invest. More positively, these considerations necessitate a complete revision of the concept of 'infant' industry and its extension to whole countries and regions. Cf. 'Some theoretical problems of post-war foreign investment policy', *Oxford Economic Papers*, March 1945, reprinted Section 6, No. 17.

---

[1] Dr. Prebisch's concept of a Latin American Common Market is based on this type of consideration; it came under the unreasoning and bitter attack of the International Monetary Fund in their neo-classical frenzy. World-wide free trade could only come into its own after equipoised areas have been created which could make full use of foreign aid, instead of remaining permanently dependent on it. Cf. footnote 3. p. 58.

[2] The importance of these conclusions is emphasised by the periodic repetition, in the context of highly topical present-day discussions (such as complex practical proposals establishing customs unions) of conclusions based on the all-pervasiveness of increasing costs. The conclusion inevitably follows that union between competitive, rather than complementary units is likely to *increase* benefits and that union between complementary areas necessarily cause losses through trade diversion towards ' less efficient ' producers. This is palpable nonsense. Though the scope for increasing returns, say in Europe, might be limited, they are extremely important in Africa, Asia or Latin America. And, as we have said, the impact on the dynamism of the system and each of its units on its level of employment and growth will, of course, be decisive. 'Estimates' of ' benefit ' through customs unions by the ' cheapening ' of supplies based on hypothetical cost schedules, without attention to the consequences of the accelerated growth (or the reverse) are being peddled by experts from Europe to Asia, the Caribbean and South America. They are completely irrelevant. Cf. e.g. *The Free Trade Proposals*, Oxford, 1960, and the illuminating review by P. P. Streeten, *Oxford Magazine*, Oct. 20, 1960. Cf. also Part II Historical Sequences, Sec. 3. Thus the futility of a *general* distinction between trade creating and trade diverting union is palpable: the effect of the union depends on whether the complementary areas are poor, and whether their union opens up scope for large scale production, increasing *their* efficiency and income. One might justifiably oppose the European Common Market (though largely competitive in character, because one might fear that increased dynamism might displace imports from areas poorer than Europe (however much European and ' world ' income were increased) Trade diversion might be justifiable:

    (*a*) because, eventually, lower cost production may be achieved;
    (*b*) because (alternatively) the terms of trade may be improved;
    (*c*) because currency is available to buy the (possibly dearer) products inside.

linked, industries, making for increased productivity and returns, there looms a more general source of what might be called *general external economies* due to and accelerating, growth in fully industrialised countries. This latter is, in my opinion, destined to be of decisive importance in the struggle for victory in the competitive coexistence between the totally planned economies and the communities based on decentralised decision making. I hope to treat this vital problem in detail in a different context. Here I shall confine myself to a summary of the argument.

Neither individuals nor even corporations can fully realise the potential gains which would occur if their investment and growth were speeded up, because their successful realisation would depend on other people's actions, especially on their investment and savings decisions. Thus there is likely to be an objective failure: the rate of growth might fall to a lower level than it would be if all concerned knew the reciprocal consequences of each other's actions and could plan them jointly. On the investment side, entrepreneurs settle down to a decision-making pattern which is influenced, if not determined, by the historical level of their previous investment which proved successful. This follows from the fact that those controlling the majority of investment will decide whether all other investment (even if well-planned) will be successful. One investment justifies another. The ' marginal productivity schedule ' is not fixed. Investment does not ' exhaust ' opportunities, except in a short run sense. It does not ' shift ' upwards automatically, either. The historical upward shift is the result of coincident investment decisions. If a majority refused to invest, those who would, would lose out. The penalty of over-eagerness is failure and losses.[1,2]

If investment plans are not coordinated, no rise in investment will be expected and none will then take place. In order to create the conditions of high domestic profit and progress, the opportunities have first to be created. Paradoxically, the existence of an overall plan might be needed precisely in an economy not subject to central planning to speed growth. Otherwise risk might increase and opportunity be wasted.[3]

[1] The consistent unscientific propaganda of the I.M.F. suggesting that a 3 per cent growth rate—grossly inferior to the Soviet one—is ' realistic ', might have decisively contributed to the slowing down of growth in the non-Soviet orbit. It has done the work of Mr. Krushchev.

[2] This view is in no way inconsistent with the fear that in *weak* countries, the expansion of investment in the rich countries is likely to cause havoc (except in the case of endowment with natural resources the demand for which rises with increased investment). The problem is one of the likelihood of complementary rather than competitive (and destructive) investment. It is my contention that these probabilities are not symmetrical in weak and strong countries.

[3] This is the sound basis of the sudden and rather unreasoned rush at the end of 1961 towards ' French ' ' planning ' by the very people who destroyed the mechan-

Equally important is the incapacity of a system based on decentralised decision-making to match increased investment by increased savings, in the sense that no cumulative inflation originates[1] and the attempt is frustrated by a premature increase in consumption. Ex-post, (as the Japanese and German case clearly shows) Trade Unions realise the benefits of increased investment and growth. But ex-ante they cannot connive at what would in fact have to be a redistribution of income towards profits, especially if the policy has to be inaugurated (as in Eisenhower America and in Tory Britain) *after* decontrol and the free-for-all has been made the cornerstone of Government policy— in the name of accelerated growth! Only a national compact, backed by appropriate tax reform might be able to perform this task.[2] But, until Mr. Kennedy's victory, the trend was contrary to such solutions. The German, Japanese, French and Italian cases demonstrate *a contrario*, each in its way, that under a system of decentralized decision-making the inauguration[3] of a regime of high investment and growth depends on some special factor paralysing or weakening Trade Union bargaining power and the possibility of achieving expert surpluses without inviting retaliation.

The traditional approach by assuming *given* factor endowments excluded this supremely important point from its purview. For weak or less developed areas this might be a decisive consideration. To make recommendations on the basis of *any given comparative cost position*, without due enquiry as to how that position has arisen, and how it might change, or might be changed, in future, is a completely unjustifiable inference from the illicit assumption that resources are given and determine trade. The need for planning and coordinating investment so as to be able to reap maximum benefits and spread them equally counsels the formation of wide enough areas, within which free(r)

ism of planning in Britain. Neither the personnel nor the organisation of the Civil Service is such as to permit much hope for success of this belated conversion. Cf. 'The Apotheosis of the Dilettante' in '*The Establishment*', London, 1961.

[1] Mr. Kaldor's recent series of models of growth (e.g. *Economic Journal*, Dec. 1958) seem to assume that Trade Unions do not exist and that increased investment thus would lead to increased saving and not to cumulative inflation in the end destroying itself.

[2] Cf. e.g. 'Productivity and Inflation,' *O.E.P.*, June 1958. The majority of the experts appointed by O.E.E.C. have agreed on the need for a wages policy. They have, however, not discussed in detail its political precondition. Cf. 'The problem of rising prices'. W. Fellner, Milton Gilbert, Bent Hansen, Richard Kahn, Friedrich Lutz, P. de Wolff, O.E.E.C. Paris, 1961. [Since this was written in 1960 there was a general veering of 'establishment' opinion in Britain in favour of a (somewhat unilateral) 'planning'—of wages.]

[3] Not necessarily the continuance. Cf. Productivity, loc. cit. There seems to be no close correlation between money wage demands by Trade Unions and the rate of growth achieved. Thus a high rate of growth might enable the devoting of an increasing part of national income to investment.

trade is supplemented by such planned and coordinated investment, protected against competition by stronger productive units. Once opportunities have been equalised (and conscious coordination of investment can be extended) the scope of trade can also be expanded.

IV

If the effects of accumulation and increasing returns were excluded by the assumptions of the traditional approach, so was the related *problem of technical progress* by postulating a ' given state ' of technical knowledge. Rather it was also treated as an outside, autonomous, once-for-all change to which there was a slow adjustment in an otherwise completely changeless system. The model conceived in terms of unspecified countries A or B, and so on, suggested a principle of symmetry or of random, unbiased impact of such limited change. No doubt it was admitted that some countries or areas *could* be hurt by change.[1] But the impression conveyed insistently by the exercise was that this was a rather exceptional case. There was no stress on the continuity of this process, its close connection with capital accumulation. Thus the systematic bias exerted by the strong against the weak through displacement of the products of land and labour by the invention of synthetic or refined products, and the consequential disturbance of the comparative advantage of the poorer areas which have to rely for exports on primary products, was disregarded.

The suggestion was that new technical knowledge would spread and thus increase income also outside the initiating focus of progress. This disregarded the basic differences between international trade between unequal partners and interregional trade within modern, highly integrated societies, within welfare states, to which allusion has been made.[2] In the absence of a deliberate intervention by a sovereign agency; in a framework of disparate economic strength, technical progress seems not merely to have widened disparity historically, but acted as a positive deterrent against the development of the poorer areas.[3]

The competitive power of the ' old ' (and old-fashioned) producers

[1] These admissions were more pronounced in earlier writers such as Edgeworth, Wicksell or Sidgwick than in contemporaries.

[2] Prof. Williams' famous essay ' The Theory of International Trade reconsidered,' *Economic Journal*, June 1929, reprinted in A.E.A. *Readings in the Theory of International Trade*), was a striking exception to this neglect. He also showed that in a ' night watchman ' state even interregional differences might be startling. Its warning was almost totally disregarded.

[3] Cf. the reply to Prof. Samuelson (1948) reprinted Section 5, No. 15. Prof. Myrdal in his *Economic Theory and Underdeveloped Areas* (1957) called this the ' backwash effect '.

And through monetary disturbances which also act as a general depressive factor. Cf. below (4).

was reduced by the increase in technical knowledge, and the consequential cut in costs, and the introduction of new and superior (or better advertised) products in the same way, but often to an even more dramatic extent than by the effects of capital accumulation.[1] Technical progress is, in these terms, likely to bring a net benefit to the dominant initiator of change—even if *some* of the victims are within its political boundaries.[2] It will proceed through two continuous processes:

(1) refinements in the production of existing commodities and services, probably also produced by other countries:

(2) the discovery and development of new or radically improved products.

The former will enable a cut in prices at home and abroad; the influence of the second is more far-reaching: it will lead to a displacement of older products and thus might force either dangerously drastic price-cuts or wholesale structural changes on the former suppliers of the same or highly competitive products. But if the new process is drastically different from the old (e.g. the mechanical loom) then the displacement due to the former cause will not be less damaging or less violent: the price might well be reduced below the level yielding subsistence standards for the workers of the non-rationalised industries elsewhere.

In both cases it is probable that the technical improvement (embodied in new investment)[3] will reduce the labour requirement of

[1] The emergence of such products invalidates price and productivity comparisons as a measure of productive superiority. Had the Americans continued to lead rather than follow the world in car production their ' superiority' might have continued, despite unchanged productivity statistics. Cf. above, pp. 10–14.

[2] The fact that Britain was a large *net* beneficiary of change might explain why this did not penetrate classical writings during the unchallenged reign of English economics. The speed with which knowledge spreads among highly industrialised countries has increased, and the monopoly profits of the dominant area have decreased. But the increase in the rate of invention has largely offset this advantage and the discrepancy between industrialised and non-industrialised countries has increased considerably.

[3] The attempt of Mr. Kaldor (in the latest version of his theory, *O.E.P.*, Feb. 1961), to subsume technical progress and capital accumulation into a ' technical progress function ', is subject to the same objection as he levels against the even more primitive ' production function '. One cannot know whether relationships observed statistically represent shifts *of* his curve (a change of the ability to ' absorb ' technical changes) or shifts *on* his curve (leading to a change in the capital-saving or labour-saving character of investment). The predictive value of this device is therefore no greater than that of the tools, the uselessness of which he has so brilliantly demonstrated. M. Salter's objections (*Productivity and Technical Change*, Cambridge 1960, p. 43–45), published after my essay had been written, against the assumption that entrepreneurs stimulate 'labour saving inventions', are mainly verbal: he prefers to call it intensive research for ' substitution'. On the other hand, the scarcity and bargaining power of labour make it specially important to save labour beyond the simple price effect.

output. Labour will be relatively scarce in the dominant country and entrepreneurs under strong incentive to use technical progress to displace it. Thus, in the nature of things, research will tend to be concentrated in the dominant country on technical problems which —if solved—are bound to decrease the value of the productive factor relatively more readily available elsewhere. The fact that research expenditure tends to be cumulatively concentrated in the ' richest dynamic ' country intensifies this bias. The form of invention is dominated by the labour-saving propensity of high wages and labour shortage. If parallel improvement in productivity does not take place in the poor country, producing labour or land intensive goods, its cost will be undercut by the dynamic country. This will put pressure on the income of the poor trading partner.[1] Once the technical revolution has been accomplished, there are a number of reasons why it will have become, in practice, irreversible. Protectionism is only one (if at times potent) reason. A subsequent reversal of the situation through the adoption abroad of the technique of the dominant country will not much help foreign suppliers to regain their lost markets in the dominant country (though it might help them in third countries): once an industry has established itself it is unlikely to be allowed to disappear— the concept of asymmetry, of a ' kinked ' demand ' curve ' has to be accepted. There is, moreover, a grave danger of the inventions overshooting the mark and further weakening the poorer area.[2]

The former comparative disadvantage of dominant countries in the production of originally labour intensive products disappears. Once this happens, superior marketing techniques and other institutional factors which will be mentioned below may, in the end, even transform the industry[3] into an exporter.

The consequences of this tendency might be exceedingly disconcerting: these—continuous—improvements might be able to alter repeatedly the international distribution of economic activity, due to an unequal original factor endowment. There is, in other words, no reason to assume that inventions will not transform processes which depend on the availability of labour or land intensity into production whose cheapness depends mainly on capital investment. The opposite

[1] E.g. the invention of artificial fibres or rubber depressed the relative price of the natural product. The improved refining process of edible oil manufactures impoverishes olive oil producers. The development of glass wool has reduced the market for cork. Most of the gain accrues to the manufacturers.

[2] Cf. Section 4, No. 12. The relative volatility of the price of primary products in combination with this asymmetry produces disconcerting displacement effects.

[3] Or indeed agriculture, e.g. rice in U.S. The devastating effects of the rise of the British textile industry on India is a good example. Apart from Hong-Kong (and the Southern States of the U.S.) there is hardly a case where 'cheap labour', without initial protection, led to the rise of competitive industry.

is, for the reason already given, more likely. The fact that the (labour or land intensive) foreign goods are known to supply an existing need will be an added stimulus because the existence of a market is known and entrepreneurs in the dominant country need only to concentrate on solving technical problems.

This means that in a dynamic setting the mechanism equalising factor remuneration postulated by Ohlin and Samuelson might work ' perversely '. Trade might not equalise, it might widen the discrepancy between the remuneration of existing factors.[1] Technical progress raises the productivity of capital instead of its being diminished by accumulation. The absolute marginal product of labour in the advanced country will grow while the impact on the prices of the poor countries' produce will leave the factor incomes there unchanged or even diminished. This impact will be aggravated by decline of the ability and willingness to invest in poorer areas.

In the context of international economic relations, the usual hypothesis that technical progress, on the average, will neither be labour-, nor capital-saving is not justified. Technical progress is not evenly distributed over the world. Thus the locus (and the direct gain) of innovation will also tend to become concentrated. The non-arbitrariness of the geographic incidence of progress not merely separates the dominant from the dominated, but also imparts a bias against the less developed (and less dynamic) countries. Technical progress becomes institutionalised and, in international relations, like a factor of production itself. The advantage of advanced countries will consist in systematic innovation. The fate of erstwhile dominant countries which fail to keep up innovation—like Britain since about 1900 and the U.S. of the nineteen fifties—seems to demonstrate this point eloquently. Yet the really poor, the non-industrialised, will not be able to benefit by this change in the fate between the more and less dynamic of the advanced countries: there is yet another case of asymmetry here. For the stagnation of the latter will lessen their demand for imports and might lead to their being curtailed by protection. Thus both innovation and stagnation will oppress the poor.

Here then we have a force of great importance. Technical progress, far from making the dominant country less competitive with the world as a whole, makes it rather more so. It lessens, in a haphazard way, the scope of profitable trade of the dominant country with (a possibly increasing part of) the rest of the world.[2] Thus the contingency of a failure of increases in demand for certain (imported) goods (and a

---

[1] I.e. the factorial terms of trade of the poor are worsened.
[2] The agricultural revolution in the highly developed areas provides a good illustration for this process.

concommitant fierce displacement of the same goods in third markets) despite an increase in national income of the dominant economy, a contingency which is traditionally treated as an exceptional and perverse case, not claiming serious attention, turns out to be a common occurrence of vital importance.[1]

If the superiority of the dominant country is due to higher saving and investment, and heavy expenditure on research, only emulation or greater technical aptitude can offset it. But it is likely that a considerable part of the advantage of the dominant country will originate in the possibility of large-scale production based on a large internal market. Thus the infant country or infant region argument would fully apply in trying to remedy inequality.

The time-sequence of progress results in further complication. Much confusion has been caused in analysing this problem by habitually treating *random* events as necessarily *neutral*. If there is reason to think that progress is distributed in a random manner over parts of one country (i.e. part of the system as a whole) the effects of progress are dismissed as unimportant because it is implicitly assumed that random effects always offset and cancel each other, i.e. that they are equivalent to an *unbiased uniform progress*. Yet in another field, in the analysis of business cycles,[2] Professor Frisch had conclusively proven that in a dynamic setting this is not necessarily the case.

In the context of international economic relations the assumed *randomness* in the interaction of the *parts* (i.e. countries) of the system with one another is not legitimate. On the contrary there is a *complete asymmetry* in the dynamic relations of the dominant country to the rest of the system. The former initiates shocks and reaps the main benefit. The periphery has to adapt itself as best it can to the new situation. The problem is therefore how the productive pattern of and capital accumulation in the dependent economy will be affected by the progress in the dominant country. If the technical progress is of an unpredictable character which acts through shocks unevenly distributed among the industries of the dominant economy, it is likely to impose a new risk on all other countries, and interfere with accumulation and growth.[3]

Thus the static formulation of the principle of comparative costs is inapplicable in a dynamic setting: it is not meaningful to recommend that a country should concentrate on producing goods in which it has

---

[1] The attempts to analyse the dollar shortage in terms of two commodities, full employment and given and unchanged propensities to import, can yield no acceptable answers: these terms rule the real problem out of purview.

[2] ' Propagation Problems and Impulses Problems in Dynamic Economics '. *Economic Essays in honour of Gustav Cassel*. London, 1933.

[3] Cf. below Section 4, on the precise mechanism of this impact.

' the greatest relative advantage ' when (at the margin at any rate) the *relative advantage changes all the time*, though not in a continuous way, or predictably. The losses suffered at the margin through the enforcement of repeated readjustments, may well be greater than any gains due to the marginal increase in productivity (if any) through the ' intensification of the international division of labour '. The problem is not one of identical products being produced with identical factors and identical production functions in all countries. Technical progress and capital accumulation changes products, changes factors and changes production functions. There are no once-for-all adjustments but the need for continual adjustment. The principle of comparative costs must therefore be rephrased in a dynamic setting. With it goes its pristine simplicity.

4. *The balance of payments: international oligopoly*

I

We have seen that the traditional approach, by sterilising into the anonymity of ' countries ' 'A' and ' B ' the enquiry into the economic relations between them, has completely vitiated the analysis of the impact of advanced countries—likely to be dominant initiators of technical change and rapidly accumulating capital—on less privileged areas. The inequality of partnership suppressed by this analysis does not end there. The bias against the weak is further sharpened by the working of the monetary mechanism.

Conventional theory avoided the politically awkward results of this analysis by treating the monetary problem completely separately from the ' real ' model based on barter, and by stereotyping it into a set of rules—the so-called Hume Law—which eliminated the interposition of ' states ' in the relations of ' *productive units* ', and thus created a model of a sort of monetary perfect competition in which the reactions of these units to the policy of other units could be disregarded. In fact the international monetary system expresses (and reacts to) the relation of a limited number of *countries* (states), the policy of each of which will affect *all productive units* within their territorial limits. The policy of each state, in its turn, will be influenced by the condition of its balance of payments and reserves, and in framing it, few states can disregard the policy of the rest of the system. Perfect ' monetary competition ' is a figment.

International monetary affairs are dominated by oligopoly and oligopolistic struggle. In particular, the different size (in terms of national money income, investment and trade) and power of resistance (in terms of the relative size of their liquid international reserves) of countries will have a decisive effect on the final outcome of any unbalance, however caused. The absolute balances in international payments, resulting from a given event will have different employment, growth (productivity and saving), income, and price effects according to the size, the foreign trade dependence and psychological sensitivity of countries. The size of reserves will have a decisive influence in this respect, as only reserves—including, of course, large short term credit owed to the country[1]—can guarantee freedom from foreign interference and from having to give in to bluffs.[2] But a holding of large reserves will represent a costly loss of investment opportunities. The disregard of these problems is the more serious as anticipations of a repetition of trouble might itself bring on trouble, and exclude certain types of policy (e.g. depreciation or flexible exchanges) because of the risk of destructive anticipatory speculation.[3]

The complete disregard of the impact of these monetary factors on the long run outcome explains much of the futility of the conventional treatment of the dynamic problems.[4] The traditional analysis cannot deal with the importance of bluff or the psychological atmosphere which might change the direction of the readjustment and, thus, also the position of the 'eventual', so-called long run, equilibrium. Nothing in this field seems to arouse greater bursts of scholarly enthusiasm than the various ' laws ' which are supposed to govern the outcome of a change in the foreign trade parameters. These ' laws ' are set out in terms of either elasticities or changes in book-keeping identities such as savings and investment (the so-called absorption approach). Thus devaluation or the payment of reparation is treated as an operation, the effect of which can be analysed on a partial equilibrium schedule, depicting the relation between the demand for exports (imports) and its price, which is assumed to be given and unchanged by the change itself. Alternatively it is assumed that simple Keynesian ' relations ' will determine the outcome, again quite untouched by the process (including policy measures) itself.

[1] On the attractiveness of this arrangement for London, cf. above and Vol. II. Section 6, No. 21.
[2] Cf. e.g. the British situation in 1948–9. Larger gold reserves or more resolute nerves in using controls would have enabled Britain to stay on the old parity until the U.S. recovery ' justified ' its economic ' soundness '. As it was, Britain's Labour Ministers were thrust into a devaluation. What were the ' elasticities ' then?
[3] I tried to deal with some of these problems in the essays of Vol. II. Sections 5 and 6, and also the ' Dollar Shortage Once More ', Scottish Journal of Political Economy, 1955.
[4] E.g. the dollar shortage and of the consequences of customs unions.

II

This system or mechanism is derived straight from the classical two-country model, where one country is assumed to be infinitely greater than the other, or alternatively[1] all countries are assumed to refrain from a ' monopolistic doctoring ' of their terms of trade or to be unable to influence 'world demand'. In one sentence, countries are expected to be on a perfectly or atomistically competitive basis: the policies or aggregate actions of any one country have no noticeable effects on the situation, objectives or policy of others.

Now foreign trade itself leads, as we have seen, to specialization, and it is only in the most trivial of cases that the assumptions of perfectly competitive behaviour can be considered meaningful. The interposition between (small) *productive units* of the monetary or commercial policy of the *state* renders international trade relations monopolistic, even if on the entrepreneurial level there was (as there is not) perfect competition. Thus a large-scale change in the volume of demand or in the foreign value of an important currency represents, *ipso facto*, and inextricably, a change in ' world ' demand. During the dollar shortage, in the late 1940's for instance, United States demand represented almost half of the total world demand, supposed to be infinitely large! This was perhaps an extreme case. The German export surplus and its absorption of world demand, however, is not negligible either. Exports of Cuban sugar or of British machine tools are sufficiently important to render the assumption of atomistic competitive relations invalid, and conclusions based on it fallacious. Nor are the price ' elasticities ' independent of one another or of the level of demand, and especially of the relationship between demand and productive capacity. It is here that the theory of the balance of payments merges into a theory of growth and development.

Edgeworth's treatment of Marshall's ' static ' geometry of reciprocal demand curves implicitly recognised this fact, although it failed to realize the decisive importance of the consequential limitation. He compared reciprocal supply-demand curves with the hands of a clock which are activated by a mechanism behind its face. 'A movement along a supply-and-demand curve of international trade should be considered as attended with rearrangements of internal trade; as the movement of the hand of a clock corresponds to considerable unseen movements of the machinery.'[2] This simile brings out clearly that both Marshall and Edgeworth thought of the relationship between a causal initial change and the resulting new ' equilibrium ' *as something given and enduring*. The clock can only go at a predetermined pace and move the hand in a predetermined way.

---

[1] Cf. the essay on 'Welfare and Foreign Trade', Section 1, No. 3.
[2] F. Y. Edgeworth, *Papers Relating to Political Economy*, Vol. II, 1925, p. 32.

The relationships between the initial change in the balance of payments and consequential developments is, of course, of an entirely different, and much more tenuous character, and will also depend on the historical position which will determine anticipations, i.e. the reactions of the countries, producers, etc. involved. This fact is of decisive importance. If this mechanism is a ' clock ' at all it is a very peculiar one. The movements of the hand necessarily have an influence on the working of the ' machine ', and it is equally possible that the ' off-scene ' happenings will have varying effects on the working of the hands with a change of the situation or psychological climate. The *ex-ante* schedule and its elasticity is not necessary relevant as it might (and is highly likely to) change as a result of the development through time. It is wholly illegitimate in any case *a priori* to assume its fixity. The *ex-post* schedule, on the other hand, depends on the historical sequence of events (e.g. the impact on the level of demand in each country, and its urgency), on the influences (through anticipations) of previous historical sequences, all of which will influence accumulation and, with it, vary the competitive power of the country. If there is a causal relationship between the original, and these further, changes or autonomous impulses, these latter can no longer be ignored as of ' second ' order of importance.

The analysis can proceed no longer by talking of countries A and B without specifying what type of a country, of what size and of what endowment (and indeed with what sort of international reserves) is under discussion, and without specifying the relationship which is to be analysed. *A given reciprocal demand curve* would thus only be applicable *ex-post* to a *single change*, from which it is constructed. This is implicit theorising with a vengeance. The contribution to general economic insight of this type of analysis is trivial. Historical situations and developments are unique. The interrelation between initial change and effect will vary accordingly.

Quite separately from (and quite inconsistently with) this approach, and partly as a result of our attack[1] (which was, of course, completely unsuccessful) on the illegitimate use of the concept of elasticity in the theory of international trade problems, a different analysis was started. What it had in common with the first was its serene conviction that all would be well, provided wicked inflationary practices were not permitted. It was based on a simple, quasi-Keynesian analysis, by which it could be shown that consumption, investment and exports added together are equal to expenditure on consumption, savings and imports. The fact that this was a book-keeping identity was (conveniently) not emphasised.

[1] Section 5, Nos. 13 and 14.

The price/demand schedule and its elasticity were replaced by income/import schedules and propensities. These were assumed to be fixed and uninfluenced by the process itself. In this way the identity between consumption and consumption expenditure dropped, in the second round, and the writer asserts that if exports were to increase and imports fall, either savings have to be increased or investment reduced. There follows a learned disquisition on the effects (via the multiplier) on the various countries' incomes, and it is triumphantly demonstrated that investment must be reduced as savings ' would not by themselves increase '.

The manipulation of these identities conceals the fact that these relations are exceedingly unstable. Technical progress or a change in taxation can shift import propensities as much as the variation of employment at home. When a country approaches full employment the historical relationship between the price and quantity of imports abruptly changes to increases in income. Imports of the fully employed country might increase even if prices abroad rise; though a decrease in prices abroad might induce very large increases in imports of that country, because price competition from abroad in a fully employed economy might be extremely effective. The result is a ' kinking ' of the ' curve ' if one must have a curve (such curves are applicable momentarily only to the given situation). The usefulness of the concept of elasticity of demand seems doubtful, as it is also only fleetingly applicable (and not independent of the historical process). On the other hand it is not true that consumption depends entirely on income and that it could not be cut by direct credit measures aimed at consumers' credit or restrictions on imports of certain types of goods, for instance, which would result in an ' autonomous ' change of consumption (and savings) which cannot be expressed in the identity. Thus the simple absorption approach is hardly less misleading than the Marshallian analysis.

In order to evade this issue the ' absorption ' approach has copied the neoclassical pretence. It was based on a sort of (Keynesian, in contrast to neo-classical) ' perfectly competitive ' *monetary* model of the world economy. It is assumed that the surplus or deficiency of a country can not affect ' *world* ' demand (because if it did the outcome will be uncertain).[1] Thus the absorption approach is just as cavalier in

[1] A number of ' other ' countries might, for instance, not feel in a position to permit an increase of their exports relative to imports, for fear of inflation. In that case export surpluses might continue so long as a ' strong ' deficit country permits itself a deficit. On the other hand, weak deficit countries might be not able to continue to have deficits while the surplus countries might not wish to have their export surplus cut, and might match the deflation of the debtor countries. There would be a cumulative downward spiral. This would inevitably be the case if there was an absolute shortage of international liquidity in terms of the value of international trade. Cf. Vol. II. Section 7, No. 24.

disregarding the 'autonomous' effects of policies (which are implicit in the situation) on Keynesian relations (say of devaluation or of currency restrictions on the 'propensity' to consume or import) as the elasticity approach was in neglecting the impact of change on the Marshallian ones. It is by no means true, *ex-ante*, that the sole condition of success of devaluation is the reduction of demand to accommodate the consequential increase in exports (which was assumed to be automatic) and enable cuts in imports.

The impact of policy on the terms of trade must be explored. It is not true that any increase in demand will increase price, or lead to a shortage and affect demand for imports and exports identically in all circumstances. No doubt the balance of trade is identical to the difference between home production and home demand. It is illegitimate, however, to assume that it will react in the same way under all circumstances: the identity can be brought about in *various alternative* ways, including an increase in production, among which, within limits, indeterminacy exists. Full employment is not a sharp divide which is unaffected by the composition of demand, thus by policy. The muddle is complete.[1]

Thus both *ceteris paribus* approaches are fallacious. Except in trivial cases, all changes in the terms of trade affect income, and all changes in income will affect prices, and change in income also affects the sensitivity of demand to price changes. In fact the two are inseparable, though not identical.[2] There is, as we have said, a twilight zone in which increases in money income will begin to have disproportionate effects, irrespective of price changes. As full employment is approached, as home supply begins to be deficient, imports rise; the sensitivity of demand to increases in prices abroad decreases. But it would be foolish to regard this relationship as something rigid. The development of productive capacity and the dynamism of the economy which determines the point of shortage plays a dominant part in *determining the balance of payments*.[3] If the traditional rigid quantity theory mechanism is quite irrelevant, because it cannot account for the effects of an increase in productive capacity, the primitive Keynesian absorption approach is no more sophisticated.

Analysis, therefore, has to proceed to show what the consequences

[1] An excellent example of this complete muddle is the altercation (*Economic Journal* 1960–1) among Chicago professors about flexible exchanges and the 'stability' of exchange markets conducted entirely in terms of constant 'long run' schedules. Cf. also Section 4, No. 11.

[2] Just as wages are (a large part of) the demand for labour, but an increase in demand for labour can initiate wage increases, and an increase in wages an increase in demand. The difference is vital. Attempts a mathematical separation of increases in wages from increases in the demand for products are futile.

[3] Section 4, No. 11.

of any primary impact will be. These will depend on the comparative
relation between income and output capacity in each country, and
might be far greater than the primary change and, in the long run,
offset, or much more than offset, the primary impulse.[1] The generalisa-
tion of such conclusions is inevitably precarious and, more often than
not, illicit. Only the most tentative rules can be made.

Imports and exports will seem to be related to:

 (i) relative money income at home and abroad,
 (ii) the relative price at home and abroad of goods and services which
      enter international trade, which will again be related to the
(iii) relation of demand to productive capacity at home and abroad
      (itself strongly influenced at the margin by the rate of investment),
      and
(iv) the policy aims of the dominant countries.

It should also be noted that relative income at home and abroad are
inextricably inter-related to prices. Equally, the interaction between
price, income and demand will differ according to the historical con-
figuration of a particular situation, because international trade and
the money economy make prices depend not only upon wants but
also upon price expectations. Thus stability itself becomes co-determined by historical antecedents. This introduces a second fundamental
kind of indeterminacy.

Equilibrium theory postulates that if all individuals take the right
decision in some sense, equilibrium and optimum will prevail. This
presupposes that there is an independently given and determinate set
of right decisions. But there is no such set. What will happen depends
on what people do now, and what people do now depends on what
they expect to happen, which in turn depends on what has happened
in the past. Where prices are the function of price expectations, the
optimum is not only clouded by the ignorance of the future, but it is
indeterminate. Finally, as we saw, all this is related to accumulation
and technical progress which are also historically determined.

If, for instance, we wished, with Marshall, to analyse the effects of
a ' change of the urgency in demand ' of one country for the goods of
another ' unaccompanied ' by a change in the second ',[2] the first effect
will be to change the balance of trade.[3] This will affect the balance of

---

[1] Cf. Section 1, No. 2. Professor Kindleberger attributed the dollar shortage to
such over-compensation.

[2] The whole concept is extremely muddled, because the change in the first cannot
leave the demand in the second unchanged.

[3] And this cannot be assumed away by uttering magic incantations about long
run positions because, as it must be repeated over and over again, the locus of the
'long run' equilibrium, if such a concept is at all meaningful, will be co-determined
by what happens as the result of the disturbance in the balance of trade.

trade of the trading partner directly, and also through, and separably from, the price change. What will happen in consequence is—as we have seen—in the lap of the gods. The emergence of the balance might, or might not be, followed by counter-action in all participating countries, which offsets or frustrates the direct consequences of the original impulse. Cumulative movements will ensue. Total demand, i.e. demand in both countries taken together, might start to fall or rise and the balance of trade might become the object of an oligopolistic struggle. To analyse this on the basis of diagrams setting out the final equilibrium position without inquiring whether (and how) the intermediate stage leading to that position is feasible (and will influence the process) is to prejudge the outcome of the exercise. It does not add to knowledge.

If one wanted to depict this through one of those abstract pictures it would have to be in terms of a series of demand curves according to each monetary demand position, the relationship between which was historically determined. Each of these demand positions would correspond to a monetary balance of payments and terms of trade position.[1] The shape of the process will be determined by the impact of the balance of trade deficit (or surplus) and the consequential income changes and policy decisions on the countries' foreign trade. In this particular case it would be necessary to know the size of the countries, the fraction of their trade with each country in the system, their attitude of employment and prices, their gold reserve positions, their capacity (within these outside limitations) to implement any policy, the availability of policy-means (e.g. controls, taxation machinery): all these factors will determine, should the policies of the member countries of the system differ, which of the countries can bluff and which will have to give in if bluffed because of shortage of reserves, or the inability to influence the incomes of their trading partners; or whose economic development will be dominant and whose will be dominated.

All this will happen between countries in the process of growth. To talk about ' stable ' situations and ' elastic ' ' demand ' and to arrive at ' formulae ' *on the basis of given elasticities and propensities,* is a turn of phrase by which the writers conceal from themselves the nature of the problem. As we have pointed out,[2] these elasticities are either based on the past, and are therefore not applicable to the future without further simplifying assumptions and specifications, or they are to be derived from the change under discussion. In that case they will have to be

---

[1] The conduct of the analysis in terms of complex ' bales ' treated as single commodities is in itself absurd. Cf. above.

[2] Cf. above, pp. 27–29.

E

derived *ex-post*: then they represent implicit theorising of no value: the equilibrium will have been co-determined by factors which this procedure is intended to eliminate, and whose analysis is essential for the understanding of the mechanism.

The problem is one of income effects due to changes in investment and growth, the introduction of new methods of production and new products, as well as in demand, which may well carry the system—at any rate for a time—away from the ' original equilibrium '. There will be employment effects and terms of trade effects which will impinge on each other, and which might start cumulative movements which in their turn might well overshoot ' changed equilibrium ' position. If the country in which this happens is the dominant one (e.g. if it is more dynamic, bigger, and has large liquid reserves relative to its foreign trade sensitivity) it can impose readjustment on its partner, and carry the latter with it, away from the old towards a new position, which might, or might not, be an equilibrium position in the traditional sense. In addition, a permanent deflationary pressure might emanate from the greater flexibility of a more dynamic system.[1] All these consequential changes are far from being in a negligible order of smalls. They all create further shifts and as changes are continual, and adjustments take time, no position of ' eventual equilibrium ' will in actual fact ever be reached, or need necessarily be conceivable. The system might be in continuous disequilibrium ' chasing ': the series of consequential adjustments might lead towards or away from a steadily receding and changing ' equilibrium ' position.[2] Equilibrium in fact will mean no more than mutually compatible development or policy. Every historical case must, therefore, be analysed separately.

When Mrs. Robinson,[3] in discussing the effects of devaluation asserted the existence of a stable equilibrium on *a priori* grounds, she was completely oblivious of this reciprocal relationship. The same applies to Professor Metzler's discussion of the (pure) ' elasticity ' of

---

[1] Cf. above p. 24. Professor Viner groped towards an understanding of this phenomenon, explaining the difference by an unequal ' efficiency ' of gold. Inequality in this sense was due to a lessened velocity of circulation. The nature of the prices of exports will also play an important role. The administered prices of the dominant exporters have e.g. imposed a grave once-for-all burden on primary producers except in rare conditions of restocking booms such as was experienced during the Korean War. Cf. 'Economic Policy and the Price System', E.C.L.A., *Bulletin*, March 1961.

[2] Prof. Haberler could not be more mistaken in criticising Prof. Nurkse, by claiming (*Review of Economics and Statistics*, 1960) that in the absence of a completely satisfactory theory of dynamic growth, all analysis has to be conducted in terms of comparative statics. The divergence in the rate of growth and bias in its character is alone sufficient to destroy comparative statics and necessitate great restraint in generalisations.

[3] *Essays in the Theory of Employment*, Oxford, p. 201.

international demand[1] in terms which suggest that he thought of them as increasing with the passage of time, and invariant to income (hence price). Here, then, is a hopeless muddle between short term considerations (increasing the 'price elasticity' of demand) and long term ones (long term 'equilibrium' of full employment determined by real output capacity in the Vineresque sense).[2]

Thus propositions such as 'devaluation will improve the balance of trade if the sum of elasticities is such and such' are either trivial (in the sense of being descriptive and meaning 'if the balance of trade improves on devaluation, it will improve'), or not more meaningfull than had the author suddenly startled us by saying 'Bow-wow'. For we must know the reaction of world income and demand to the measure proposed, and its relation to world productive capacity (itself one of the determinants, and at the same time not independent of the measure) to know what will happen. In a 'world' near full or over-full employment 'elasticities' as we have seen might be 'perverse'. In other words, increases in price of any one country might still not prevent an increase in its exports.[3] Changes of income both shift and alter the shape of the 'schedules' thought to be 'given' by traditional analysis. The elasticity-mongers assume things constant which must necessarily change. In fact 'world' demand for imports is not determined by 'real' factors and its price 'elasticity' is subject to violent variation due to employment variations. Nor does it necessarily improve with the passage of time. In periods of intense oligopolistic struggle for reserves it may worsen as time passes, even so far as single countries are concerned.[4] It will, as we have demonstrated, depend on

[1] *A Survey of Contemporary Economics*, H. S. Ellis (Editor), 1948, ch. 6.
[2] Cf. above p. 4, note 1.
[3] Hence the absence of transfer difficulties in the case of U.S. aid in both peace and war. Thus the Rueff-Ohlin-Keynes discussion took place on a completely fallacious plane. The first two entirely ignored (in 1929 of all years) the possibility of falls in 'world income' induced (or at least aggravated) by the payment of reparations. Keynes, by arguing on the basis of a Marshallian curve could not defend his thesis, as he had implicitly accepted the static framework. Later on, neo-classical economists (though not Rueff) would angrily deny that they had ever believed in Say's 'celebrated' law in an 'operational sense'. Devaluation in Britain did not cause inflation: it caused deflation abroad. Cf. Vol. II. Introduction.
[4] The conflicting claims made by the heads of the Federal Reserve System in the 1920s, on behalf of their efforts to 'sterilise' the gold inflow in order to preserve a 'new era' of stable prosperity, and the consequential difficulties caused elsewhere by this one-sided distortion of the classical gold standard mechanism, foreshadow problems which are still with us. The continued difficulties of Britain, moreover, demonstrate the clash between the need to maintain investment and thus to protect the increase of productivity, and the *modus operandi* of the classical mechanism which works by restricting demand and thus interrupts growth and (in a dynamic world where wages are not instantly in 'equilibrium') imperils competitive power: the classical mechanism could only be conceived to work satisfactorily in a static world. Only in that world, a world without capital accumulation and changes in productivity, will restriction not prove self-stultifying after a short time.

the (historical) monetary relation of income to productive capacity and the anticipations attached to each of these factors.

Once full employment is approached, 'flexibility' in a single country falls, unless there is rapid growth. Yet if full employment is not maintained, growth will slow down and the country suffer in the longer run from a relative eclipse in innovation and investment.[1] Devaluation, which has been advocated to render full employment possible without express international agreement, turns out to be a broken reed. Not only might its 'effectiveness' be wrecked by repetition through the creation of a fixed pattern of anticipations, but its effects on a fully employed economy are stultifying its function as they engender inflationary pressures increasing home demand and imports. These are difficult to resist, even on the first occasion, and almost impossible to resist on repetition.

Moreover, the school which sees in fluctuating exchanges a means of smooth readjustment ignores the fact that these fluctuations, together with the sluggishness of the productive system, will prevent, rather than promote, physical readjustment for which new investment is required. Currency depreciation will enable the 'wrong' industries to continue to exist. The optimistic conclusion is the outcome of confusion between the relationship of long and short run, between the 'real' and 'monetary' sphere.

This analysis demonstrates that the assumption that international trade is conducted by individual firms, with the role of the monetary mechanism being restricted to transmitting automatically impulses originating on the 'real' side, depends on the acceptance of the existence of rigid rules governing that mechanism. This was, perhaps, accurate, in the first instance, with a coin standard.[2] So long as Central Banks were 'politically' independent, and merely registered gains and losses of gold, the Hume mechanism could still be thought as, to some extent, effective. It was already being increasingly modified by the differences in the 'efficiency' of using gold,[3] the rate of growth of international liquidity (gold and formerly also silver), and the rate of growth of capital (which was considerably influenced by it). This phase of development ended already before 1914, even in Western Europe—and in large parts of the world it was inapplicable even earlier. Since the First World War the theoretical framework became com-

---

[1] E.g. U.S. after 1953: Britain well nigh since 1914.

[2] Including the colonial Currency Boards which had a 100 per cent coverage. The implication of this arrangement for the development of these territories cannot be discussed in this context. Cf. 'Malayan Monetary Controversy', *Malayan Economic Review*, 1959.

[3] Which comprehensibly exercised Dr. Viner. (Cf. *Studies*, op. cit., pp. 365–74.)

pletely at variance with reality.[1] Conclusions based on it are thus fallacious.[2]

When monetary and fiscal policy become subject to volition, single producers and consumers in any one country will be affected in the same way (though of course not to the same degree), and their action depends on those policies. The rigid framework of the quantity theory disappears. Consequently, *countries* rather than micro-economic entities, entrepreneurs, become the proper object of study. Unfortunately the Keynesian revolution miscarried before it had influenced doctrine in this vital field. Its propensities and multipliers became conventionalised.

Once it is recognised that the first effect of changes in international trading will affect *countries* (through their balances of payments) and it is countries that will react, the whole problem appears in a new light. If the relationship of individual producers in highly developed areas cannot be analysed in terms of atomistic, perfect competition, how much less is it applicable to relations of a very restricted number of countries to one another, each of which is exporting a more or less limited speciality of products of which it is an important supplier.[3]

The reaction of a country to, e.g., a balance of payments deficit, will be determined partly by the automatic effect (both price and income) of that balance on domestic economic affairs, partly on the deliberate reaction of the Government (including the Central Bank), and the degree of its liberty of action.

The latter will be influenced by:

(a) the principles of policy; does the Government want, for example, to:
- (i) stabilise employment,
- (ii) maintain reserves,
- (iii) maintain the stability of prices;
(b) the latitude of choice open politically among policy means in carrying out its policy, e.g. whether restricted to ' global ' monetary controls or capable of instituting direct controls;
(c) by the degree of dependence of the country on foreign trade (because great dependence might make compensatory policies difficult, if not impossible) and on the relative availability of liquid reserves.

Generalisations will be difficult. It might be suggested that if the majority or the most powerful and economically independent countries

[1] Cf. e.g. The League of Nations. *International Currency Experience*, 1944.
[2] Cf. Section 2, No. 3.
[3] It is of course possible that even a diversified exporter is in oligopolistic relationship to other countries because of its exceptional importance.

are bent on (*a*) (ii) or (iii), i.e. do not primarily aim at maintaining employment, a deflationary bias is likely to be imported to the world system as a whole. It is, generally speaking, easier to enforce deflation than employment stabilisation. *The risk of losing all reserves before the world situation changes is obvious and immediate. There are no obvious and immediate financial risks incurred by toleration or promotion of gains of reserves.* The risk consists of forgoing growth and that will become obvious in the longer run only and responsibility for it can be explained away.

It takes deliberate action to counteract a gain in reserves by an increase in demand when the world as a whole suffers from deflation, from a general deficiency of demand; while passivity will probably lead to further gains. Thus in an oligopolistic struggle or game situation, the ultimate retreat will always be towards maximising reserves and minimising gold losses. The traditional language which talks about the ' strength ' of currencies, the need for ' conserving reserves ' and which greets the inflow of gold as a favourable balance, and the exchange of non-income bearing gold for high income bearing assets as a ' crisis ' will strengthen this bias.[1] It could be overcome but probably only by supranational action.[2]

We may conclude therefore that the impact of foreign trade on the development of weaker countries will depend

(i) on the relative size and character of the leading country (i.e. whether it is foreign trade sensitive);

(ii) on its economic policies, especially whether it is primarily aiming at stabilising reserves or employment;

(iii) on the intensity of technical progress and its bias relative to international trade;

(iv) on the absolute magnitude of comparative cost differences;

(v) on the existence of international agreements or institutions to mitigate international inequality through increased investment in poor areas, and adequate means to aid them.

It will depend on the same factors how much international liquidity will be needed for international stabilisation of employment and growth.

So long as Britain, with its great international sensitivity and sluggish industrial performance, was the leading financial power, the need for liquid reserves was less than in a world in which the U.S. (or Germany and its Common Market partners) are dominant.

---

[1] The American ' crisis ' of 1960 was mainly caused by the acquisition of foreign assets by private individuals and firms.

[2] I still adhere to our original 1943 proposals in this respect, as the most satisfactory solution all round. Cf. Section 3, No. 3 and Vol. II. Section 7, No. 23.

Looking at these questions from a sane point of view, it is evident that the so-called ' elasticity ' pessimist can most happily be defined as a person who fears that the policy-recommendations of the ' elasticity ' optimists will be implemented. The ' elasticity ' optimist could be described as someone who works hardest to defeat his own predictions. Anything resembling the usual concept of ' elasticity ' is not involved. Expectations about the behaviour of the balance of payments represent, in the main, expectations about monetary policy of leading countries combined with the more basic factors such as relative technical progress which have been discussed.

The conclusion suggested by these considerations[1] is the vital importance of avoiding the spread of deflation due to a shortage (or an anticipated shortage) of reserves, hence of the establishment of a strong central organ which guarantees the feasibility of creating sufficient international reserves to obviate such cumulative deflation. The gravity of the crises experienced by the United States prior to the establishment of the Federal Reserve System, due to the absence of such an institution, seems sufficient to prove the point. By making provision for creating reserves, the value of, and need for, accumulating reserves is immediately reduced. Thus the likelihood of a cut-throat competition for reserves is obviated and the pressure on the world economy is relieved. It is only to be hoped that it will not take quite as many crises to bring this reform about as were needed in the U.S., and that once established, the new institution can be prevented from bringing about the conditions by deliberate policy (again, much like the Federal Reserve System or the International Monetary Fund), the avoidance of which was the aim of its foundation. At the same time a sane code of international behaviour would be required to lessen the need for its intervention and prevent deliberate inflationism.[2] Mechanical gadgets will not work. Those ' schemes ' which are sufficiently ' liberal ' in the sense of providing adequate liquidity to parry deflationary shocks during confidence crises would prove to be too ' inflationary ' in happier general circumstances. Those ' tight ' enough to cope with speculative outbursts and over-expansion are bound to lead to general ruin in a deflation. Institutional reform without the adoption of sensible policies is unavailing to restore the weakened dynamism of the non-planned areas of the world.

---

[1] Cf. *International Liquidity and Reserves*. Section 7, No. 24.
[2] It is this consideration which inclined me against the Keynesian Clearing Union Scheme, which was based entirely on creating liquidity (cf. Section 7, No. 23.) In an inflationary atmosphere it would have created excessive international demand, while in a deflationary environment it might still have failed.

III.   THE OUTLOOK: LESS UNEQUAL PARTNERS

I

The proud structure of neo-classical international trade theory, with its confident, if slightly shrill, admonitions to politicians to free trade from all ' harmful encumbrances ' is no more. Like the Cheshire Cat, all disappeared but the smile. The hurray words only remain, without content.

Does this mean that systematic economic analysis has lost its importance in this all-important field? On the contrary: the failure of empty generalities, the exposure of the grand abstract designs and diagrams as signifying nothing, depicting non-existent relations; the recognition of the historical uniqueness of macro-economic problems, all this increases the need for careful and detailed economic analysis, for the painstaking investigation of each case and its peculiarities. The acknowledgment of the complexity of inter-relationships, of the impossibility of coming to snap-judgments on the basis of simplified assumptions and general models, expands the scope of international economics. The choice between ways of life or the fate of social classes and great regions which are involved, will no doubt necessitate intimate collaboration with historians, political scientists and socio-logists. This surely is an advantage rather than a drawback: at last a meaningful attack can be launched on problems in which the persistent complete failure of ' pure ' economic advice was not a sign of the venality of the public men but the incomprehension, if not worse, of the economists.

Scepticism about *free trade* as the sole way to salvation must not lead to the conclusion that a *wide international division of labour* is not an essential condition of material advance, or that regional organisation, especially among the newly-freed countries (but also among the long independent units of South America) is not vitally needed for their prosperity. Indeed, denial that free trade can serve as a means of obtaining a fair division of labour is the most striking recognition of the vital importance of the right kind of division of labour. What is opposed is the parrot-like reiteration of faith in the beneficent role of *current* comparative costs in determining the future direction of domestic production and international trade. Scepticism about free trade acknowledges the vital power of direct and indirect economies of large scale production to promote growth. It acknowledges the decisive importance of the size of countries and their balanced development in promoting prosperity. It does help in understanding the threat to the weak implicit in the uncontrolled sway of market forces between unequal partners.[1]

II

What are the basic conclusions which should govern our attitude?

1. The decisive importance of growth in determining the fate of countries cannot be gainsaid. *The compound influence of capital accumulation* embodying technical progress far outweighs the gains attainable from a *once-for-all 'reallocation'* of resources as a result of liberalising, if, indeed, the impact of trade can be conceived of at all as a ' reallocation ' of *given and intact*, ' unchanged ' volume of resources, as a once-for-all-change. The growing importance of specific capital investment is only one of the reasons for the inapplicability of the neo-classical comparative static approach to the analysis of dynamic problems. Trade will be beneficial if its expansion at least does not impede growth on account of its impact on the division of income and investment while enabling even the weaker partner to make use of the advantages of specialisation.[2] In a choice between growth and trade the former must, in all but exceptional circumstances, carry the day. This is so, even if the psychological gain of belonging to a dynamically expanding community and the feeling of uncertainty and risk attendant to increased vulnerability through trade are disregarded.

Economies with centralised decision-making have a considerable structural advantage in this respect which, if not recognised and consciously counterbalanced, might establish their crushing superiority in the long run.[3] Only if investment and savings plans of individualist economies could be made consciously and mutually consistent, can this fatal drawback be overcome. International trade, over too wide an area, and too loosely coordinated, might render such cooperation impossible. This is a decisive argument against negative liberalisation without safeguards and effective institutional arrangements to enable the maintenance of the growth of the lesser partners and the promotion of greater equality of opportunity. Only the complete and wilful disregard of the biased nature of growth and the non-random impact of technical progress could have led to any other conclusion. The overwhelming importance for the fate of the poor, of effects of the dominance of the strong, and the historical uniqueness of the relations

[1] The reversal of the comparative real advantage of Russia, which attended her rise to second place as an industrial giant, shows the futility of basing policy on short term advantage.

[2] The failure of the Soviet satellites in Europe must be mainly attributed to the disregard for the need for specialisation.

[3] Cf. Preface and Vol. II. Section 9.

between the dominant and dominated countries in different periods which shapes the path of economic readjustment, and determines its character, direction, and speed, must be recognised in order to be able to deal with the problem of ensuring the balanced growth of *all* partners. The approach on the basis of 'countries' 'A' and 'B' sterilises analysis of all relevance. It is the particular shape of oligopolistic relationships between countries which give each epoch its character.

2. If, of course, trade between unequal partners could be combined with undiminished pace of growth in the weaker countries, it might speed their development through the gain in productivity, income, and investment capacity, on the basis of full utilisation of comparative advantages. Trade might also stimulate growth if it breaks down monopolistic restrictions, or entrepreneurial backwardness. But care must be taken that the general background is conducive to expansion rather than stagnation or contraction. Hence the *planned* development of wide areas (e.g. Latin America or West Africa) might provide the setting for optimal development unimpeded by the depressive influence of exceptionally strong or dynamic partners in the region itself (or the world at large) on the rest.[1]

3. Convertibility, and/or non-discrimination, which in fact secures a free field for the superiority of the strong, is likely to be pernicious economically and worse morally, unless means for equalising the opportunities of unequal partners are provided, either (i) by redistributive unilateral investments grants aiding investment in the weaker country (or region), or (ii) by securing favoured terms of trade; the former is likely to be more effective when highly developed areas have to deal with subsistence economies encumbered with the remains of feudal land tenures, where 'trade' will give rise mainly to increased profits and heavy spending, rather than accelerated accumulation; (iii) sufficient international reserves are available, or their smooth creation provided, for the multilateral system to obviate all risk of an insufficiency of liquidity causing an all-round deflationary pressure; (iv) rules for good international neighbourly behaviour are accepted which (*a*) ensure that dominant leaders maintain full employment demand so as to offset the deflationary impact on the weaker partners of technical progress; and (*b*) also permit unilateral protection of regional 'infant' industries (or rather of infant regions) until their equalising grants have ended the inequality of the partnership. This implies that the

[1] The establishment of the European Common Market with its discrimination in an important market against the industries of (weak) outside areas is therefore likely to be iniquitous to the world distribution of income. This pernicious effect will be increased if the Common Market countries insist on negotiating 'associated territory status' with African countries singly, and not treat Africa as a unit.

problem of inflation can be solved without large-scale unemployment and the slowing down of growth. An abandonment of the exclusiveness of monetary controls seems an essential condition of success. A reform of the personnel and structure of the international organisations dealing with international trade, monetary arrangements, and finance is surely also overdue. Their abject failures in the Mediterranean as well as Latin America (not to speak of Britain) have amply demonstrated their incapacity for dealing successfully with the problems of the non-Soviet orbit.

4. Long run terms of trade of primary producers are not likely to improve unless the Soviet Union begins to turn massively to trade with under-developed countries, buying primary products in exchange for manufactures. There is as yet no indication of this. Thus under-developed areas must try to break the constriction on their development and trade, imposed by the feudal land tenure, and the consequent distribution of opportunity costs detrimental to industrial development, and increase in the standard of living by land reform, resettlement and protection for industry. They would have to combine into regional units in order to form potentially equal trading partners to the highly developed areas. The present division of the poor areas into small states each incapable of providing, even potentially, markets large enough to enable full industrial development must defeat all efforts to assure international equality of opportunity.

5. Without a systematic attempt to eliminate a number of further causes which vitiate the working of the price system, a successful and equitable widening of trade is unlikely to succeed:

(i) Unemployment and depression are equivalent to discrimination by the depressed country against those maintaining full employment; means can be found to offset this consequence of their depression either by isolating them by commercial policy or by neutralising the impact through international ' open market operations ' restoring the gold reserve of the ' debtor ' countries (which are debtors only because they are not depressed);

The importance of accumulating international reserves must be diminished to eliminate the danger of an oligopolistic attempt or game to hold on to them, or increase them, by unduly restrictive policy in a situation of threatened general unemployment.

(ii) Disparate growth based on increasing returns and higher accumulative and research power might enforce repeated adjustments to the actual loss and detriment of the poorer and weaker areas.

Provision must be made, therefore, to overcome these effects, partly by the strong countries undertaking to maintain a slight excess of demand and partly by the reforms indicated above; in default, the improvement of the terms of trade of the poorer areas might give the U.S.S.R. its chance for trade expansion and political influence.

(iii) The obstruction to growth and increasing returns in poor areas are not mainly economic, and are unlikely to yield to economic measures alone.

III

The forces of obscurantism have received a setback. I have no illusion, however, about the permanency of the victory of a sophisticated approach over the naive Free Trade or simplistic Keynesian ' theory '. The resilience of exploded fallacies is infinite. When Professor Tinbergen was told in Keynes' critical review that, perceiving the futility of what he was doing, he would ' engage another ten computers' to 'drown his sorrows in arithmetic ',[1] he did better. He engaged them by the score and drowned *us all* in elasticities and correlations and least squares calculated on the basis of data stretching over two dozen years, and meaning nothing: and gained world renown. Keynes' warnings are forgotten. Doctoral theses will follow professorial articles, learnedly discussing the effects of customs unions or economic development, like Prof. Viner, in a strictly static and wholly irrelevant context.

I fully expect the cheerful grinding out of new and ever-newer models,[2] with umpteen parameters, elasticities and propensities and related multipliers which, on closer analysis turn out to be more unstable than the multiplicand. Misleading schedules will still be pitted against imaginary curves. Increasing returns will continue to be ignored.[3] Book-keeping identities will persistently be used to give weighty policy recommendations,[4] as if they represented reversible causal connexions. Rigour will still be prized, even if it really means the *rigor mortis* of reality.

---

[1] *Economic Journal*, 1939.

[2] Having regard to all signs, the next will be an attempt to constrain international economics to fit a linear programming model.

[3] The International Economic Association dedicated a whole session to the denial of the obvious (Lisbon 1959). (Cf. *Economic Consequences of the Size of Nations*. Proceedings of a Conference held by the International Economic Association. St. Martin's Press, 1960.) This followed a Conference in Rio where much the same thesis was preached by a selected band of faithfuls.

[4] Cf. Sir R. Hall's pithy remarks about the illicit use for policy advice by I.M.F. of the book-keeping identity between the balance of payments and the difference between savings and investment. *Economic Journal*, 1959.

In practical advice, however, I think the sway of comparative static analysis is less likely to recover. The Communist challenge has begun to drive home the lesson preached in vain in those spacious days when Russian growth had not yet got visibly under way. It is likely to keep policy orientation fixed on the need for stable expansion, shared by all. Western political economy will have little to claim for its role in spreading enlightenment or speeding human progress. But at least it will accommodate itself to a reality which it can no longer successfully deny.

SECTION ONE

WELFARE AND TRADE

1

THE CONCEPT OF A DOLLAR SHORTAGE

THE breakdown of the policy of convertibility of currencies, provided by the Bretton Woods agreement, within a few weeks after its first test in 1947 undoubtedly caused some discomfiture among its erstwhile advocates. They had failed to appreciate the grievous state of the European economy, and had hoped, rather naively, to be able to emerge from the breakdown of the world economic system of 1938 simply by trusting to the 'free' market forces. Fortunately, we did not have to pay the full penalty for their advice. The worsening of the international political situation resulted in a reconsideration of U.S. policy. The rigid dogmatism of Mr. Cordell Hull and Mr. Clayton was superseded by the more flexible approach of General Marshall and his advisers. A catastrophic fall in the standard of life and shrinkage of world trade was avoided.

Instead of admitting that they were wrong in their estimate of the magnitude of the disequilibrium in the world economy; and that the elimination of that large-scale disequilibrium is a matter totally different in kind from the maintenance of equilibrium once it is attained, orthodox economists continue to assert that the excess[1] demand for dollars ' is merely a consequence of the fact that many countries are unwilling or unable for one reason or the other to live within their means. The propensity to spend and to inflate is so strong that the equilibrium in the balance of payments is constantly upset '.[2] The opposite view, i.e. that the rise of the United States through two world wars to a position of pre-eminence has created problems of an unparalleled character, is dismissed by a pained imprecation: ' Evidently even in the land of Adam Smith, Ricardo, Marshall, and Keynes it is necessary to point out again and again that trade is governed by comparative not by absolute cost! '[3] The possibility that the United States might

---

[1] Professor Haberler, ' Dollar Shortage ', in *Foreign Economic Policy for the U.S.*, ed. S. Harris, Harvard, 1948. Also Professor H. Ellis, ' Dollar Shortage in Theory and Fact ', *The Canadian Journal of Economics and Political Science*. 1948, p. 358.

[2] Haberler, op. cit., p. 435. Identical views are expressed by Mr. MacDougall, ' Britain's Foreign Trade Problem: A Reply ', *Economic Journal*, 1948, esp. p. 92; also R. Harrod, *Are These Hardships Necessary?* 1947, p. 42.

[3] Haberler, op. cit., p. 436.

undersell the rest of the world, if perhaps not 'all along the line', over a sufficient range to create large-scale disequilibrium and impose unemployment, is regarded as rank heresy. It is argued, therefore, that inflation outside the United States should be stopped, and currencies devalued. 'Equilibrium' would then be restored, and all would be well.

These complex arguments continuously switch between 'pure' theoretical considerations and advice of the most highly practical character. Professor Haberler's 'equilibrium' position, implicitly taken as an 'optimum', discloses his view of the nature of the 'world economy' which underlies his policy recommendations. It demands that a country's international payments (perhaps excluding capital flight[1]) should be made to balance without any direct controls over payments, without quantitative restorations, and without 'resorting to crude protectionist policies which, even if they succeeded in alleviating transitional strains, would do so only at the cost of permanently impeding the international division of labour and preventing the optimum allocation of resources'.[2]

The proof which has to be furnished by Professor Haberler in order to establish his case is not whether the United States is able by retaliatory action to enforce convertibility and non-discrimination. No one doubts that threats by the United States with her overwhelming military and economic power would be effective. *The problem is whether there is any ethical justification for the United States to use her power to enforce the rule of the unfettered price-mechanism on other countries.* An attempt will be made in this paper to show that the 'model' which underlies Professor Haberler's policy recommendations has no conceivable relation to the world we live in.

Let us first turn to the so-called long-run problem, i.e. disregarding, for the moment, monetary disturbances. We need not suspect Professor Haberler of having a physical maximum in mind when he discusses the goal of his policy: though the phrase 'optimum allo-

---

[1] Professor Haberler at some points gives the impression that even capital flight should be permitted ('Dollar Shortage', op. cit., p. 430). He rejects the current balance as a measure of disequilibrium, insisting on what he calls the current balance minus 'Equilibrating capital movements'. It is, however, difficult to attach any significance to this emotive concept. Capital movements even from low to high interest rates areas might well be 'disequilibrating', in the sense that they permit the maintenance or intensification of 'disequilibria'. They end in bankruptcy. In any case, whether or not a country's borrowing is 'sound', so much depends on the creditors' subsequent policy as to rob the concept of 'equilibrating' capital movements of all sense. Efforts to combine a 'real' (barter) equilibrium analysis of foreign trade based on absolute factor immobility with monetary analysis (usually through a primitive quantity theory) in the hope of obtaining a truly dynamic theory are doomed to failure. Cf. below (2) on the importance of the path of readjustment.

[2] Op. cit., p. 440.

cation of resources' might be interpreted in the sense of the point yielding maximum physical product, in the sense that the same output could not be achieved with less effort or a greater output with the same effort. This concept has no economic relevance without reference to the distribution of the product. Should he think of maximizing some quantity of 'utilities' or reaching 'higher' 'indifference levels' his difficulties are not less. Only if the following conditions were fulfilled —as they patently are not—would his optimum have any meaning (and we shall see not much meaning at that):

(1) The original endowment of the units participating must be given, unchangeable by policy and *distributed optimally* (whatever that may mean). There must be full employment.
(2) There must be *given* tastes and technical knowledge in the widest sense of the term; they must not be subject to alteration by conscious policy involving international trade.
(3) Perfect competition must prevail within (and between) countries; moreover, there must be free internal mobility of factors.
(4) The relatives between social and private costs must be proportionate and must not be influenced by risk induced by foreign trade, i.e. comparative advantages must be large and unchanging.[1]
(5) Absolute international immobility of all factors including capital.

If these conditions are not fulfilled, 'non-discrimination', commercial and monetary, would certainly not bring about an 'optimum'.

The first condition is certainly not fulfilled because—quite apart from any other difficulty—of the vast increase, during the war, of inequality of opportunity and means between the United States and the rest of the world. Professor Haberler confounds total and marginal conditions and neglects increasing returns. He also falls into the pit, against which Marshall warned, of failing to inquire into the distribution of original endowments. Indeed, one might say that almost any position which resulted from some discriminatory action turning the terms of trade of the United States against her, would seem to fit the description of 'optimum' better than that which would be brought about by 'non-discrimination'.

Moreover, and this is perhaps even more important, every single one of the other conditions required to justify Professor Haberler's 'optimum' is violated in such a way as to load the dice cumulatively in favour of the United States. Thus the 'optimum' of Professor Haberler and his colleagues must be rejected as false.

---

[1] Quite apart from anything else, tariffs must not be imposed by the (temporary) surplus country against an increase in imports. There is no suggestion that the U.S. will not protect itself against depreciation. The I.T.O. certainly permits raising tariffs in this case.

The concept of a *definite* ' long-run-equilibrium ', ' towards which the system is tending ', is itself subject to the gravest doubt. Professor Haberler, as we have seen, invokes high authority for, instead of proving, his dictum that it is *comparative* and not absolute costs which determine trade. If taken literally, this statement is obviously untrue. Comparative costs are unknown to entrepreneurs or governments conducting trade. They act (in the absence of direct controls) on the basis of *money prices* and *exchange rates*. It is wholly illicit to assume that *money prices* are proportionate to *long run social real costs*. We know that private money costs are not proportionate to social real costs, and neither are prices proportionate to private money costs. Moreover it is illicit to assume that the free market system possesses an inherent mechanism which would restore proportionality between these three sets of variables, e.g. maintain full employment. Comparative costs might be said in any meaningful sense to determine foreign trade only if equilibrium in the sense of conditions (2)—(5) of the previous section has *already been reached* and *therefore no balances arise in the current account of any participating country*. But these conditions rob the argument of such relevance as it might still possess.

If a large-scale disequilibrium has arisen the concept of the eventual ' equilibrium ' position has no sense *independently* of the *path* taken. Its position will be co-determined by the path of readjustment. The path itself, however, is determined by absolute costs and monetary factors. Sustained inflation (or deflation) e.g. in a leading country will decrease (or increase) its competitive power and lead to structural changes (in comparative costs) which are likely to persist after the original dis-equilibrating effect is removed. In any case the enforcing of secondary readjustments by the restoration of the equilibrium of the country originally responsible for the disturbance, might well depress opportunity costs to zero in other countries.[1]

There is no earthly reason, for instance, why a country could not ' undersell another all along the line '[2] provided loss of reserves takes place on the part of the deficit country. The short-run elasticities, which seem extremely low (whatever they may be in the long period), will further impede readjustment, and may result in substantial lowering of the standard of life—through a worsening of the terms of trade—of those on whom readjustment is imposed, i.e. of the dominated, i.e. the weaker, economies.

[1] Cf. my article ' Exchange Depreciation and Economic Readjustment ' in *Review of Economics and Statistics*, 1948, pp. 277–285, and J. J. Pollak, ' Exchange Deprecia-tion and International Monetary Stability, ' ibid., 1947, pp. 173–82.

[2] Cf. my paper ' The U.S. and International Economic Equilibrium ', *Foreign economic policy*, op. cit., as well as Professor Samuelson, ' Disparity in Post-War Exchange Rates ', ibid., p. 407.

F

The dominant economy in addition might cause a further and unnecessary lowering of the standard of life of its partners by imposing unemployment through employment effects inseparable from the price-movements,[1] income effects, which could have been avoided had different, more discriminatory means been used to restore the balance in international payments.[2] Any shock in the dominant economy by its multiplier effects and reactions is bound to cause fluctuations much greater in extent than the original cause. On the other hand the repercussions of ' readjustments ' on the surplus countries must not be under-estimated. The richer a country, the more difficult it is for her to maintain monetary equilibrium, and the more dangerous shocks from the outside.

It is for those who, from time to time exhume Say's theorem[3]— having periodically busily interred it—to prove that employment effects are not bound to arise and thus to affect the eventual position of ' equilibrium '. The growing uneasiness of the ' orthodox ' school is reflected by the fact that they have without exception refrained from recommending the observance of the ' rules of the game ' to the United States. According to orthodox canons the United States should now inflate (while the deficit countries deflate) until the resultant rise in incomes and prices helps to wipe out her surplus. In this way the extent of readjustment abroad would be lessened. The realisation that this procedure would in fact aggravate the European crisis (apart from inducing a domestic cumulative disequilibrium in the United States)[4] has begun to dawn. Yet its corollary, that orthodox measures cannot minimise the lowering of the standard of life of the poorer countries, is still being fiercely resisted.

It has been argued that the cumulative processes induced by monetary 'readjustment' are merely short-run phenomena, and that if protective measures are introduced, the long-run opportunity costs will rise by more than the gain from the employment effect. Whether or not this is so cannot be decided on general *a priori* grounds. It will depend on the extent of the long-run comparative cost differences and of the degree of unemployment. If unequal dynamic progress in two

[1] On the monetary mechanism, cf. my paper ' The International Aspects of Full Employment' in *Economics of Full Employment*, Oxford, 1944. [Reprinted Section 2 No. 3 and Vol. II. Section 7, No. 23.]
[2] Moreover, if Say's law is thus dropped at any moment through the ' path of readjustment ', as it must be, comparative costs become meaningless: for the ' country ' suffering from unemployment opportunity cost of a commodity sinks to zero or below.
[3] E.g. Professor Haberler, *The New Economics*, ed. S. Harris, p. 173.
[4] As in 1927: it is interesting to see how little reference is made nowadays to the colossal failure of the Norman-Strong attempt to master a disequilibrium similar to the current problem by orthodox methods.

regions makes a periodic recurrence of the 'shifts in equilibrium' probable, and thus necessitates periodic readjustments, the opposite is more likely. Moreover, the risk of such recurrence itself will undoubtedly influence 'comparative costs', retarding economic development—to the detriment of the weaker exporting nations. This was precisely what was threatening by the growing dominance and faster progress of the United States, if suitable measures had not been taken to bring about a better distribution of factor endowment between the Western countries, so gravely upset by the war.

The volume of trade—and this, e.g. Professor Haberler seems to forget periodically—is the result not merely of cost differences (comparative or otherwise) but also of international lending. Lending will, moreover, tend to decrease comparative cost differences due to the inequality of original factor-endowment and thus tend eventually to reduce the *proportion* of trade to national income (though not necessarily its absolute volume). At the same time lending or grants will tend to decrease the inequality of opportunity in different parts of the world. *Thus loans or grants represent an alternative to discriminatory commercial policy as a means of reducing inequality.* Thus, *provided* grants and loans continue, a larger scope for non-discrimination would be compatible with the welfare of the less-well-endowed countries. But this conclusion is entirely beyond the models of the orthodox economists which in basic matters disregard capital (and other factor) movements (though mentioning them whenever convenient for their argument).

Thus we may conclude that the denial of the problem of a dollar shortage in the sense

(1) that discriminatory methods will lessen the required extent of readjustment of the weaker countries, and

(2) that discrimination will also produce a more equal international distribution of income and opportunity

is based on a model of the international economy which *a priori* excludes a discussion of the problem which the writers set out to investigate.

2

WELFARE AND FREER TRADE—A REPLY

I

Professor Harberler in a recent article[1] returns to the discussion of 'certain elaborations and applications of the now familiar and widely

[1] Some Problems in the Pure Theory of International Trade (*E.J.*, June 1950, p. 223). The word 'pure' in the title seems a device—repeatedly used in the article—to disclaim the intention of making inferences which, it is quite obvious from the

used presentation of the theory of comparative costs in terms of opportunity cost.' He writes in terms to suggest that he considers this type of analysis highly relevant to current problems and tries to cast general aspersions on some of my concrete policy recommendations.[1] I am forced, therefore, to attempt once more to show:

(a) that his treatment of the problem of welfare is so unsatisfactory as to invalidate most of his conclusions, and

(b) that his assumptions do not justify his belief that his presentation of the case can be applied to problems of the real world; indeed most of the questions at issue are *a priori* ruled out by his treatment; some at least of his deductions are, moreover, inconsistent even with his limited model.[2]

I shall now proceed to deal with the shortcomings of Professor Haberler's welfare-economic approach which in themselves are fatal to his case.

In an 'individualistically organised economy,' says Professor Haberler correctly, '. . . what is to be regarded as a better position, a larger national income or a superior welfare position must be defined in terms of individual incomes and welfare positions.'[3] He goes on, however, to define an 'improvement' solely by reference to *physical* output, valued on the basis of arbitrary weights, i.e. based on exchange rates determined by the *existing* distribution of income.[4]

'Modern welfare economics had, however, shown that in the following sense the situation after trade can be said to be better than before, if income were appropriately distributed every individual would be made better off than before. *It is not necessary* (my italics) that income will actually be redistributed so that every-

context, are intended to be drawn. Professor Haberler, rightly, stresses the fact that his essay is largely in welfare economics, i.e., political and applied in character (p. 223 and especially note 1 on p. 227). 'It should be clearly realised that such a statement necessarily implies a value judgement on the part of the scientist, and in that sense is not necessarily objective.' Note the emotive word 'scientist' and the emotive qualification of the disclaimer of being objective 'in that sense' and 'entirely'. Either a statement is made by a scientist, in which case it must be objective, or the statement is made as an expression of an ethical attitude, which is not scientific.

---

[1] 'The Concept of a Dollar Shortage', *Manchester School*, May 1949, reprinted in *The Dollar Crisis* (Blackwell, Oxford, 1949). [Reprinted in the present volume, Section 1 No. 1 above.]

[2] All this is not merely not new but has recently received ample attention, cf. the bibliography quoted by Mr. R. F. Kahn, 'Tariffs and the Terms of Trade' (*The Review of Economic Studies*, 1947–48, p. 14).

[3] Haberler, op. cit., p. 226.

[4] Thus he cannot avoid dealing with income distribution. He merely selects his weights arbitrarily.

body will in fact be better off. There will practically always be some individuals who are worse off than before. But it is sufficient that everybody *could* be better off. That is the definition of what is meant by saying that one situation is better and constitutes a larger national income.'[1]

Now 'modern welfare economics' has shown precisely the opposite. It is not merely sufficient to show that every loser ' could ' be ' compensated '. It must be shown that everybody who *should* be compensated *has been* compensated and[2] could and will be compensated in all conceivably relevant situations; and that the measures necessitated by such compensation will not detrimentally interfere with allocative efficiency of the system,[3] not merely actually but potentially. It is, of course, entirely possible to take the view in concrete cases that losers should not be compensated because the ' change ' itself leads to a better distribution of income or for other stated reasons. Certainly no *general rule* can be laid down about *disregarding losses*. The change must not exclude future, even more favourable policy options: a qualification exceedingly important in the case of problems of highly dynamic character, as problems of international adjustment and development invariably are. It should be noted that these measures of compensation would be not merely internal but international.

Professor Haberler's conclusions automatically follow from this disregard of the problems of distribution.

(1) He thinks first of all that he can prove his case in favour of non-interference without showing that non-interference (and not merely the absence of protection)[4] will produce a unique point, a *maximum*

---

[1] Haberler, op. cit., pp. 226–7. [The fundamental point is that to measure an increase in income certain assumptions about prices *have* to be made; these must rest on some distribution of income. Now, where the increases are vast, it is perhaps excusable to avoid this point. But are they? 1961.]

[2] Cf. Little, *A Critique of Welfare Economics* (Oxford 1950).

[3] Cf. Samuelson, 'The Evaluation of Real National Income' (*Oxford Economic Papers*. N.S. January 1950).

[4] It is entirely characteristic of Professor Haberler's way of argument that he asserts that I believe that I have ' proved something by a loose and inexact enumeration of possible deviations from the competitive ideal '. In the article quoted I argued that Professor Haberler's position in favour of non-intervention into economic relations with the U.S. could be supported on if a *maximum maximorum* were achieved without intervention, i.e. if the initial distribution of wealth internally and internationally were ideal, a stationary state existed, and competitive conditions prevailed. As this was not the case and *as the conditions of competitive equilibrium are violated in such a way as to benefit the U.S., ethically*, any policy, *i.e.* discrimination which would *lessen the discrepancy of wealth* between the latter and the rest of the world would be *justified*. I never claimed that in certain circumstances measures increasing trade might not be needed. On the contrary, a large part of the article was devoted to advocating such measures. I was merely at pains to demonstrate that his concept of ' optimum ' was an emotive concept lacking objectivity, and based on personal values.

maximorum.[1] This, of course, he has not done. Indeed, it would be impossible to do so. There are an infinite number of maxima unless one special distribution of income is accepted as ' ideal '.

It is therefore entirely sufficient to show, in order to controvert him and to justify interference, that the conditions for such a maximum (*i.e.*, *an initial distribution of wealth and income accepted by all as optimum*; perfectly competitive conditions; as well as the absence of dynamic disturbances or of development and of employment problems) are not fulfilled. In that case measures which turn the term of trade against the rich countries, and thereby decrease the disadvantages suffered by, or secure advantages to, the poor countries, are perfectly justified. Attempts to ' enforce ' freer trade by insisting on the dropping of protective devices which the poor use, and, especially of non-discrimination against the rich, without countervailing concessions by the rich, cannot be supported by welfare economic arguments. We shall presently see in what manner Professor Haberler hopes to escape this rather obvious conclusion.

(2) The second consequence of his peculiar definition of what constitutes ' superior welfare ' in his contention that perfect mobility is not a ' necessary condition for the ideal classical model '.

Once we assume that a heterogeneous collection of goods will stand for ' welfare ', that this collection can be ' increased ' by trade because the terms of trade are more favourable than internal transformation ratios: that, in other words, the terms of trade are fixed, then it follows that if we disregard distributional effects, trade will ' increase ' ' welfare ', unless *trade* can be shown to *cause* a *shrinkage* of production. Such shrinkage can be caused only by unemployment. Immobility might cause a fall in the remuneration of the factors. It does not, says Professor Haberler, cause unemployment, if there is ' flexibility ' so long as their price (imputed value) is positive. Unemployment, under the assumption of Professor Haberler's static model, can be caused only by factor-price rigidity. Hence it *implicitly follows from the definitions* that trade will be beneficial, *unless factor prices are rigid*, and thus cause

---

[1] It might be suggested that Professor Haberler is conducting his argument in terms of a single country, and not of the world as a whole. And thus he need not show a *maximum maximorum*; he merely has to show that the single country gains even if it causes a bigger loss elsewhere. If this were the case one would merely have to show in order to controvert him, that under certain assumptions, a policy which turns the terms of trade in favour of a country would be preferable to ' free ' trade, and refer him to the large literature on this subject. But, though he tries to protect himself by several footnotes (some of which are wholly out of context), Professor Haberler, by assuming that the terms of trade could not be altered, in effect conducts his argument in terms of the world as a whole. In that case, however, he falls foul of the *maximum maximorum* condition.

unemployment.[1] Thus, according to Professor Haberler, factor mobility is not a condition of the ' free trade case '.

The fact is, of course, that nothing general can be said about welfare under these conditions. Some people will lose, some will gain. In some countries total loss might be large in relation to total gain, in others small. But, unless we assume a *group mind*, or specify that we regard the *losers* as *less deserving* or less capable of enjoyment (and this Professor Haberler expressly condemned), *we cannot, in the case of factor immobility, equivocally say which position is ' more favourable ' a priori*. This does not mean that we cannot say in any concrete case what the consequences of any given policy will be and under what value assumptions it would be desirable.

We may conclude that Professor Haberler's obviously insufficient definition of welfare accounts for his disregard of the real problem involved in his defence of free trade (or freer trade than is actually taking place), and for his view on the consequences of an imperfect mobility of factors. On any reasonable definition of welfare he would obviously fail in establishing his case in either respect.

II

We must now turn to the assumptions underlying Professor Haberler's ' model ' in order to show that—even if his welfare economics were at all tenable—their utterly unreal character would still rob his conclusions of all pertinence.

1. ' The external terms of trade will be assumed to be given.'[2] This procedure is entirely justified.[3] Provided the conclusions are not applied to the real world where the facts of international specialization and of the unequal importance of countries (especially since 1914 and even more since 1946), rule out the assumption that countries (apart from unimportant and isolated cases) *can*, even with the best of will, be in atomistic competition, all would be well. An entirely consistent and really ' pure ' model would have been constructed.

Professor Haberler however, continues:

' This does not mean that what will be said applies only to a country of so negligible a size in the world economy that it literally cannot by its action influence its terms of trade. It only means that the country is supposed to act competitively and that

---

[1] [But this is very odd. For if the prices of factors employed in import competing industries are depressed far enough, and they are wholly immobile they will displace imports. Trade will lead to no-trade, but merely to income redistribution! (1961.)]

[2] Haberler, ' Some Problems, etc.', op. cit., p. 224.

[3] Cf. above on its welfare implications.

the possibilities of monopolistic doctoring of the terms of trade and oligopolistic or bi-lateralistic complications will not be discussed in the present paper.'[1]

Little if any meaning can be attached to this qualification. Once a country's economic potential has grown beyond a certain critical relative size it cannot *help* acting non-competitively. Whether it is a question of tariff protection, or of subsidies, or of monetary changes, anything which a country may do (or, what is less realized, *may fail* to do) *cannot help* influencing its terms of trade (a depression, e.g. has the same influence on the demand for imports as tariffs). The international division of labour—because it leads to specialization—tends to reduce the critical limit beyond which a country cannot act competitively.

Fortunately the whole problem has received an exhaustive treatment in recent years. Mr. R. F. Kahn[2] in particular has shown the quantitative importance of the advantages (or rather the avoidance of disadvantages) which can be obtained by protective measures. Thus in this context there is no need to do more than to refer to these papers. Whether measures of protection on this ground are justified depends on the details of the concrete case. It must be known who protects what and under what precautions. The policy can certainly not be ruled out by introducing a highly coloured emotive appellation ' monopolistic doctoring of the terms of trade '. What is involved is the highly complex problem of the international distribution of wealth and welfare. The ' doctoring of the terms of trade '—by the poorer and weaker countries—might represent the only way in which a growing discrepancy of wealth and a growing instability of the world economic system might be mitigated—as a system of unilateral grants by the rich, having the same effects, may not always be possible. In so far as the whole discussion of the dollar shortage, in which Professor Haberler took so influential a part, and his advocacy of the abandonment of discrimination against the United States is entirely based on this point,[3] a restatement of the ' free trade reasoning ' in terms of the assumption that changes of the terms of trade can be safely neglected, is misleading.

2. The exclusion of the dynamic aspects of the problem (' dynamic aspects will also be ignored ')[4] has equally far-reaching consequences.

(a) We have already pointed to the peculiar way in which the

---

[1] Haberler, ' Some Problems, etc.', op. cit., p. 224.

[2] R. F. Kahn, op. cit., and also ' The Dollar Shortage and Devaluation ' (*Economia Internationale*, Geneva, February, 1950), in which the influence of the terms of trade is analysed from the point of view of the present position.

[3] Cf. Kahn, ' The Dollar Shortage ', op. cit.

[4] Haberler, ' Some Problems, etc.', op. cit., p. 224.

problem of unemployment is treated in Professor Haberler's essay. His unemployment is not the result of balance-of-payments disequilibria however induced.[1] It is the consequence of the refusal of certain productive factors to accept an 'economic' remuneration. What would happen if these factors accepted this price, and suffered a violent fall in income, is not analysed. This procedure allows the attribution of all evils to the rigidity of factor prices, i.e., in practice, to the rigidity of *wages* or, in other words to trade-union activity. At the same time it gives the impression that he had dealt with the problem of unemployment as it occurs in real life, and thus had, in an objective and broadminded manner, admitted, however much qualified, an important case for protection. This, of course, is not the case.

Comparative statistics rule out a discussion of the path of adjustment. But once a large-scale disequilibrium has arisen, the concept of the 'classic' eventual equilibrium position has no meaning *independently* of the *path of readjustment* because its position and character will be largely influenced, if not determined, by the path pursued.

The problem is very much that of the Marshallian analysis of moving equilibrium of which Mrs. Joan Robinson has wittily remarked ' the resources of mathematics fail us if the dog (the short-term position in pursuit of the moving equilibrium) is likely to bite through the tyres of the bicycle when the man slows his pace '. Comparative statistics will not tell us anything about the relative merits of policies. Once involuntary unemployment is admitted opportunity cost sinks below zero. Thus countries which are less likely to experience depressions might gain more by a system of protection which prevents the overlapping of depressions from richer and more unstable countries than they lose. The developments of 1949 (and of 1929–33 and 1937) are a case in point.

The same is true of unequal technical progress (quite apart from the 'infant industries' aspect of the problem). If we can expect swifter economic progress in one country periodically to require readjustments in the others which cannot in the short run be undertaken without unemployment (though devaluation might decrease the severity of the crisis)[2] a limitation of intercourse will not result only in losses (due to less perfect division of labour) but also in gains (avoidance of unemployment). Whether or not protection should be resorted to then will depend on the circumstances of the case.

(*b*) Equally obvious is the limitation of Professor Haberler's

[1] 'It should be observed that no adverse multiplier effects depending upon a temporary excess of imports over exports are involved. The balance of payments is in equilibrium all the time.' Haberler, ibid., p. 231.

[2] The improvement of the terms of trade of the protectionist group will represent an additional gain.

treatment of decreasing cost. He now at last admits that in Professor Graham's famous case of ' wrong ' specialization (and also in the somewhat similar and long-accepted case of ' infant ' industries) protection is justified. He merely casts doubt on the practical applicability of these theoretical constructions in real life. Current private money costs in his view do reflect long-run social real cost ratios.

So long as we assume that all areas under consideration are at an identical stage of technical development—e.g., in the late eighteenth century—this argument seems convincing.[1] Even then historical accidents might favour one country against another, and start it off on a career of technical supremacy which feeds upon itself; and, unless intervention then took place the countries left behind would not be able to restore their position. Thus current costs relationships do not reflect the long-run social cost relations which *could* be achieved on the basis of *present* technical knowledge, provided a *large-scale, conscious development programme* was instituted in the less favoured area. The cost of investment in technical education which he quoted is only one of these obstacles. The immense cost of basic public services which no single entrepreneur can afford, but which sharply decrease as development takes place, is another. Finally, there is the risk of competition of established (and thus low-cost) foreign industries.

Professor Haberler seems unaware of the deterrent effects on the supply of entrepreneurship in weaker countries of the existence of all-powerful giant industrial combines backed by the government of a very large country. In consequence it is hardly likely that industrial development in the poor area will follow the commands of *long-run* social costs. Professor Haberler sees the risks connected with foreign trade exclusively in the deterrent effects of trade restrictions on established or prospective export industries in dominant countries. From the point of view of the overwhelming majority of countries and populations the former case is infinitely more important and less manageable.

It will simply not do to treat the international economic problem under assumptions which disregard the differences in social and technical development and economic power between countries. The inhabitants of different countries do not have and hardly ever have had an equal chance. Nor has he any right to believe that he has demonstrated the case for *free* trade by a *reductio ad absurdam* by showing that

[1] Professor Haberler having admitted the case for protection for these cases arguing that ' *in principle* ' (my italics) ' the shifts (in the production opportunity curves) may be in either direction '. Diseconomies in the scale of production or in the case of industrial development of an underdeveloped area are hardly as *likely* (though no doubt they are ' possible in principle ') as economies. It should be stressed again and again that we are not discussing the division of labour between two *similar* areas at a *similar* stage of development.

' the possibility of favourable shifts ' in production opportunity costs may be ' in either direction '. The free-trade case is a case against intervention and not merely against import restrictions.[1] Some of the measures most sharply attacked in Haberler's writings, e.g., reciprocal trade and bulk-purchase agreements, preferences, aim precisely at securing a chance for ' infant ' export industries in third markets and increase the volume of trade beyond the point which would in fact be reached (due consideration being given to risk) if there were no intervention.

(c) This brings us to a further and hardly less-important point. Professor Haberler's model concentrates on the accomplished (static) equilibrium position. He does not ask whether it is likely that it will ever be realised or whether measures could be taken to speed it up. If ' objective ' cost relations are favourable their immediate exploitation is assumed (or if they are not exploited it is assumed that this must be due to the ' refusal ' of the workers to move or some other sort of malevolent-state-restrictionism or intervention). This emerges clearly from his treatment of ' mobility ' (which as we have already said has little to do with what is usually meant by that term). In his model *all* mobile factors are remunerated at a unique equilibrium rate, and no movement takes place, either of these factors, or by definition, of the immobile ones.[2]

In fact, there is movement; the problem is, however, not merely of the *width* of the gap between the remuneration of various factors but also the *speed* at which the movement takes place. In underdeveloped agricultural countries industrial development will, e.g., be handicapped by the fact that the earnings of agricultural labourers will be much higher than the marginal productivity of labour (which might well be zero or negative) because labour power is organised as a family and they share their earnings. Where labour is moved to the cities it has to be paid more in terms of money, though their effective standard of life remains low because they can no longer take recourse to the family in the same way. Thus protection will be necessary in any case to restore the proportionality between social and private costs in agriculture and manufacture. By *ensuring* movement real income is increased.

Admittedly in many cases (especially in mainly industrial countries) countries *protect* industries in which wages are low (e.g. British agriculture) in order to permit factors to remain in that occupation. In these cases, theoretically, subsidies to imports might be more appro-

---

[1] As he seems to think, e.g. p. 238, note 1.
[2] This is clear from note 1, p. 234. Earlier (p. 228) he gives the impression that he is going to deal with the problem of immobility as generally understood.

priate to cause movement towards high-productivity industries.[1] In any case, the argument based on income distribution is weakened by the consideration of productivity through a reallocation of resources. Professor Haberler is certainly right to call attention to the evils of an unthinking application of protection in these cases. But his condemnation must not be extended to include the efforts of underdeveloped or war-damaged, or for other reasons, less favoured countries to protect their *industrial reorganisation plans* from the stifling influence of the competition of technically more advanced countries.

(*d*) It should be emphasised, however, that in all cases in which intervention does take place to effect large-scale industrial reorganisation, measures must be devised to prevent its abuse by the protected interests. It is not, however, sufficient to point to the limits of human intelligence to argue that all intervention will *necessarily* result not in a quickening industrial development but in growing abuse. The *laissez faire* policy adopted by most Colonial Administrations, however incorruptible, in overseas territories has resulted in far less favourable conditions (when all allowance is made for the natural handicaps including the population problem of these territories), than were achieved by way of industrialisation by an admittedly corrupt and inefficient bureaucracy in Eastern Central Europe (e.g., Poland, Hungary, and Rumania) in the period of economic nationalism.

There is no *a priori* rule for maximising international welfare. We must by patient and detailed work establish the solution of each new problem or situation as it emerges. Far from decreasing the attraction of economics, the growing realism of our approach should enhance it, lifting it above the scholastic disputes about *a priori* tenets.

III

Professor Haberler's attempt to demonstrate the ' superiority ' of ' freer ' trade shows up the weakness of the foundations of his advocacy of policy measures which, e.g., the dropping of discrimination against dollar supplies, would inevitably decrease the standard of life in Western Europe. The recent change in economic trends has perhaps lessened the importance of this issue. It is to be hoped that when the further explosive expansion of United States productive capacity stimulated by rearmament will once more pose the dollar problem, this fact will have been realised not merely in Europe but

---

[1] But before such a policy is decided upon it might well be worth while to investigate the effects on the terms of trade of the increase in exports necessitated by the increase of imports consequent on the shift of factors from the liquidated ' low wage ' industry. Cf. e.g. Professor Robinson and R. L. Marris, ' The Use of Home Resources to Save Imports ' (*Economic Journal*, March 1950).

also in America. In that case we might expect that a renewed crisis of the Western World can be avoided by suitable measures through a greater consensus of opinion on international economic policy on both sides of the Atlantic.

POSTSCRIPT

Professor Haberler in his reply to my article was constrained to say that ' we should experiment with alternative hypothetical valuations ' in devising policies, blissfully ignoring that his whole case rested on being able to assume that ' in the following sense the situation after trade can be said to be better than before: if income were appropriately redistributed every individual would be made better off than before. It is not necessary that income should be redistributed.'[1] In his latest 'Survey of the Theory of International Trade' (Princeton, 1954, p. 16), he has virtually given up his case with a graceful reference to Professor Samuelson's essay showing the contradiction inherent in efforts trying to establish community indifference curves.

More recently economic freedom has been advocated and not because it leads to ' superior welfare position ' but because (without quoting Professor Galbraith) an ' affluent society ' can ' afford it '. The application of this argument to international trade would seem to mean that the poorer society ' ought ' to ' afford ' to adopt a system which favours the affluent. I would not exclude the possibility of some economic ' theorist ' making this somersault and arguing what amounts to the reverse of the original case for free trade. There is, of course, a perfectly good case against tariffs or any other policies by rich countries—including tolerance of unemployment—which would worsen the terms of trade of the poor.

My articles pointed out that the conditions in which nondiscrimination, convertibility and generally freer trade would promote welfare (even in the conventional sense) were not fulfilled, and that, therefore, liberalisation would increase inequality and limit the expansion of the national income of the weak partners. At first the protagonists of 'Free' Trade (e.g. Professor Haberler) called this an 'irrelevant catalogue ' of conditions for perfect competition, as if the ' Free Trade ' case had not been based precisely on that assumption. Subsequently, and without acknowledging my article on the dollar shortage which paid due debt to Professor Kahn's paper on 'Optimum Output',[2] a

[1] G. Haberler, 'Some Problems in the Price Theory of International Trade', *Economic Journal*, 1950, p. 226.
[2] *Economic Journal*, 1937.

large literature grew up under the misleading title of ' Second Best '.[1] This seemed to imply that if the ' best ' i.e. free trade (optimal distribution of resources under perfect competition, etc.) was not attainable at least there was a ' second best ', also based ' scientifically ' on the price-mechanism. This was misleading in the first place because the ' best ', as implicitly or explicitly assumed, *does not and could not exist under conditions such as characterise the world economy*, and which have been discussed in my article, e.g. unequal factor endowment and nonidentical ' production functions '; possibility of increasing returns; losses from repeated readjustments in productive pattern imposed on the weaker partner, etc. The expression ' second best ' is also misleading because it implies that at any one moment there is *a definite* system of factor allocation which is to be preferred. This is fallacious. There are as many patterns of allocation as time-horizons considered. It depends partly on how fast development can be enforced and how far the ' population ' (if such a concept were permissible), when made aware of the relevant facts, would wish to forego consumption. Recommendations require political decisions and cannot be deduced from ' economic ' considerations.

Thus, this further attempt to secure a second wind for a solution based on a ' modified ' form of ' free trade ' or at least methods of control ' conformable ' to the price mechanism, even though more sophisticated than the original case, fails equally.

[1] Cf. e.g. P. G. Lipsey and K. Lancaster, ' The General Theory of the Second Best ', *Review of Economic Studies*. 1959.

FULL EMPLOYMENT AND TRADE

3

THE INTERNATIONAL ASPECTS OF FULL EMPLOYMENT

PREVIOUS studies have considered the problem of how to create and maintain conditions in which the resources of a closed economic system would be both fully and efficiently employed. We must now turn to analyse the consequences and implications of the fact that the world economy is not a homogeneous system. It is, and will in the foreseeable future remain, a collection of some scores of sovereign national or regional units of widely different economic, social and political constitution, at widely different stages of economic and technical development. It does not possess common executive organs which can evolve and pursue a coherent economic policy in order to solve the problem under discussion: even if all units had identical views about the broad character of the common policy to be adopted.

The classical theory of foreign trade was based on an economic model which was supposed to function automatically in response to changes in demand and supply acting through free markets on the profit motive. Under its assumptions, foreign trade does not in essence differ from inter-regional trade. In that system *ex hypothesi* no conscious policy is needed: in that system any Government ' interference ' with ' unseen ' economic forces of adjustment is assumed to result in economic *malaise* only. Given these assumptions, the economic consequence of the existence of national units was taken to amount to no more than that divergences in economic changes were more marked, the relative immobility of factors, especially of labour, greater, and differences in productivity resulting from the uneven geographical international distribution of resources larger between, than within any one of the national units. It may be objected that the ' classical ' theory recognized the difference in monetary adjustment between and within countries and evolved the analysis of gold movements. This is undoubtedly correct. But on the gold coin standard identical gold movements take place between and within countries. The establishment of Central Banks must, from the ' Liberal ' point of view, be regarded logically as the first step to ' State interference '. The really logical followers of that school, of whom Professor Mises may be mentioned, in fact advocate ' free banking ' linked by gold automatism.

As soon as it is recognized that the community organized as a State can, and in certain cases, must, take conscious action to secure the optimum exploitation of its natural resources and manpower, the scope of the study of international economics is completely altered. The non-existence of appropriate world organisations and executive organs immediately raises new problems: the scope of international, as contrasted with national, problems must then be defined as embracing that field of economic activity in which appropriate executive action cannot be taken without affecting relations with economic units over which the executive taking the action has no constitutional regulative or coercive power.[1]

The strength of the challenge of so-called ' Liberal Internationalism ' is derived from this fact. Its slogans are clear-cut and decidedly attractive: the abstention of states from entering into commercial quarrels; the refusal to use sovereign power to grant privileges to private people by way of the innumerable methods of protectionism; the clear distinction between profits and politics; these considerations must appeal *a priori* to all who wish to further international amity and general progress. The argument that nations should be so closely knit by commercial ties that each should be unable by itself to lift the sword sounds more than plausible to a generation which has become sceptical about the efficacy of formal pacts in preventing hostilities. Free economy and free trade, however, may mean—and in the inter-war period have meant—economic dependence and insecurity for the majority of the population and a standard of life well below the potential level corresponding to the increase in productivity. If considered in this light, the moral precepts of the Liberals, however attractive at first, appear somewhat artificial and false.

In the present essay an attempt will be made to analyse: first, the conditions in which full employment can be maintained in a world economic system consisting of different national units following divergent economic policies; secondly, the methods available to a single country to enable her to pursue a policy of full employment if the prerequisites of an international full employment policy cannot be attained.

Derived and spontaneous balances in international payments

The international balance of payments of any country can be un-balanced for two kinds of reasons. The disequilibrium might, first, be due to the failure of other countries to maintain ' full employment '

---

[1] These economic units might therefore either passively comply with the regulation or induce another equally sovereign executive to take retaliatory steps.

effective demand; or to its own failure to do so while others maintain such demand; or finally to its own efforts to secure full employment when others fail to do so. We shall call active or passive balances which are due to this cause ' derived balances '. Balances which would persist in spite of all countries having attained full employment—balances which were the *sole* object of analysis under classical assumptions—we shall denominate ' spontaneous balances '. It is not necessary to point out that actually recorded balances are composed of both elements. Any action, moreover, taken to adjust such actual balances will have repercussions which will, in all probability, change not only the magnitude of the balance but also its composition.

Derived balance due to slumps abroad

Let us start from a position in which all countries are fully employed and there is equilibrium in the balance of payments. We understand under this term the position in which the short-term capital position, i.e., the liquid reserve, of a country is unchanging; any long-term borrowing, however, is offset by an increase in the productive capacity of the country.[1] If we now suppose that a slump starts in any country, all other countries will immediately be affected—and this in two ways. With home demand sagging, industries of the depressed country will increase their sales pressure abroad (after a time probably aided by a fall in money wages). The fall in effective demand in the depressed country will, secondly, mean a fall of its demand for foreign products. Thus the balances of payments of all countries will be thrown out of equilibrium by the slump, even if they had balanced before its occurence. The depressed country will improve its balance: all others not immediately affected by the slump will experience a worsening.

Two consequences follow: first, if the deficit countries do not *increase* their home demand, the depression will automatically spread. A deficiency in the balance of payments is equivalent to a fall in demand, because relatively more goods are bought from abroad whose production does not create incomes at home, and/or relatively fewer home-produced goods, whose production would have created incomes, will be exported.[2] If, in order to stabilize employment at home, the deficiency in effective demand caused by the slump in foreign demand is

---

[1] Our definition is unsymmetrical in the sense that equilibrium cannot be said to exist if the country is getting potentially poorer, but only if it gets potentially richer.

[2] The slump in demand will have a disproportionate effect, for the apprehension caused by it will immediately curtail expenditure. It will start a secondary deflationary spiral.

G

offset by an expansion of home demand, while the slump abroad continues, this will mean a further worsening of the balance of trade.

If the deficit countries possess sufficient liquid reserves, they may be willing and able to tolerate the deficit without taking steps to restore the balance. If the depressed country is more or less of a size similar to that of the other countries; if the liquid reserves of the world are more or less equally distributed; and if the forces of expansion in the rest of the world are strong enough to offset the fall in the world effective demand due to the slump in any one country, the export surplus acquired by the depressed country may be sufficient to overcome the original disequilibrating force, the export surplus having replaced the original fall in home investment (or consumption). If, however, the depressed country represents an important fraction of the effective money demand of the world, and/or if the liquid reserves of the world economy are not spread evenly among all countries, but are concentrated in a country which is liable to spasmodic deep depressions, and is unable to achieve such internal conditions and international economic relations in which it would periodically disgorge the liquid reserves accumulated in slumps, then a deflationary bias will be imparted to the whole world economy. In that case other countries will not in the longer run be able to tolerate a loss of liquid reserves.

But if the deficit countries take measures to prevent the worsening of their balance of trade this must, for the same reasons, aggravate the slump in the country where it started, since it was the growth in its foreign balance which had initially mitigated the fall in home effective demand.[1] A grave danger arises, moreover, that each country, because it possesses only limited liquid reserves, will try to remedy the diminution of external demand, not by measures increasing home demand, but by operating on the foreign balance, by cutting imports and stimulating exports. The beggar-my-neighbour policy[2] will extend the area of deflationary pressure to more and more countries and will reduce the maximum scope of the international division of labour at full employment. Yet because retaliation will follow with a decreasing lag as the slump deepens, such measures will fail to increase the actual employment in any one country appreciably at any given moment.[3]

---

[1] As would also the origination of an ' autonomous ' slump in the deficit countries through the shock to expectations. The ' spilling ' over of the deflation to the other country will cause more or less ' automatic ' unemployment in the world system. The shock caused by this deflationary impact and the secondary autonomous unemployment caused by it might be quantitatively more important than the primary derived unemployment.

[2] Cf. Mrs. Joan Robinson, *Essays in the Theory of Employment*, 1947, p.210 et seq.

[3] In the great depression Britain was for some time faced with countries which were by their financial prejudice prevented from retaliation.

Derived balance due to full employment policy

An attempt to achieve full employment at home presents to some extent identical problems. The country—which might be supposed to be in short run and intermediate equilibrium—by increasing its own effective demand will tend to export less and import more than hitherto. Unless other countries fall in with the new policy the country attempting to pursue it will be forced either to desist, or to increase its degree of self-sufficiency, or to borrow from abroad.

An attempt to increase employment accompanied by increasing self-sufficiency would, of course, not represent a beggar-my-neighbour policy because the *absolute* foreign demand of the country would remain unchanged (or might even increase) even though the ratio of its foreign to its total demand would decrease. But while in the short run this attempt would be justified as it would increase real income, and while no retaliation ought to be feared, as increased protection in these circumstances (and other things being equal) would not involve a net increase of employment abroad,[1] the potential maximum real income attainable *if stable full employment were achieved all round without protection* would be higher.

Autonomous disequilibrium and the prevention of inflation

Deficiences and surpluses in the current balance of payments might occur even if all countries pursued full employment policies. Such a deficiency will represent a primary net ' expansionist ', and a surplus, a primary net ' contractive ' influence in the world system. The deficit country derives an import surplus from other countries, i.e. receives from them part of the fruits of their current productive effort. Three possible cases should be distinguished:

(i) If the maintenance of full employment is the policy of each of the member countries of the world economic system such deficits must be cancelled by a surplus which represents a voluntary reduction of effective demand (saving) in the creditor countries.

(ii) If it is not accompanied by such voluntary reduction, corresponding to consciously planned loans, the spilling over of the effective demand of the ' inflating ' (deficit) country (on the basis of its gold reserves or of excessive loans) will result in true inflation in the surplus countries and in an involuntary fall in their available home real income.

---

[1] It might, however, involve a shift of the demand of the full employment country for foreign exports, hence of employment from one foreign country to another as the greater autarky results in an increase of import demand for certain (primary) products while it leads to the fall in demand for others. Even such a shift of demand might, therefore, result in retaliation.

The inflating (deficit) country, by using its accumulated reserves, will compete with the home consumers of the (fully employed) surplus country for its home supplies, and by bidding for its own exports reduce the supplies available to the surplus country.

(iii) The export surpluses at full employment might represent the servicing of foreign loans. The deficit then is the means by which payment is effected and must be accompanied by a decrease of the effective home demand of the repaying, and an increase in effective demand above full employment level in the receiving country.

Deficiences and surpluses in the balance of payments of member countries which do not in the first instance arise either out of international long-term development schemes or out of depressions, must be dealt with by direct readjustment in the countries who have acquired an unfavourable balance themselves, with a co-ordinated policy in other countries, lest the readjustment should lead to a general deflation. An attempt to deal with autonomous deficits by general monetary expansion would lead to general over-employment.

Balances in the current account of international payments and the intermediate equilibrium

Both autonomous and derived balances may be associated with long-term foreign lending. This would re-establish 'short-term' equilibrium in the sense that there would be no change in the liquid reserves of the countries concerned. Only if the long-term borrowing is paralleled by at least an equivalent increase in real productive capacity can we regard intermediate equilibrium as assured, in the sense described above, (that no subsequent fall in real income will be produced in the long run by the obligation to service and repay the loan). We must distinguish, moreover, between the ' capacity to repay ' of a country and its ' capacity to produce real income '. If the creditor country does not accept repayment by permitting an import surplus (i.e. in all probability, unless it can maintain an over-full employment internal demand), no a priori criterion can guarantee that borrowing, however used, will be paralleled by at least as great an increase in the ' capacity to repay '. An effort to repay, as we have shown above, would result in a cumulative deflationary process. The second criterion is somewhat less elusive. Unless the borrowing is accompanied by an increase in the capacity of the community to increase real income, i.e. unless its productivity increases, pari passu, either because of an increase of capital equipment or labour skill, the cessation of loans will result in an abrupt fall in the national real income.

If it could be assumed that full and stable employment is maintained in the world economic system as a whole, the problem of international borrowing would be relatively simple.[1]

As soon, however, as we drop the assumption of general and partial equilibrium new complications arise. Which country will develop a deficit and be forced to borrow[2] will depend on the foreign trade multiplier, on the investment multiplier, and on the degree of employment. A further influence will be exerted by the historical position in the countries concerned. This will determine the rapidity with which excess capacity is absorbed by increasing employment. As long as confidence is maintained, foreign investment, once it starts, will tend to justify itself. During the continuance of the upward movement the import of capital might sustain a deficit in the ' wrong ' direction, i.e. by mature countries. If the ' lending ' enables the surplus country to maintain its own employment and income by increasing exports, an interruption of the process would evoke resistance. Yet this lending may well result in a growing disequilibrium in the deficit country which in the longer run might lead to a sudden fall in its real income when the process can no longer be sustained.

If, however, certain rich areas were unable to maintain full employment without far-reaching reforms for which they are unprepared, induced deficit balances on the part of developing countries, if carefully directed to avoid over-borrowing, could at one and the same time decrease the discrepancy in capital intensity between different areas of the world and maintain employment, i.e. utilize for world development resources which would otherwise remain unemployed.

Readjustments in the balance of trade and full employment

In order to analyse the international implications of a full employment policy we were forced to distinguish between derived and autonomous balances in the international payments of a country. The classical doctrine of foreign trade did not recognize this distinction because it was based on the assumption that general equilibrium, i.e. full employment, in the system as a whole would continuously be maintained or at least automatically and rapidly regained. The problem of the international repercussion of business fluctuations in any one country, i.e. the problem of international fluctuations in the employment of the system as a whole, was neglected. All deficiences (though not equally surpluses), which may have been the result of other countries and thus the whole world economy, losing equilibrium, were regarded as a sign of disequilibrium of the country suffering from it.

[1] See O.E.P. article reprinted Section 6, No. 17.
[2] Cf. Knapp, 'International Capital Movements and Verifications', *Review of Economic Studies*, 1944.

So long as business cycles were regarded as an inevitable phenomenon this attitude was completely consistent. But it imparted an *a priori* deflationary bias to the world economic system.

The existence until 1914 of vigorous expansionist forces prevented this bias from exerting its basic influence. The peaceful development of the world economy enabled countries to undertake readjustments gradually. Even when these readjustments were aggravated by the cyclical fluctuations of the system as a whole there was no question of the complete reshaping of the international economic relations of important countries.

Once a model is investigated in which full employment is preserved, or restored automatically, the analysis of the problem whether certain methods of readjustment are more or less compatible with the maintenance of full employment are implicitly excluded. The classical approach by its assumptions prevents the investigation of the question which it sets out to answer, i.e. the maximization of output or welfare in a system of independent economic units. Without admitting that changes through time are not merely possible but highly likely and that they might be caused by the dynamics of the system itself, economic theory cannot provide a useful basis for determining policy. Static analysis is applicable only after all adjustments have been made and long-run equilibrium reached. In actual life, however, the establishment of equilibrium takes time and if the system as a whole or any of its parts are non-stationary, a policy, the aim of which is to establish equilibrium as prescribed by the conditions prevailing at the initial moment, may result in a maldistribution of resources on account of the changes which have occurred in the meantime.[1] If the quantity and quality of productive resources in the system as a whole changes or if the degree of the employment alters, the classical argument cannot be applied.

The ways of readjustment

We may now turn to the more systematic analysis of the ways in which a deliberate alteration in the balance of current payments can be brought about. Action can be taken to cut imports, visible or invisible, or increase exports, or both. The two general methods available for the purpose, i.e. acting through variation of total income either in terms of the home currency or of foreign currencies are

[1] It may, for instance be claimed that industrial protection in agricultural areas reduces the real income of the system as a whole, and each of its constituent parts. But this conclusion follows only if we assume given existing resources, i.e. given existing skills and given, what is even more unreal to assume, the existing capital intensity per head disregarding, moreover, the redistribution of income which results from State interference.

deflation and the depreciation of the currency. Specific methods to achieve the same ends are the limitations of imports and stimulus to export (a) indirectly through the price mechanism, i.e. by duties or subsidies, and (b) more directly by quotas or discretionary licensing, bulk purchase and reciprocal trade arrangements respectively.

Each of these methods will have two effects, both internally and abroad. First, they will influence employment at home and abroad. We shall term this the employment effect. This effect itself is not simple. The elimination of deficiency or surplus will in itself represent a fall or increase in the effective demand at home and abroad. This change may have an impact effect on the general employment position, i.e. start a secondary inflationary or deflationary spiral. Secondly, the readjustment will influence the direction of the productive effort at home and abroad, i.e. productivity.

The problem of minimizing the adverse effect of any readjustment both for the country undertaking it and for the world as a whole, depends therefore on (a) prevention of unemployment and (b) the minimization of the interference with the optimum international division of labour. These two effects in practice unfortunately often constitute alternatives, i.e. either unemployment can be avoided at the cost of limiting the effective international division of labour or *vice versa*. The optimum degree of the international division of labour, however, is itself an elusive concept. The state of employment and demand co-determine it. If, i.e. the demand for a country's products falls sharply and irrevocably, part of the readjustment will consist in replacing imported products by home output. It may well be, however, that the inherent sluggishness of reaction, monopolistic elements, the imperfections of markets, risk and other vital factors, traditionally relegated from economic theory as frictions, will prevent a rapid readjustment. State interference in this case, though it may appear to be wanton would, in fact, merely speed readjustment.

The danger of secondary spirals will be minimized if the extent of readjustment is minimized. The maintenance of the total short run effective demand in the system as a whole will be facilitated if the worsening of the real terms of trade is minimized by co-operative steps sustaining effective demand in the system as a whole. Thus—in the short run—the interest of the country undertaking the readjustment coincides with the interest of other countries.[1] If she is, moreover, not permitted by suitable international arrangements to undertake the readjustment partly by expanding her exports without undue worsening

---

[1] In the long run the worsening of the terms of trade will benefit other countries. This contradiction explains the favour which import quotas enjoyed in importing countries such as Britain, though they deliberately worsened the terms of trade.

of her terms of trade, she will inevitable be forced to rely mainly, or even entirely, on the alternative of excluding imports.

Yet the reduction of the real income of the world as a whole will be greater if the readjustment were achieved by cutting imports rather than by increasing exports. The more favourable the terms on which a country is permitted to increase her exports (e.g. if she is permitted to use discriminating methods), the less she will rely on the decrease of her imports as a method of achieving balance. A discriminating policy thus may well result in a smaller alteration in the short run in the international division of labour and less violent repercussions in other countries. One of the most important arguments in favour of the establishment of an international currency and investment authority is that it might enable the deflationary impact of a given readjustment upon other countries to be minimized through co-operative action. The risk of cumulative retaliation would thereby be reduced. It should, of course, be borne in mind that in the *longer* run it will be more important and necessary to induce a shift of factors from obsolete industries than to prevent such shifts from having deflationary effects.

(*a*) *Deflation.* Readjustment by deflation is obtained by reducing effective money demand in terms of home currency. This reduction will *pari passu* depress the demand curve for imports while cutting the demand for home products. Unless the degree of monopoly could be appropriately changed, or all money incomes can be reduced by general agreement or legislative action proportionately in each case, the eventual readjustment, i.e. the fall in the money cost of home products, must come through a pressure on wages, i.e. unemployment.

This method must *a priori* be excluded as a means of full employment policy. Yet, as we have seen, it is impossible to avoid at least the *primary* impact of a deflation which affected a foreign country, if *positive* steps are not taken to counteract the fall in effective demand at home which the unfavourable balance implies. The consequent fall in the expected rate of profit would in all probability start a further secondary deflationary spiral which might in the end carry the economic system further than even the depression in the country where it started would warrant.

Under the orthodox gold standard ' rules of the game ' a country suffering from an excess of out-payments had to protect its gold reserve by increasing the bank rate. If it possessed short-term balances abroad (or if the confidence in its ability to pay was unshaken) this mechanism in the short run led to a withdrawal of (or influx of foreign) capital from abroad. Provided the disequilibrium was of a minor character this influx, together with the consequences of the automatic lessening of the effects of the original relative over-investment (or increase in consumption) through the worsening of the trade balance, was sufficient to restore the short-term balance of payments without having to rely on a secondary, consciously generated, fall in effective demand. If, moreover, the long-term expectations were favourable, the increase in the short-term rate of interest did not result in a further fall in the level of effective demand.

If a further change in the current balance of payments was required it depended on a complex set of factors whether the terms of trade would be worsened or improved in these circumstances, thus increasing or mitigating the extent of the required readjustment. If the internal deflationary pressure in the depressed country was very great and the elasticity of supply low, its terms of trade would worsen sharply. Past experience, however, is no clue whatever as depressions in important countries hardly ever coincided with full employment. With falling demand which, therefore, hardly responds to price changes the terms of trade were mainly determined by the elasticity of supply.[1] In a partially fully employed world economic system changes in the terms of trade are likely to mitigate rather than worsen from the point of view of the world, the effects on depression on the balance of payments of the depressed country. How important this effect is likely to be depends on the respective price elasticities of demand and supply and on the ratio of the effective demand of the world as a whole to the effective demand of the depressed area. In this analysis it is, of course, assumed that the depression is not permitted to overlap into other countries.

The original theory of foreign trade, by assuming that purely competitive conditions can be applied to relations between countries, excludes this problem from its purview.[2] It has long been recognized that a country can, by protective devices, ' make the foreigner pay '. An analysis of the economic consequences of measures or policies which influence the volume of effective demand in a country has only recently been undertaken.[3] Even this analysis has not made it explicit that a variation in effective demand can have the same result on foreign countries as tariffs. If the price elasticity of demand of a country for

[1] The terms of trade therefore went regularly in favour of industrial countries in depressions and moved in their disfavour in recovery. The United States unfortunately is not merely the strongest industrial country but also an important primary producer, so that the net effect of a depression on its balance of trade cannot a priori be taken as a mitigating factor.

[2] Without quite recognising the fact that the subjects of international trade were countries having sovereign policies. Beginning with Mill, the monopolistic character of foreign trade became apparent. The revision of the theory began by considering the problem of tariffs. Cf. N. Kaldor, Economica, 1940, and T. Scitovszky, Review of Economic Studies, 1942.

[3] An adequate treatment of the problem can only be found in Mrs. Joan Robinson's two essays on Foreign Trade and Exchange (op. cit., pp. 183-231).

foreign products is less than unity, if its income elasticity is considerable, and if, furthermore, the country represents an appreciable part of the world supply or demand of certain commodities, the fall of its effective demand would have a similar effect on its terms of trade[1] as the imposition of tariffs. The effect on total real income of the country will, of course, depend on whether the loss resulting from the consequent decrease in employment is bigger than the increase due to the change in the terms of trade.

Measures which enable the increase of the national income of a country either by internal expansion or by technical progress, while at the same time not involving the abolute worsening in the total real income of the rest of the world, cannot be said to be exploitative. This is true even if these measures involved a worsening of the long run position of foreign countries relatively to the state which would rule if the increase in the national real income would have been brought about automatically, i.e. without a deliberate (protective or discriminatory) policy. We may thus contrast exploitative and constructive measures of protection, at least in the short run.

The exclusion of deflation as one of the methods of readjustment in a world pledged to maintain full employment does not absolve us from analysing its consequences on the foreign demand and supply of a country. Deflation will cause an immediate downward shift in the demand schedules of the country. This will increase the price elasticity of supply of exports and potential exports given demand abroad. Conversely, once a deflationary spiral has started it may produce further downward shifts of the home demand and the supply schedule. We are here confronted not with a single demand curve but a family of demand and supply curves whose positions are determined by the level of income. Yet, these unavoidable shifts in the home demand curves for potential exports and the resultant shifts in the supply curves constitute a vital element in the situation. The shifts will be most marked in the case of capital equipment. The demand for foodstuffs and essential raw materials will be more stable. The demand for luxuries might remain inelastic to income changes up to a certain point and then fall steeply when people can no longer strive to maintain their previous standard of life.

[1] The exclusion of an analysis of fluctuations has prevented classical economists, e.g. Mill, from applying the analysis of reciprocal demand to this contingency. An attempt (cf. Viner, *Studies in the Theory of International Trade*) to explain obvious disequilibria caused by the transfer of gold from one country to another by reference to differences in the final velocity of circulation had to break down because this explanation involved a change in the total effective demand of the system as a whole according to whether funds were transfered from high to low velocity areas. The resultant general fluctuation could not be analysed by the conceptual tools of orthodox theory.

The consequences of simultaneous changes in the degree of employment in more than one country are similar if not identical to those which can be observed in a closed economic system. The analysis applied to the probable consequences of price and wage changes during fluctuations in business activity in a closed economy, can with increased force be used in an international system consisting of inter-connected economies, because of the greater uncertainty about the future policy and behaviour of sovereign countries. The effects on the demand for any one country's produce of a fall in price are highly conjectural. They will depend on the reactions of competitors in other countries and also on the state of expectations in each of the countries which again are inter-connected. All countries may well sink and rise together without their international balance, in distinction to the volume of total trade, altering in a significant manner. Any readjustment, therefore, which involves a deflationary shock must, because of the severe consequences and strains evoked by a fall in effective demand, be guarded against. This should be carefully borne in mind when considering the readjustment even of autonomous disequilibria. In a world economy which naturally or consciously tends towards full employment, the readjustment will be relatively easy and it is this case alone which has been analysed by classical economists. But the case in which readjustments are accompanied by foreign depression should be very carefully differentiated from cases where they are not so accompanied. The reaction of foreign countries to an effort to increase exports will in the two cases be totally different.

(b) *Devaluation*.[1] The second general method of readjustment consists in altering the equivalent of the total effective demand of the country by changing the value of its currency in terms of other currencies, without changing its volume or distribution in terms of the home currency. It is, therefore, a special case of a policy of export premia and import duties of a uniform proportion. If we could assume that effective home demand, as it asserts itself in the market, is a sufficient criterion from a social point of view for judging the urgency of needs, and that therefore an unrestricted play of the price mechanism will on the one hand choke off the least import demand and will stimulate the most effective production, devaluation would seem not only the fairest method of readjustment, but would also minimize the losses and maximize the gains for the community. The efficacy of devaluation as a method of readjustment will depend on whether the relative price elasticity at home and abroad is substantial enough

---

[1] [This problem has been treated in a more expanded form below. Section 3. Enough from the present text has been included, however, to retain the thread of the argument.]

to enable the necessary shifts in production and consumption to take place without causing *considerable* frictional unemployment.

What are the conditions for these hypotheses being fulfilled? We shall have to differentiate strictly between systems which are generally fully employed, partially unemployed and generally under-employed.

The first and not least important case to be investigated is the readjustment of autonomous disequilibria in single countries when others are fully employed. The foreign price elasticity of demand for the particular countries producing under these conditions might be assumed to be high.[1] There is no *a priori* reason under these circumstances to fear that competitive countries would immediately take steps to counteract the stimulus of the devaluation to exports of the readjusting country. Thus, even that part of the effect of the devaluation which is due to the substitution of the commodities exported by the devaluing country for identical goods produced elsewhere will not be neutralized. Thus depreciation might be able to neutralize the effects of over-employment in any one country on the balance of payments, even if, as we shall see presently, it may not under all circumstances be an appropriate method of dealing with unfavourable balances induced by a depression abroad. This is the only case envisaged and investigated by the classical school under their assumptions of full employment and/or automatic and quick readjustment abroad.

The effectiveness of depreciation as a method of stimulating *exports* will depend (i) first and foremost on the price elasticity of foreign demand abroad, (ii) secondly, on whether and to what extent two internal effects are likely. Of these the first is that depreciation, by increasing the internal price of potential exports, discourages home demand and thus increases the proportion of the currently produced output which is available for exports. The increase of exports is reinforced by the second effect, which consists in the investment of new resources in the export industries and in industries competing with imports.

An effective depreciation implies the adaptation of the structure of industry. Such adaptation is bound to be slow and it is even questionable, moreover, whether in violently changing conditions, which slumps and booms imply, it would be desirable. If changes in the balance of payments originating in developments abroad are due not to a trend but to cyclical fluctuations, if therefore the causes to which the change in the state of the balance of payments is due are not permanent, and if subsequent movements are not in the same direction, the accomplished readjustment—i.e. the loss of the old investment

[1] This is the most important reason why the close co-ordination of employment policies internationally through appropriate organs is so important.

undertaken as a result of the readjustment—will turn out to be unjustified and the new investment misdirected.

The theoretical advantages of the depreciation as a 'long-term policy' in that it represents an equal 'impartial' stimulus (and hindrance) and that therefore it is supposed to select the 'most productive' industries for stimulation (either for exports or to replace imports), render it unsuitable as a policy to deal with cyclical fluctuations, where, in the short run, it would leave the 'less' productive specific factors wholly unemployed. A more flexible policy which would enable a more gradual adjustment of available factors in the export sector would seem to accord more with the needs of a general full employment policy. In the long run, nevertheless, measures must be taken to shift those factors which have permanently lost their previous productivity on account of the change in conditions into more productive use. But the current net private returns are an insecure guide in this respect.

The same conclusion emerges if the effect of depreciation on *imports* is analysed. As long as full employment is maintained, price elasticity of home demand for imported commodities (even luxuries) may be very low. In consequence readjustments may be forced on the country to secure sufficient exports to pay for these imports at the cost of lowering the standard of life of the whole community by an adverse turn of its terms of trade. A non-selective method of repressing effective home demand for foreign products such as depreciation would in these conditions involve unnecessary sacrifice. This would be increased, the greater the difficulties in the way of an increase in exports.

As Mrs. Robinson[1] pointed out, foreign assets (and income from them) and foreign debts (and their burden) can be treated as exports or imports. Their repercussion on the balance of payments will depend whether they are contracted in terms of the home or foreign currencies. Debts in terms of home currency 'may be regarded as an export of which the home supply is perfectly inelastic'. They would tend to respond favourably to depreciation. If, however, a country is the centre of a network of foreign payments—e.g. Britain—the threat of repeated devaluation will cause foreign clients to withdraw their working balances (which in effect amount to a cheap credit from the point of view of the debtor) or demand a 'gold guarantee' which in effect transforms them into liabilities in terms of gold.[2] But if the debt is fixed in terms of foreign currency 'they may be regarded as

[1] Ibid., p. 196
[2] The Joint Plan of Experts does not specify whether the Fund or the debtor country (the debt takes the form of a sale of the home currency to the fund) will shoulder the loss consequent on the devaluation of the debtor's currency. The U.S. proposal (White Plan) which was the basis of the new draft provided that the debtor indemnified the Fund (para. IV, 4, p. 9).

an import for which home demand is perfectly inelastic '. The position of the country will be aggravated by depreciation. The same is true (except if otherwise the assets would depreciate because of default) of foreign assets in terms of the home currency.

As long as fluctuations can be assumed to be small, or if any initial readjustment required on account of the break in the economic development is not considerable, general internal measures, e.g. taxation, might safeguard the interests of the community. The same applies to a completely collectivized system or to a system which reserves foreign economic transactions to government monopoly.

We conclude, therefore, that in a world economic system in which sharp economic fluctuations in important countries continue, other countries wishing to maintain full employment can ordinarily not rely on depreciation of their currency as a short-term method by which external fluctuations are made compatible with internal stability. Depreciation as a method suffers not merely from the drawback of causing a deterioration of their real income through an attempted— yet partly unsuccessful—stimulus of export and consequent ' unnecessary ' worsening of their terms of trade, but also from the decisive disadvantage of not being subtle or potent enough to prevent unnecessary frictional unemployment.

The reasons for the failure to realize these limitations of depreciation as a means of readjustment are threefold. First, prior to the British return to the gold standard and its reversal in 1931, devaluation was practiced by weaker overseas countries where conditions for its relatively successful working obtained. Secondly, the amount of readjustment required in most of those cases was relatively small. Thirdly, where the extent of the required readjustment was large the depression of the domestic economy was not avoided, i.e. effective demand declined and the consequent under-employment of the domestic economy ' helped ' the readjustment of the foreign balance by changing the relevant home price elasticities. The application of past experiences to problems of fully employed economies is misleading.[1]

---

[1] Lord Keynes (*Hansard*, House of Lords, May 23, 1944, col. 844) affirms that the liberty of changing the value of the currency and the management of the rate of interest permitted by a control of capital movements would ensure the conditions necessary to maintain full employment at home, irrespective of conditions abroad, and without further direct control of foreign trade. As we shall see, legitimate doubt may be entertained whether the monetary plan accepted by the experts permits full readjustment by devaluation. In any case his hope is justified only under the implicit assumption that foreign elasticities of demand for British exports are high. In conditions such as will presumably prevail after the war, this tacit assumption is highly unrealistic. Devaluation as a method of readjustment thus will at best be ineffective, at worst it will aggravate the problem. Moreover, if the new plan is accepted it will not be possible to devalue all currencies of an interrelated area, e.g. the sterling area, together, if some of the constituent members are not

(c) *Direct Control*—(i) *Method and Aim.* The effectiveness of devaluation has been found wanting as a method maintaining balance. The reasons which render devaluation ineffective seem to originate in the low price elasticity of foreign demand for a fully employed (industrial) country's exports when under-employment is prevalent elsewhere. Measures in two directions can therefore be expected to be helpful, directions which were not sufficiently differentiated from one another in analysis because they were in practice necessarily intermingled.

The first method takes the effective demand abroad as given and attempts to minimize the disequilibrium in the balance of payments by diverting trade from its normal channels, and/or by turning the terms of trade by specific measures in favour of the readjusting country. To this extent it might be termed exploitative. The second method is to increase by conscious action the foreign demand for home products. We must finally analyse the technical arrangements which permit a country with a given economic system to utilize these methods.

The first method will utilize the fact that neither the elasticities of foreign demand for various export items nor the elasticities of home demand for various import items are homogeneous. The effect upon the balance of payments and of appropriately differentiated export premia and import controls (tariffs, bulk purchases, etc.) is more favourable than a depreciation equivalent to the *average* of the export premia and import restrictions. The direct regulation of imports permits the exclusion of those which appear to be least urgent from a social point of view. The pressure to export is relieved. Thus in cases where depreciation cannot succeed in improving the balance of trade easily, differential methods may still sometimes do the job.

This amounts to a direct control of the home propensity to consume foreign goods and of the supply of exports. A reduction in foreign demand in such a system would find its expression not in the unemployment of industry, but (i) in a smaller fall in the value of exports achieved by decreasing the price to the foreign buyer, and (ii) in the restriction or direct control of imports.

The utilization of the second method is somewhat limited by the fact that the country which is contemplating the policy will be suffering

suffering from a deficiency in the balance of payments (partly because of the deficiency of Britain herself). Thus Britain may suffer from a worsening of the terms of trade to these countries and the devaluation of sterling may not improve the position unless full employment policy is discontinued and the price elasticity of demand increased. The attempt to impose on economically interrelated but politically sovereign economies ' rules of the games ' which do not apply *within* sovereign countries must lead either to political union or to the economic paralysis of smaller political units.

from an excess of outpayments and thus the *laissez-faire* method of promoting effective foreign demand by the granting of foreign loans does not come under consideration. To be successful the method must automatically ensure that an increase in the demand for foreign products will be matched by an increase in the foreign demand for home products, or rather that the maintenance of the home demand for foreign products in the teeth of a depression abroad will result in a re-expansion of the foreign demand for home products.[1] It does not represent a mere diversion of existing foreign demand from the cheapest market, but the creation of conditions in which foreign demand can be induced to increase to the mutual benefit of all participants.

(ii) *Modification of the Current Balance of Payments through Direct Action not affecting Total Effective Demand directly*. The first method of achieving readjustment is to stimulate exports and to restrict imports by measures which are not ' monetary ' in character.

If the Government has full monopoly over foreign economic relations it can directly secure this aim. Economic systems based (at least mainly) on private enterprise, which wish to maintain full employment, will have to achieve similar results by tariffs, quotas, exchange restrictions and export subsidies. *Unilateral* bulk purchase or sale agreements which use the monopoly or monopsony position of the initiating country to secure better terms than would result from the ' free interplay ' of market forces and thus redress the balance of payments, come under this heading, except in so far as they are not supplemented by (or do not give rise to) arrangements in the partner country which permit an increase in that country of effective demand and real income. Such agreements can be discriminating or non-discriminating.

Export Stimuli. The selective stimulus of exports can be financed, and thus the real burden of the worsening of the terms of trade can be borne, in different ways. It will in all circumstances be less than that caused by devaluation: this because we assume (rightly) heterogeneous elasticities. One of the methods is to finance exports by a levy on home trade. This is both inefficient and inequitable.

A second and more efficient method of finance would be to employ direct grants to private firms from the Treasury to stimulate exports. This policy is not without its internal and external dangers. It is, however, not more dangerous than devaluation of equal effect. Any increase in exports in the teeth of declining foreign demand represents

---

[1] This method, therefore, consists in consciously re-establishing the high elasticity of foreign demand which otherwise would obtain and on which the hopes of the devaluationist *laissez-faire* school, which *implicitly* assume it, are really based.

a pressure on foreign countries and will be resisted. By trying to concentrate the increase in exports to industries the price elasticity of demand for whose products is relatively high, the full employment country might at least hope to avoid running foul of the most depressed of its foreign competitors who are likely to put up the bitterest fight. The relatively high price elasticity of demand for any one country's products is *a priori* an indication that competitive foreign excess capacity in that industry is not too large.

The stimulation of exports—whatever the means employed, apart from measures which increase effective demand abroad—will tend to depress prices abroad. The change of relative prices will change the differences in opportunity costs which render international exchange of goods profitable. If then exports are maintained by ' intervention ' productive factors will be diverted from their optimum current use. As a weapon of employment policy a stimulus to exports must be condemned because of the unnecessary loss in real income. Whether in any given situation it should nevertheless be used to permit the continuance of a certain level of imports depends on the *ex-post* opportunity cost differences. These will be determined also by the possibilities of re-employing the non-specific factors engaged in the export industries for other purposes.

Control of imports. The control of imports must accompany the stimulus to exports. Failing this it is possible that exports will have to be undertaken beyond the optimum.

The control of imports can be indirect, through the price system (tariffs), or direct through the fixing of quantities either by way of quotas and exchange licences or by centralized buying. All protective measures[1] tend to improve the terms of trade and thereby—at least temporarily and partially—to offset the fall in real income of the community (which finds its expression in the increase of the price). In principle[2] a level of tariff can be found exactly equivalent to any given direct restriction of imports. On closer analysis it appears that this equivalence is severely limited to the effect on the balance of payments. Unless the tariffs are wholly prohibitive (in which case there is, of course, no difference between indirect and direct ' restriction ', as it is absolute) their influence both on employment and on the distribution of the national income differ from that of the ' equivalent ' direct restriction. A direct control will give a far greater security to home producers than tariffs (and *a fortiori* than depreciation) because the

---

[1] Except for the system of granting quotas or licences practised, e.g. by the British Agricultural Administration before (and the Exchange Control in the first few months of) the war by which the increase in home prices could accrue to the foreign seller.

[2] Cf. League of Nations: *Quantitative Controls of Foreign Trade*, p. 20.

H

entrepreneur will know in advance the effect of the quota on the home
market while the effect of the duty—unless prohibitive—will depend
also on the readjustment of foreign competitors to the new duty.
One of the main difficulties in isolating a fully employed economy from
fluctuations abroad will be encountered because the loss of confidence
will tend to overlap to the full employment country (i.e. the consequent
rise in the risk premium and a fall in investment). Some control of
imports will probably have to be an integral part of full employment
policy in an unstable world system. The difference between long and
short run cost might be so substantial as to render stability at home in
the face of fluctuations abroad difficult, short of State investment or
guarantee against losses on new investment.

Unilateral Bulk Purchase. Unilateral bulk purchase agreements use
the monopolistic bargaining power of a country with respect to its
imports to secure better terms and thus reduce an adverse balance of
trade. American writers, e.g. Professor Viner,[1] hold that all direct
transactions involving a monopolistic influence on markets are discriminating and exploitative. A differentiation between exploitative
and non-exploitative readjustment on the basis of static concepts is
not legitimate. Whether such bulk purchases will be exploitative or
not will depend on whether or not the national real income of the
partner country will rise or not. This cannot, as we shall presently
see, be determined by price relations alone. Long-term purchase
agreements eliminate the risk inherent in producing for an uncertain
market. It is clear, therefore, that the purchasing country performs a
service to the selling country which might be, and mostly is, of considerable importance. The producers in the selling country, especially
if they are small and weak producers, as a result of the purchase
agreements will be enabled to tap cheap sources of credit and modern-
ize their production. The possibility of such reorganization of their
production was, without the agreement, completely closed to them.

An industrial country which undertakes to purchase a considerable
part of another at a fixed price will be unwilling to commit herself if
she is not assisted more directly than any general monetary arrangement might succeed in doing, not only that she will be able to pay for
the supplies, and on terms which will not subsequently be rendered too
onerous by events over which she has no control (e.g. deflation in the
supplying country), but also that other countries will not be able to
obtain the same goods at better terms elsewhere at a subsequent date.
The supplier of the (primary) products, on his part, must have the

[1] *Trade Relations between Free Market and Controlled Economies,* League of Nations,
1943.

assurance that once the sale is concluded the purchaser will not insist on unreasonable prices for his exports.

In the absence of an international monetary agreement which safeguards the interest of the purchasing country a wide extension of unilateral bulk purchase is not very likely.

Methods influencing Foreign Effective Demand. Both monetary and non-monetary means are at the disposal of a full employment country to influence effective demand abroad for its products. The non-monetary method consists of reciprocal bulk purchase; monetary expedients are clearing agreements and payment agreements. The need for such auxiliary methods in helping the readjustment of the balance of payments arises because the maintenance of full employment in a country results in a maintenance—or rather increase—of the purchases of that country relative to the purchases of the depressed countries abroad. If more orthodox methods of readjustment were followed, the resulting disequilibrium, a fall in national real income, could hardly be avoided. As long as employment (and/or investment) policies are not co-ordinated in such a way as to balance international payments, the purchase or sale internationally of commodities without the assurance of a reciprocal transaction cannot be taken as the equivalent of the same transaction undertaken with the certainty that a reciprocal transaction will in due course automatically follow. The neglect of the reciprocal transaction as a factor determining the advantage of the transaction implicitly rests on the assumption that the system as a whole is fully employed, i.e. that ' Say's celebrated Law of Markets' operates internationally,[1] and that therefore the reverse transactions take place automatically and without any further adjustments, on the basis of the existing comparative costs which are taken to remain unchanged by the original transaction. This assumption could only be accepted if some comprehensive international agreement were to be arrived at which would allow for the maintenance of full employment in all member countries. The success of multilateralism depends on full employment and not *vice versa*. If such agreement is not arrived at, then the gains from foreign trade can no longer be judged by *current* comparative cost differences. All secondary effects of every transaction, including its effects on total demand in the member countries (exerted via the necessity of global readjustment) must be taken into account. In the absence of the application of special measures no, or much less, trade would take place as the emergence or increase of induced balances towards countries which failed in or had no full employment policies would force all countries to cut down their

[1] Lord Keynes' plea (ibid.) in favour of the restoration of full convertibility was, oddly enough, based on precisely this fallacy.

imports because these balances might be spent anywhere, i.e., also in areas which by their deflationary pressure absorb liquidity without increasing their demand for foreign goods and services.

All reciprocal agreements eliminate the necessity of having sufficient internationally acceptable liquid reserves prior to the purchase of goods and services. Unless the counter-party to the transaction does not utilize the credits standing to his name for an immediate contrary transaction an automatic credit is provided. In the case of countries, therefore, which suffer from a lack of liquidity and whose economic systems tend to produce a bias towards deficiencies in their balances of international payments, this arrangement permits the maintenance of full employment and the maintenance of supplies from abroad. A country which has a bias to export its unemployment through export surpluses, i.e. a country which has a tendency to absorb international liquidity, has no need to fall back on this device. It is the means at the disposal of countries which do not wish to submit to deflationary pressure from abroad.

The prevention of reciprocal agreements on the basis that they imply discrimination amounts to a unilateral acceptance of the bargaining power of unstable export surplus countries.

Non-monetary Reciprocity. The non-monetary form of such agreements are reciprocal bulk supply contracts. Whether they will in fact modify foreign total demand depends on the internal policy of the partner country. They provide a possibility for expansionist policy which without them would possibly result in a worsening of the balance of payments. The practical limitations of reciprocal bulk purchases lie in the character of the economic system of the countries concerned. Reciprocal bulk purchase can be practised easily by two entirely collectivized countries. It is difficult to arrange it between countries whose economic system is based on individual enterprise. It is then not the State, but the individual traders who export and import, and those traders who export are not also necessarily in charge of imports. It might, therefore, be difficult and clumsy to force traders to conclude direct barter agreements.[1] Nor must it be forgotten that ' voluntary ' barter arrangements in so far as monopoly and monopsony powers are brought to bear in arranging them, can be

---

[1] This will be the case especially with respect to manufacturing countries trading with primary producing countries. Bulk purchases of raw materials and food stuffs are easily arranged, but it will be much more difficult to force importers in a primary producing country to buy from the country to which the primary country exported, an equivalent amount of manufactures, if the purchasing country is not as cheap a market as a third country to which sales are impracticable. Yet, without forcing them to do so the primary producers may not be able to export at all and both that country and the manufacturing country would be forced into unnecessary autarky.

exploitative. In fact, as the exchange of definite commodities will have to be arranged, which is a clumsy method and restricts the choice of the weaker partner, both in the range of commodities and in time of purchase, it is liable to more abuse than arrangements by which the proceeds of exports are earmarked for purchases in the same country but without such restriction of choice.

Monetary Reciprocity. Monetary reciprocity takes the form either of payment or of clearing agreements. Under payment agreements a country undertakes to use a certain proportion of the proceeds of her exports for certain predetermined purposes. Under clearing agreements all payments are credited or debited to her on a central account; payments from that account can only be made with the permission of the authority controlling the account. Both can be voluntary in character. Forced blocking presupposes that the country undertaking it is a debtor country, otherwise no country needs to continue deliveries. No one needs to sell to the country which earmarks (blocks) the proceeds of the sale and permits their use only for internal payments. Such reciprocal payment or clearing agreements should be rather *less* discriminating than direct reciprocal bulk purchases, as they interfere less with the choice of the trading partner. Provided that only one of the partners maintains full employment (and therefore imports) such agreements automatically provide, or rather create, international liquidity to finance imports and thereby impart an expansionist bias to the economy of the selling country. It is true that by restricting the choice of the selling country they also create market imperfections in favour of the industries of the purchasing country. Without the purchases of that country, however, the seller would not be able to buy at all. To talk of exploitation in *every* case is therefore unjustified. Whether exploitation takes place depends not only on the *prices* ruling in the purchasing and selling country and elsewhere and the rates of exchange, but also on the ratio of the *volume* of the transactions passing as compared with the volume which would be possible if the agreement had not been concluded.

The main purpose of these agreements is to prevent the leakage of liquidity reserves into depressed areas, i.e. to maintain the liquidity of the full employment areas. The alternative to such agreements, if

Given the restricted initiative on the part of most government departments, at any rate in Britain, it is almost impossible to visualize that extended use will be made of direct ' voluntary ' bulk barter. Lord Keynes' interpretation (*Hansard*, May 23, col. 870) that the prohibition and discriminating monetary arrangement exempted ' voluntary ' barter agreements from its operation, while in severe conflict with the official American thesis, as expounded by Professor Viner (op. cit.), does not in fact offer any scope for maintaining international exchange of commodities between full employment areas irrespective of the state of trade elsewhere.

unemployment prevails in important countries, may well be national autarky. Full employment would then lose liquidity to under-employed countries because their full employment policy makes them good countries to sell to, but unfavourable markets to buy in. This process could obviously not continue indefinitely.

It is often suggested that the exploitative character of *clearing* agreements is due to the fact that the ' clearing ' countries ' overvalue ' their currencies in terms of the currencies of ' free ' countries. If only they devalued, it is said, their problem would be solved. But by their policy of ' over-valuation ' they ' exploit ' their partners as they turn the terms of trade in their favour. As we have seen, the actual elasticities of demand and supply and thus the balance of payments as well as the rate of exchange are a function of the degree of employment. There is no *a priori* reason to suppose that an equilibrium rate of exchange need exist without direct controls (including tariffs) between a full employment country and areas which suffer from underemployment and where effective demand is still falling. We understand under equilibrium rate of exchange in this sense a level which would balance international payments without a change in the short-term (liquid) capital account. This merely means that *if* a country wishes to retain its international equilibrium in an under-employed world it might, in the absence of direct controls or increasing autarky, have to give up full employment policies.

Thus, if a country refused to follow the rest of the world into depression and maintained effective demand unchanged (i.e. increased home demand to offset the fall in international demand) this would *ipso facto* ' over-value ' the currency. The discriminating subsidies and tariffs which would enable the stabilization of the trade balance towards the outside area would indeed lessen the relative worsening of the terms of trade in comparison with devaluation of an identical effectiveness, (if such a rate of devaluation existed). But it would be rather fanciful to speak of exploitation in this case.

If, then, the country concludes clearing agreements and continues its full employment policy, this ' reflation ' itself will now render all clearing countries ' over-valued ' and respect to depressed ' free exchange ' countries. Thus relations between the countries are likely to become *ceteris paribus* more intimate than before the slump as they will constitute an oasis of full employment in a desert of underemployment and thus *both* their currencies will be ' over-valued '. To charge the full employment country that it has exploited its clearing partner would surely be a complete *non-sequitur*. It was the depression abroad which is the *fons et origo* of the whole process. If the depression lifted quickly, no ' block ' would be formed.

What might constitute an objectionable discrimination are not such agreements but the exclusion, for political reasons, of countries willing to enter into *similar* agreements *on the same terms.*

Thus reciprocal arrangements, if properly managed, represent nothing less than an exchange of products of countries which could not otherwise be sold and probably would never have been produced at all in the absence of such agreements. They can be utilized not merely to secure an approximation to a state of affairs which would rule if ' free ' trade is obtained. They can be a basis for the development of the production and exchange of goods which could not have been produced and exchanged even under conditions of free trade. The existence of risk would have narrowed the scope of profitable trade, and neither the knowledge nor the capital for trade would have been available, though *ex post* the production and exchange is perfectly justifiable and profitable according to all canons of classical theory. There is no reason why both partners should not share the benefits of such agreements; the producing country, by being able to sell more, and the purchasing country by being able to buy more (by obtaining supplies at cheaper prices) than she would otherwise have been able to do.

Clearing arrangements thus permit the planning of full employment at home, which offers stable and expanding markets at favourable prices to countries having complementary economic systems. They provide in an unstable world the assurance that exports will be practicable to pay for imports without deflationary adjustment. In such a world imports might otherwise not be permitted and the exchange of goods would be further restricted.

4

A NOTE ON THE ECONOMICS OF RETALIATION

1. The fear has been expressed that an attempt to organise deliberately the production and exchange of goods and services between different countries would evoke retaliatory action on the part of those countries which are intent to maintain individualistic market economics as the basis for their economic organisation; and that these countries could impose their economic system on others, by insisting on multilateral monetary and commercial agreements outlawing ' discrimination ', including all direct reciprocal long-term agreements. It is to be hoped that these fears are exaggerated. Differences in economic and social background of the diverse nations might make it

impossible to establish a fully world-wide trading system which could combine multilateralism with stable full employment. In that case regionalism—the organisation of countries which agree on domestic economic policies into wide regional blocks—might provide the optimum international division of labour, that is practicable at this stage. The prevention of such blocks by the threat of retaliatory action would be an act of economic aggression not likely to benefit the country threatening action while harming everyone. The prohibition of bilateral agreements within the full employment block or between that block and third countries would merely mean that all other countries would have to follow the trend of employment in the ' non-discriminating ' country, or else would have to pursue fully autarkic policies to defend themselves against the effect of economic fluctuation in that country. In either case the loss of potential real income would be greater than if the establishment of a full employment block were permitted. The threat of retaliation against policies which are ' discriminatory ' only in so far as is necessary to maintain full employment in the countries practising it, is therefore akin to the behaviour of the dog in the manger.[1] It would be a different matter if foreign trade controls and bilateral agreements were used for the purpose of enforcing more favourable terms of trade against the ' free ' market countries. In practice, unfortunately, it would be difficult to establish whether or not such ' exploitative ' use had been made of the controls. Actual price comparisons, or comparisons of exchange rates could not necessarily be adduced as proof, since they might hide the cost of readjustment that would be incurred by one ' free ' country in finding new markets in another. The *social* cost of importing from that country might be much higher than obtaining a nominally dearer article by bilateral agreement elsewhere. But a rough measure of equity could in most cases be established by inisting on the right to sell on the same basis (including the terms of payment).

2.   We must now consider what retaliatory action might be taken against countries which decide to form regional blocks in order to

---

[1] This has also been recognised in an official publication of the U.S. Government. Cf. *The United States in the World Economy*, 1944, p. 13. 'A world economic structure organised on the basis of equal treatment and with large scope for free enterprise cannot be maintained in the face of such reduction in the supply of dollars as have occurred in our international transactions in the past. Unless the supply of dollars is more adequate to meet the requirements of other countries, they assuredly will insist on their rights to exercise a close selective control over the use of the amounts available and to promote more intensive relations with third countries under preferential trading arrangements. And unless dollars are made available with greater regularity than in the past it would be both unjust and unwise to demand the removal of restraints and controls largely designed to protect the internal economies of other countries against external shock and pressure.'

maintain full employment internally and are, therefore forced to 'discriminate' against the exports of countries which are unwilling to join the block on this basis. We shall designate the 'non-discriminating' free market country, as (A); the full employment block as (B). We assume that both (A) and (B) are highly industrialised. Among third countries we shall differentiate between a (C) type, which we assume to be relatively thinly populated primary producing countries exporting a large fraction of their output and (D) countries which are underdeveloped areas with a high density of population and low productivity.

3. We assume (A) to engage in retaliation against (B) because the latter has, in order to eliminate her debit balance of payments with (A), discriminated against imports from (A). Retaliation might take the form of an embargo on (or penalisation by differential duties, etc. of) the products of the block (B) in the markets of (A). This would also result in an embargo on the exports of the retaliating country (A) to the block (B) as the block could no longer pay for these exports. Several cases must be examined.

(A) can have a current export surplus only if:

(a) she absorbs international liquid assets

(b) she grants foreign loans

The second possibility will be examined below. If (A) is currently absorbing the liquid reserves of other countries, the consequences of its retaliatory action cannot normally be formidable. Its bargaining power, i.e. its capacity to inflict losses on other countries by cutting its purchases is relatively weak. Its own economic system would suffer more by reciprocal embargoes as it sells more abroad than it buys.

An embargo on imports by (A) might inflict serious losses on (B) only if (A) had a strong monopoly or monopsony position with respect to the exports or imports of (B).[1] The existence of such exclusive relations is rare so far as manufactures and most primary products are concerned. The losses inflicted on certain specialised industries in (B) might, of course, be serious. But, from a global employment point of view, this type of retaliation cannot hurt a 'full employment block' very severely. The export surplus is equivalent to investment and its disappearance would represent a net deflationary impulse in (A) and a net inflationary effect in (B). This would even be the case if (A) had an export surplus with respect to its trade with (B), but import surpluses with respect to (C) countries which had import surpluses from (B). Retaliation would in all these cases reduce exports from (A) as

---

[1] This might be the case if (A)'s exports are necessities unobtainable elsewhere or if (A) provided markets for special products which, e.g. luxuries, cannot easily be sold elsewhere.

much as it reduced its imports. It is probable, if (*A*) were an individualist market economy, that the internal resistance against retaliatory measures would be strong, as the interests which exported to (*B*) would protest against the loss of their markets. Only a collectivist state could compensate them out of levies obtained from the increased profits of those entrepreneurs who now supply the internal market with goods hitherto obtained from (*B*) or who now replace (*B*)'s exports to (*C*).

The position would be different if all countries pursued full employment policies. Imports would then not represent a potential menace to domestic employment but a means to increase the pace of economic progress. The embargo on exports would then possess the same bargaining power as a refusal to ' accept imports ' has in a regime of general under-employment. But in a world economic system organised on those lines bilateral agreements for the purpose of securing imports would in any case be superfluous and harmful; the problem would then not arise.

4. Retaliation may also take the form of systematically pre-empting supplies which the ' block ' (*B*) needs from third (*C*) countries. If successful, this method would be awkward to the block as it would turn the terms of trade against her. It might even be possible for the pre-emptor (*A*) to insist that the selling countries should not spend any part of their proceeds from the pre-emptive purchases in (*B*). Provided that the retaliating country agrees to pay high enough prices, these (selling) countries will benefit from this deal even though international trade is diverted from its natural channels.

But the danger of pre-emptive buying on a large scale is not very real. The internal absorption of these supplies would create unemployment and be subject to the same objections and resistances as a general policy of increasing imports. If an expansion of imports is not entertained—and if it were, (*A*) would cease to be an export surplus country—the pre-empted supplies would either have to be destroyed or given away to other (e.g. (*D*)) countries.

These methods have been followed with varying success in the economic warfare operations of the United Nations against Germany in countries which were contiguous to her and, therefore, could not be blockaded. It is doubtful, however, whether they could be systematically pursued in peace-time by countries wedded to traditional ideas in economic matters. The losses incurred by purchasing commodities and destroying them (or selling them at cheap prices in countries which could not afford to buy them before at the previous world price) would fall on the national budget. It would imply a complete break with the canons of sound finance to maintain such expenditures as a habitual state of affairs. And if such re-orientation of policy is possible, it is difficult to suppose that the conclusions of general agreements ensuring full employment on rational lines should at the same time be excluded. The whole problem, in that case, might not arise.

Alternatively (A) could spoil (B)'s terms of trade by offering goods to (C) countries which (B) supplied hitherto, at much lower prices. Such 'spoiling' offers, however, could not alter the barter terms between (B) and (C) countries so long as (C) has no means of acquiring (A)'s currency; which again presupposes that (C) can sell to that country. The cheapness of (A)'s goods to (C) would be nominal as long as (C) has no possibility of selling goods to (A) at prices which (B) is willing to pay. In such circumstances goods from (A) could only be obtained at the cost of having to endure mass-unemployment in order to overcome the difficulties of balancing transactions with her.

5. There is, finally, the weapon of foreign lending as an instrument of retaliation. Two methods may be distinguished:

(a) The retaliating country (A) could grant foreign loans on condition that the borrowers (C) spent the purchasing power in the lending country.

If the loan expenditure is part of a general expansion programme in the borrowing country (C), the increase of its demand for its own produce (unaccompanied by an increase in the demand for foreign products other than those of the lending export surplus country (A)), is likely to turn the terms of trade against (B).[1] This effect will be made permanent and strengthened if the new productive capacity serves to replace previously imported goods from (B).

As long as export surplus countries of the type (A) suffer from under-employment, it will be impossible in practice to avoid the discrimination implied in such loan policies, quite irrespective of whether 'discriminatory' methods in commercial agreements are excluded or not. But their unfavourable effects are mitigated by the fact that world employment and demand is likely to increase as a result of the lending.

[1] E.g. the U.S. granting loans to the Argentine on condition that she purchases from the U.S., supplies hitherto bought in Britain. The increased national income in the Argentine would tend to increase the price of meat and maize and thus worsen the terms of trade of Britain. They would be further worsened by the increased competition of U.S. manufactures with potential British exports and the increase of the Argentine industrial capacity. Such 'discrimination' by foreign loans is sometimes held to be 'non-discriminatory' in the United States. Cf. e.g. statement by Mr. H. Hopkins, *Daily Express*, February 17th, 1944. [The British negotiators accepted the exemption of 'tied' loans from the general prohibition of discriminatory practices. The reason for this was presumably their complete misjudgement of the position of Britain in the post-war world, a misjudgement which was to cost dear to the country (1961).]

If the borrowing country (C) specialized in the production of certain commodities and obtained other products by importing—and in the case of primary producing countries, this is always the case—it is not likely to absorb *all* the produce which it has hitherto exported. The increase of its standard of life will undoubtedly tend to increase its consumption of its own produce; it is unlikely to increase it sufficiently to render the markets of the import surplus country (B) of no importance.

(*b*) Foreign loans could, secondly, be combined with pre-emption. The procedure would be simple. The lender (A) might grant foreign loans to undeveloped countries (D) on condition that they purchase the produce of primary producing countries (C), which may have hitherto been selling to the import surplus country (B).[1] At the same time, (A) arranges to sell under better conditions, possibly on credit, to the primary producers (C), supplies which hitherto have been bought by (C) from (B). Both kinds of loans could furthermore be made dependent on the beneficiaries cutting their commerce with (B) altogether. In this case the immediate position of the latter might be seriously endangered. Equaly dangerous are, for the latter, the long-run consequences. The grant of loans opens up new channels for future exports to the lending country because of the close business connections to which the loans give rise. At the same time the lender is enabled to maintain a higher level of employment by means of export surpluses, while her terms of trade would remain favourable, or even improve despite the increase in exports.

A policy of this sort might be preferred by the lending country— quite apart from its aspect as a retaliatory measure—to those alternative ways of increasing home employment which rely on public works or the stimulation of home consumption by budgetary deficits. It does not increase the burden of the public debt—or rather, the increase in the debt, in this case, might be thought to be offset by the acquisition of a foreign asset. And it does not interfere with the internal distribution of income.

It would not be possible for (B) countries to extricate themselves from the threatened isolation by a mere willingness to absorb supplies from (C). For its prospective customers, both (C) and (D) would now be able to dispose of their production on excellent terms, and at the same time would receive the benefit of long-term loans. We must conclude, therefore, that (B) countries could only counter this threat by matching the loan offers of the export surplus country (A) in

---

[1] E.g. U.S. grants loans to China for the purchase of Argentine meat or wheat, and at the same time opens credits to the Argentine to enable her to purchase U.S. machinery on better terms than are obtainable in Britain.

addition to offering reciprocal purchase agreements. If the full employ-ment block (B) is poorer than the export surplus country (A), it would have to have an internal economic organisation which would permit it (in case of need) to increase the rate of saving above the level which would result from the voluntary decisions of the inhabitants and thereby release resources for the purposes of foreign lending.

There is a further advantage, however, which (B) countries could offer to their prospective customers; and that is long-term stability. For in the absence of long-term purchase agreements, (C) countries would still remain exposed to the consequences of business cycles emanating from *laissez-faire* countries such as (A). Their gains from being able to sell in times of boom at higher prices might be far out-weighed by the losses due to the unevenness of business activity losses which affect primary producer (because of the price-inelasticities of demand) more severely than industrial areas. Hence the bargaining position of countries willing to pursue full employment is automatically strengthened by the conditions of stability which they can offer to primary producers.

6. We may conclude, therefore, that the danger of retaliatory action by individualistic export surplus countries, is not in the field of commercial policy so much as in using the weapon of foreign lending in order to cause diversions in the channels of trade. We have seen that by abstaining from 'discriminatory' trade agreements other countries could not, in fact, ensure that such a policy will not be followed by rich areas subject to depressions; for countries which intend to cure their own unemployment by means of an export surplus, a policy of this sort would offer great advantages, quite apart from its possibilities as a weapon of economic warfare. The offer of long-term reciprocal purchase agreements, on the other hand, by its promise of economic stability, would increase the advantages to third countries of trading with the 'full employment' block. Unless and until satisfactory world-wide agreements, which safeguard employment policy, can be concluded, and potential export surplus countries can be induced to renounce the right to 'tie' foreign loans, it would be suicidal for potential deficit countries to renounce the right to conclude reciprocal (bilateral) bulk-purchase agreements. They would give away the only weapon by which they can secure supplies at tolerable terms; their standard of life would suffer as they would be forced to rely on home production.

The larger and more diversified the blocks formed by countries willing to pursue a full employment policy (a) the less it will be natur-ally dependent on outside supplies; (b) the more powerful will be its bargaining strength in securing such supplies as it needs; (c) the costlier and less effective would be an attempt by third countries to interfere with full employment policies pursued by the block; (*d*) the greater would be the advantages—in terms of security of employment, high productivity and rapid economic progress—that could be offered to countries intending to join such a block. Hence, if owing to the unwillingness it should prove impossible to secure truly international policies of full employment and stability, it is very important that the countries that are willing, and able, to pursue these policies should join in regional agreements for the purpose of guaranteeing this mutual trade. Acting singly, they would be placed at a grave disadvantage.

POSTSCRIPT

Keynes writing to Kalecki during the war was exceedingly complimentary about the volume of essays (in which the main piece of this section appeared) which applied the Keynesian analysis (as it now seems in a rather simple manner) to full employment. He made, quite comprehensibly, a scathing exception of this Essay. Nor was my contribution more successful generally. Though the main ideas have been accepted at the end of the war, this essay has never been noticed. The inveterate yearning of economists for ' rigorous analysis '—despite its lack of realism—had led to the establishment of a *simpliste* Keynesian formalism complete with parameters, propensities and multipliers. In the ensuing scramble, ably led by Professor Metzler's contribution, my unfashionable offering was completely lost.[1] Imports seemed to become simple functions of exports and multipliers. In the end econometricians worked out price-elasticities on the basis of observations stretching over twenty years, full of structural change and monetary disturbance; others tried to show that these nonsense results were too pessimistic, without paying any attention to the basic Keynesian problem of change in the effective demand. We are well on the way to the rehabilitation of Hume's Law by some elder economic statesman while full employment and the rate of growth of the economies with decentralised decision-making has been severely interfered with by the reversion to control through monetary policy. In fact the U.S. not merely did not stand on the letter of the Anglo-American Financial Agreement in 1947, but initiated and actively supported the formation of a discriminatory ' bloc ' under the Marshall Plan. Only the exceptional restraint by the U.S., the ' dominant ' country, enabled the full recovery of Western Continental Europe and its rise towards dynamic leadership, to the discomfiture of the benefactor. Unfortunately by that time the British officials had been completely persuaded, or had persuaded themselves, about the advantages of unilateral convertibility (a view which was eventually to crystallise in 1952 in the so-called Operation Robot). This exceptional opportunity was thus sabotaged by the British representatives, for establishing a full employment bloc comprising Europe and the Commonwealth, with due care to the interest of the poorer areas outside, on the basis of *inter-Governmental* (as against supra-national) controls under O.E.E.C.

The consequence of the failure of Britain was the rise of ' little Europe ', of E.E.C., a problem which will be treated in greater detail in Volume II. Its impact both on the less dynamic areas *within* the new organism and on the less developed countries outside, whose indus-

---

[1] *A Survey of Contemporary Economics* . . . Philadelphia, 1948, p. 210.

trialisation and rise from poverty is bound to become more and more dependent on the export of simple industrial products, will follow the pattern suggested by my analysis of the U.S. menace. As the threat of Soviet expansion matures, my view is bound to find practical acceptance in solving the international implications of the problem of continuous yet accelerated growth of the rest of the world. The question is only whether the European countries, like the U.S. in 1947, learn rapidly enough for effective action[1],[2] in warding off the threat to the progress of the uncommitted poor countries which their exclusiveness represents. In the meantime the problem of maintaining full employment in a loosely controlled system might pose itself again and with a vengeance.

[1] Cf. Vol. II. Section 9 on the problem of the possible Soviet impact on the terms of trade of the primary producing and non-planned industrial countries.

[2] Cf. Vol. II. Section 6 on the need for a planned establishment of Common Market in underdeveloped areas.

DYNAMICS OF ADJUSTMENT I
MONETARY VERSUS DIRECT CONTROLS

5

DEFLATION, DEVALUATION AND FOREIGN EXCHANGE CONTROL

THE crisis has confronted debtor countries with two fundamental and inter-related problems. They have had to adjust themselves to the catastrophic fall in the price level; and they have had to adapt their economic structure to the sudden cessation of foreign lending and the reversal of the flow of capital.

The readjustment involves an adaptation of the balance of trade to the real transfer of that greater proportion of the national income which, after the fall in prices and the cessation of the foreign loans, represents the interest and sinking fund service. And it involves an adaptation of their production and capital values to a rate of interest which is very much higher than during the expansion period and higher than the rate which would obtain had no foreign borrowing taken place and if actual deflation were not going on. It is the aim of this note to enquire into the methods of this readjustment and to show that in the present circumstances and reactions in creditor countries this process is of a self-generating nature and one of the most potent driving forces of the spiral of deflation. That is to say, that as time goes on an increasing part of the necessary further liquidation can only be explained by the previous liquidation itself. The question is whether on the debtors' side any measures can be taken calculated to slow down this process of spontaneous disintegration.

The necessary readjustment could take the form either

(a) of a depreciation of the monetary unit in terms of gold of an extent greater than a rise (if any) in money earnings; or

(b) by a reduction of the real earnings with a concomitant maintenance of the gold value of the monetary unit;

or a combination of the two methods. In both cases the internal price level in terms of gold would have to fall and real efficiency earnings decrease relative to the change abroad. In the former the increase of the prices of internally traded goods will bring about a rise in the price level relative to efficiency earnings (which rise will be somewhat mitigated by the movement in the price level of purely home traded goods). In the second case the shifts in demand and supply are accomplished by a fall in the general price level accompanied by a greater shrinkage of efficiency earnings (the fall in the price of commodities which enter—or may enter—international trade will also in this case be somewhat less than in other commodities). The niceties of the theory of transfer under such conditions need interest us no further as their influence on the transfer is overshadowed by much more potent factors.

In order to bring the mechanism of transfer into play on the debtors' side the Central Bank of the debtor country must bring about a decrease of the volume of purchasing power in active circulation by withdrawing at least the amounts due to foreign countries. But creditor countries themselves are under a pressure of deflation. The consequence of this is momentous. The deflation in the debtor states will in no way be counterbalanced by an increase of the volume of active circulation in the creditor country. The money received by the creditor is hoarded or used to repay outstanding bank liabilities— which in international relations finds its expression in the use of gold import for the reduction of the Central Bank credit or for an increase of the cash ratios of the joint stock banks. *The mechanism will only work in one way—namely downwards*. The whole burden of readjustment is thrown on the debtor.

Under the present circumstances, moreover, efforts on the part of debtors to increase their exports is resisted by the creditors. Quite apart from any time-honoured general prejudice against foreign goods, 'unfavourable' trade balances are resisted by raising tariffs and instituting import quotas, in order to prevent the transmission of depression existing in debtor countries to the markets of the creditors. Therefore, the whole readjustment takes the form of a drop in imports and a general slowing down of trade.

With the pressure and the limitation on the volume of foreign trade increasing, prices falling, the new level of activity was pushed farther and farther from the position on the basis of which the capital and debt structure was created. The measures introduced as a result of the crisis became the cause of a further crisis. An ever-increasing need for further downward readjustment, for further liquidation was created by every step of liquidation. But already that position was fraught with dangers and disequilibria[1] which increase the amount

---

[1] On the causes of these disequilibria—apart from the monetary fluctuations which are, of course, more accentuated in debtor than in creditor nations, cf. 'Theoretical Aspects of the Central European Credit Crisis' *International Affairs*, May 1932.

of readjustments required. The forcing of the liquidation at this juncture of the trade cycle must carry the structure far below any level which could be maintained were a more normal psychology prevalent and a greater part of incomes not hoarded. At a certain point the maintenance of the pre-crash capital structure is impossible as the equity capital is exhausted by the necessity to meet debt charges. The greater the rigidity in nominal earnings, the sooner this stage must be reached.

A scaling down of fixed interest debts, both internal and foreign, becomes, therefore, inevitable. The only question which can be at issue is in what way this scaling down can best be effected, i.e., so as to minimise the impact effect on the economic life of both debtors and creditors.

In the case of debtors which previously entered into short-term *capital* obligations abroad above the limit of the quickly realisable assets[1] an automatic readjustment not involving bankruptcy was not possible. Given the amount of foreign short term international indebtedness[2] in terms of foreign currencies, and given the concentration of short term debt relations—especially with foreign countries—at the big joint stock banks, the consequences of a bankruptcy would have been disastrous and might well have caused a complete chaos with unforeseeable social and political consequences.

The internal run on the banks which develop under the pressure of the threatening foreign position and the ensuing panic necessitated a freezing of the position as normal monetary measures—restriction of credit—could not be effective.[3] All outward capital movements had to be prohibited. The banks were closed. The export trade was put under control in order to check any flight through that expedient. These measures were quite as unavoidable in the case of debtor states as the suspension of the gold standard by England, which being a debtor in terms of her own currency and having enormous foreign assets could rely on the restoration of equilibrium by depreciation.

The moratorium on foreign short term debts and the prevention of a flight from the currency equalized the position of debtors with and without short term liabilities. Total chaos was avoided but the need for internal readjustment in order to ensure collection and transfer of the interest and sinking fund service, which in the changed cir-

---

[1] The marginal flexibility of the balance of trade as compared with the amounts callable was very limited. Study of the German balance of payments reveals that even though that country was in an exceptionally favourable position as the terms of trade went heavily in favour of industrial countries, practically no repayment was effected out of current earnings.

[2] In most of the Central European countries the volume of such obligations reached a multiple of that of the Central Bank foreign reserves.

[3] i.e. without causing bankruptcy.

cumstances represent a greater proportion of the real income, still remained.

The solution by depreciation accompanied by an annulment of the gold clause would at least solve some of the internal difficulties by reducing the real burden of internal debt. It would help to avoid or at least mitigate the risk of a wave of internal bankruptcies. Moreover the other well-known frictions reducing the volume of output which make the process by deflation so dangerous and impolitic would also be avoided. But in certain expert circles there is a distinct bias against such a solution similar to the irritation some drivers feel when, in order to surmount a hill, he has to ' dishonour ' his car by changing into a lower gear.[1]

Three main objections are raised against this method. It is contended that it has a detrimental influence on the savings habit essential to a future reconstruction; that it causes a run of the banks and thereby complete disintegration; and that it upsets the equilibrium of the budget.

Undoubtedly devaluation will have the grave consequences on the savings habit especially in countries which already underwent currency depreciation. But even from this point of view there is an overwhelming case for this road of least resistance, as it is more than questionable whether the series of bankruptcies inevitable in the case of a further deflation do not have even more unfavourable psychological effects. The control of the capital movements ensures a comparative security against the danger of a sudden collapse of the exchange. A possible run on the banks, which as the American example shows must ensue also in case of deflation as soon as depositors realise that the value of the assets corresponding to their deposits is steadily whittled down, can be countered by appropriate measures. There can be no doubt that if a conservative banking policy is followed, the rise in internal prices which will probably ensue as a result of an increase of the velocity of circulation can be kept in bounds.[2] The current argument that a depreciation permanently increases the difficulty— especially of the Government—to effect payments abroad is untenable. There is no reason to suppose that a deflation of a size necessary to effect the transfer, with the inevitable accompanying shrinkage of the national output, would reduce Government incomes to a lesser extent than a depreciation of the same extent which does not influence output

---

[1] Of course, it takes some skill to change it at high speed without an ugly noise and without letting it slip altogether. [May this be claimed as one of the earliest examples of the present appalling addiction to motoring analogies? (1960).]

[2] There is, moreover, no reason to suppose that banking policy is more effective in decreasing prices (which is necessary in case of a solution by deflation) than in preventing a rise.

to the same degree. Both measures have the same effect: the segregation of a certain greater part of the national income for the purpose of debt payments than hitherto; only the deflation renders this even more difficult by actually reducing output resulting from the concomitant frictions which under the present social conditions cannot be avoided.

In fact the drain of reserves was brought to an end, not by a reduction of money earnings, i.e. by deflation, not by the variation of the price of foreign exchange, i.e. depreciation, but by refusing to furnish foreign exchange for imports not considered as vital, and by forcing at the same time the surrender of the proceeds of exports at the pre-crash parity: in other words, by exchange control.

The extremely unfavourable consequences of this measure, if applied by all countries at the same time, are apparent. The level of money earnings at the parity maintained is not compatible with the surplus on the balance of payments which is essential in order to maintain payments. The foreign exchange surplus is, therefore, not obtained by natural change in relative prices described above and consequently by shifts in production and consumption, but by the introduction of import prohibitions of an indefinite nature and by restricting payments for goods previously imported. The transfer mechanism, already hampered by the incessant interference with foreign trade and deflation abroad is now altogether vitiated by the internal lack of adaptation. All readjustment takes a form of a shrinkage in trade to an extent incompatible with the maintenance of debt structure.

The position into which the exporters of other countries were forced became untenable as they did not receive payments for their exports, and their respective countries, in their turn, proceeded with retaliatory measures.

This fight of all against all led to progressive paralysis. Thus by different subterfuges clearing agreements had to be evaded, as in fact they tended to encourage imports just of those goods the exclusion of which would have been necessary. Vital imports on the other hand were supplied by exporters only against cash payments in gold or gold exchange. At the same time in spite of the maintenance of the gold parity very varying monetary policies were followed. The increasing scarcity of goods thereby tended to increase prices of foreign goods relative to prices abroad, and make for an ever-increasing artificiality and muddle.

The clearing agreements in any case would do little with respect to the real aim, the maintenance of solvency, as they were mainly concluded between debtors and envisaged only in exceptional cases the increase of the aggregate export surplus of debtors into creditor countries. The resulting disequilibria would no doubt have long ago led to a complete cessation of foreign trade, had the natural forces not led to the establishment of so-called Black Bourses and had not private dealings in foreign exchange between exporters and importers been allowed by different countries.

The situation thus in fact means that a fiction of an unchanged exchange parity can be maintained strictly only as far as foreign debts and a certain proportion of foreign trade is concerned. Interest on foreign debts, therefore, in some cases is paid out of continuously decreasing reserves or to the detriment of debts arising out of commodity transactions; in others payment is effected only in internal currency on the basis of the unchanged parity into blocked accounts, without any provision for the ultimate transfer. A restoration of something approaching freedom of economic forces[1] without a change of the exchange parity would necessitate such deflation as to increase further the disequilibrium between assets and liabilities and thus lead to the breakdown which was avoided only at the price of such extreme sacrifice last year. A depreciation without abolishing the gold clause both externally and internally (thereby defaulting) would hardly mean less.

On the other hand the wish to maintain the fiction that foreign debts can or will be paid in full, to which in fact the maintenance of the parity without the required further internal adjustments amounts, cannot be recognized as justifying the dragging out of a solution indefinitely.

With the maintenance of the trade restrictions as time goes on they themselves and not merely the wish to pay the creditors (which, moreover, must be stultified as the parallel restrictions of the debtors largely cancel out) are the cause of further and further new restrictions and thus of an increasing shrinkage of trade. This must not only destroy all hope for recovery and for the avoiding of a complete default but actually endanger the very existence of the population. At the same time the interference with interest rates and a *de facto*, if not a *de jure*, moratorium to avoid bankruptcy internally paralyses the home business activity, and reduces economics to a state rapidly approaching barter.

It is at the present moment of extreme distrust and extreme interference with foreign trade impossible to say what part of the outstanding liabilities contracted under totally different circumstances and expectations can be paid and even more what can effectively be transferred in future. The cessation of the complete collection of the capital and in some cases also of the sinking fund service and interest may prolong the life of obligations which if collection and transfer were

[1] Excluding, of course, capital movements.

attempted would be *ipso facto* wiped out. The effect of a Government guarantee of loans which, had the economic forces left free play, would be wiped out by bankruptcy as well as the payment of interest on public loans uneconomically invested is essentially similar to reparations: it burdens the whole community thereby lastingly impeding recovery.

It is an illusion to suppose that foreign lending will, and a grave mistake to hold that it should, recommence at the pre-crash rate if the present trend in international trade policy is not completely reversed. The piling up of liabilities to pay for debts already beyond the capacity to pay, whilst the competitive restriction of trade continues, is tantamount to folly. Even if by the cessation of the free international distribution of capital the rate of economic progress is further reduced, the risk of such periodical breakdowns as the present one cannot be run. The argument that the ' credit ' of debtors must be maintained by paying to the utmost is meaningless and harmful if not implemented by a reversal of monetary and economic policy. The reversal of the trend, however, can only be brought about if debtors are not trying to suffocate markets and deflate creditors in their craving to do the impossible, to pay in goods against the wish of the creditors, and if creditors do not try to prohibit the natural consequences of the effort to pay—namely, the increase of the import surplus. A depreciation in debtor countries as a means of readjustment is *not a result of inflation but a means for reduction of their efficiency earnings*. If, therefore, liabilities of debtors and the direct and indirect transfer possibilities[1] are not brought into some relation, but the effect of depreciation wiped out by further tariffs and restrictions, then a final collapse is inevitable. But such a reversal of the monetary process in creditor states can be hoped for but not relied upon. It is questionable, therefore, whether a temporary moratorium and a using of the still available unemployed resources for an increase of trade activity would not be preferable, even from the point of view of the creditors, to a more or less passive waiting until the slow attrition of foreign trade and assets makes a default inevitable. As the import surpluses in creditor countries are not sufficient to cover all liabilities of the debtors, it is evident that the free fight now going on will solve only the question which of the debtors is to default first. At the same time, however, the very basis of recovery of the economic system is endangered. A temporary stoppage of payments which might allow for a restoration of internal

---

[1] Which must be increased by appropriate measures, like the granting of preferences, forming customs' unions, or preferential schemes whereby the trade of the debtor ' blocks ' is made more favourable with the outside world—especially creditor countries.

equilibrium without an unbearable lowering of the standard of life is preferable to the risk of complete breakdown. Without an agreement, however, the process of disintegration cannot be arrested, as no single country can take—save *in extremis*—such a decision. At the same time formulae could be worked out enabling the automatic flexible resumption of payments as soon as the restoration of a more normal position is accomplished, and an unobstructed transfer is ensured. There can be no doubt that at this juncture we have passed the stage when a settlement of Government debts can provide relief. The whole complex of the economic and financial relations of debtors and creditors will have to be solved in order to permit lasting recovery.

6

A New View of the Economics of International Readjustment

To European economists who are impressed by the unsatisfactory state of the theory of international trade, which was left far behind the revision of economic doctrine initiated by the late Lord Keynes, Dr. Triffin's paper[1] certainly represents some encouragement. The grave errors both in policy and in institutional planning due to the persistence of older views and exemplified by the Final Act of the Bretton Woods Conference and first two drafts of the International Trade Organisation might be mitigated, if not remedied, by the development of a new international ' case-law ', based on a suitable re-interpretation of the rules.

After an analysis of the mechanism of the gold standard prior to the First World War and in the inter-war period, Dr. Triffin comes to three important conclusions:

(1) That even prior to 1914 the gold standard did not work, as it is assumed to have worked by the classical theory, through a see-saw movement of simultaneous inflations and deflations in the gold losing and gold gaining countries respectively. If there had been any tendency for changes in the liquidity position to engender consequent—contrary —income movements, in the two types of countries, which is by no means proven, they were certainly drowned in the basic fluctuations which were world wide and spread from a dominant country to the

---

[1] Printed in the same issue. [Dr. Triffin subsequently joined the ranks of those who demanded a fundamental reform of the powers of the international organs to create international liquidity. He still does not seem to perceive the need for a reform of policy-making. Cf. Vol. II. Section 7].

weaker nations (though sometimes disequilibria in the latter did in-fluence the former). Readjustment of unfavourable balances of pay-ments arising out of business cycles in accordance with ' rules of the game ' by deflation will, therefore, tend to intensify and spread the depression without bringing about ' equilibrium '.

(2) That even devaluation, as a method of readjustment, though less inimical to stability than deflation, will not in these circumstances, necessarily or sensibly reduce instability.

(3) That exchange control of current transactions coupled with certain non-discriminatory ' multiple currency practices ' might, in certain circumstances, prove to be less restrictive to foreign trade than the more orthodox methods of restoring equilibrium.

None of these conclusions is new. But it is one thing to come to ' unorthodox ' conclusions in an environment in which the futility of obsolete theories is clearly demonstrated as it is in Britain to-day,[1] and another to bring them forward in the less congenial atmosphere of the United States of America to-day.

Once the possibility of a serious deflationary instability in an impor-tant member of the world economy is not excluded from the analysis (as it has been excluded by the implicit assumptions of the ' classical ' school), multilateral schemes cannot *a priori* be shown to secure optimum progress for all members of a world system. The gains from an unrestricted extension of the international division of labour are offset by the unemployment (and increase in risk) engendered. Dr. Triffin admits that this problem must be analysed. But then the ques-tion arises:

(*a*) whether a considerable degree of instability should be expected and what means can be devised to minimise it;

(*b*) what measures are needed to isolate other countries from its effects?

The decision on the policy of single countries (or a group of countries) will have to depend—from a purely economic point of view —on the extent of the instability on the one hand and on the other the potential loss of productivity due to the limitation of the inter-national division of labour.

(*a*) *General Considerations*

Thus we are driven to consider the factors which in a world system will determine the degree of instability, i.e. the problem of the deter-

---

[1] [This was written in 1946. It would be rash to repeat this claim today (1960)].

minants of international employment. We can no longer assume that the *size* and *wealth* of the members of a world economic system are of no importance in determining the course of events. We can no longer assume, as it has been fallaciously assumed, that international trade merely differs from internal trade in that the mobility of certain factors, especially labour, is not perfect.

The nations of the world even in the nineteenth century were far more positive in their action than is implied in the assumption that they merely provided a ' framework ' within which individual entre-preneurs conducted trade, not otherwise influenced or inconvenienced as by political regulations. It is only when a gold coin standard exists and there are no banks of issue, that identical gold movements take place between and within countries. The establishment of Central Banks must, from the ' Liberal ' point of view, be regarded logically as the first step to ' State interference '. The really logical followers of that school, of whom Professor Mises may be mentioned, in fact advocate ' fee banking ' linked by gold automatism. But apart from the regulation of the flow of money, the imposition of tariffs, regulation of wages (negatively the prevention of Trade Unionism) all these produce effects for entrepreneurs which are homogeneous within one country but differ widely between countries. Dynamically these differences will determine the essential features of the business cycle.

If we then apply the Keynesian theory to the balances of payments we must immediately recognise how vastly important the size and especially the relative size of national units is. For small countries, even if they suffer large excesses or deficiencies which distort their economic system, cannot make an impression on the level of business activity of their big partners, especially if those partners are blessed with relatively large gold reserves. On the contrary, the instability, the competitive position and the policy of the ' dominant ' powers decisively influences the economic position of the ' smaller ' nations.

Indeed, a properly conceived general theory of international em-ployment and exchange should, starting from this asymmetry in the functioning of the world economy, explain the concrete international pattern which economic fluctuations assumed in history It will give a clue why, e.g. economic development before the First World War in France, was slower yet more smooth than in the ' English orbit ', includ-ing Germany. It will also reveal why a world system in which England was the ' leader ', though also suffering from sharp fluctuations, could be expected to recover more quickly and with less damage to the ' peripheries ' than the new system in which the U.S. is the ' leader '.

The degree of instability in a multilateral and nondiscriminating system depended in the past (and will depend in the future) on:

(1) the rate of decline in demand in the leading depressed country relative to its national income

(2) the rigidity (or fluidity) of its cost structures

(3) the size of the surplus in its balance of payments and its relation on the one hand to domestic saving (determining whether the slump can be cured by an excess of exports) and on the other to total world demand (determining the degree of pressure exerted abroad by the excess of exports).

The size of the export surplus of the 'dominant' country will depend *initially*, partly on its own foreign trade multiplier and the relative domestic elasticities of demand and supply, partly on those of foreign countries. Once the export surplus has materialised, the outcome will depend on the reaction of foreign countries. This will again be influenced by a host of factors, the most important of which is whether those foreign countries which, as a consequence of the depression suffer from a deterioration in their balance of payments, are *able* to 'carry' the deficit, i.e. on the size of their liquid reserves relative to the import surpluses which developed and whether they are *willing* to do so, i.e. whether their own policy is 'orthodox' in the 'rules of the game' sense or whether they try to attempt to stabilize employment despite the losses of reserves. This action and reaction will determine a family of world demand curves which are interrelated and determine the world position at any one moment. The larger the 'leading' country and its national income relative to the world, the greater its own instability relative to the world, the more fluid its cost structure and the more urgent the demand for its products, the greater will be the instability of the system as a whole.

If when the 'new rules' of convertibility and non-discrimination are imposed, the leading member has no employment policy (as e.g. the U.S. in 1929 or again in 1937) and is insensitive to outside influences, while the 'weak' members have no reserves, the resultant 'oligopoly position' (in which balances in international payments and the level of employment play roles similar to those played by price and quantity in ordinary oligopoly analysis) will be serious for the latter. It will involve (apart from the automatic 'deflationary' impact income effect of the emerging export surplus on the level of employment in other countries) a conscious 'secondary' deflation in the weaker member countries,[1] which will eventually hit *all* countries. The resultant shrinkage in income and/or counter measures, such as the imposition of tariffs, etc., limiting imports, will depress employment

---

[1] Aimed at maintaining their reserves at all costs.

in the whole system to a point where savings in the 'leading' member are sufficiently reduced to provide a stable basis for recovery as opportunity for investment increases.

What are the lessons to be learned?

(b) The Transition Period

The problems of the transition period must be dealt with on a different basis than the long term problems, otherwise they might prejudice the establishment of a stable system—very much as after 1920.

In the transition period itself there will be a formidable monetary strain between countries which are able during the war to preserve some equilibrium because they escape devastation and those where immediate decontrol would result in a violent inflation. This strain will be similar to that which might appear later when one or more countries are depressed while other still work fully at their reconstruction. In both cases the less wealthy or reconstructed countries will be good markets to sell to and bad markets to buy from. And this fact will produce considerable unfavourable balances in the war-weakened countries. But the solution of the longer run problem, caused as it is by a deficiency of demand in the richer, and not by a deficiency of production in the weaker areas, is—at least theoretically—easier, because the cure would merely imply bringing back into production, through foreign loans or grants, the unemployed capacity of the richer countries. This procedure is not practicable in the transition period without international planning and controls because the richer areas are themselves fully employed. Thus poorer areas have no chance of obtaining additional supplies from the richer areas except at the cost of violent price increases, which are likely to retard rather than to help reconstruction. Yet they are precluded from buying from one another if they do not buy the same goods from the 'rich' countries. The exceptions provided to the rule of absolute multi-lateralism and non-discrimination in the Bretton Woods Final Act and the I.T.O. Charter for the transition period are wholly insufficient from this point of view.

The period contemplated for the transition period, moreover, already very short, has been further shortened by the Financial Agreements which the U.S. has concluded with European countries. It can already be seen that those who warned that non-discrimination under post-war conditions will have a restrictive rather than expansionist effect on trade have been proven right. Sweden, Argentina, among others, have already curtailed their purchases from Britain in order to increase their export surplus and obtain more dollars from

Britain, thus hastening the day when Britain is no longer able to buy from them. Britain, on her side, was forced to curtail the imports from ' soft ' currency areas because she can no longer afford to buy the same goods from the U.S. In both instances reciprocal arrangements would tend to decrease the cut in world trade.

(c) The Long Run Problem

The long term outlook is also disturbing. The two wars have violently upset a world economic equilibrium which was the outcome of a slow development over a century and a half. The distribution of population had adapted itself to that equilibrium and it is impossible to readjust it even in scores of years. Moreover a brusque alteration has taken place in the relative power of Continents. The post-war economic settlement negotiated at Bretton Woods and Washington, however, by implication insists that the nineteenth century political unit should be the basis for twentieth century world economic organisation; for it rules out, in practice, new preferential customs unions (and the establishment of full Customs Unions between the main European countries is not politically or economically feasible). It also prohibits long term reciprocal purchase agreements, which represent an alternative means of regional planning, because such agreements conflict with the principle of non-discrimination and unconditional convertibility of currencies. Under these circumstances the enforced ' opening ' of economic frontiers will perpetuate the superiority of large and rich countries for the export industries of these countries are based on large and protected internal markets, reap the advantages of increasing returns through mass-production and will therefore retain their superiority in all industries in which mass-production can successfully be applied. But these are the industries on which Western Europe must now largely rely to secure vital imports by manufactured exports. It is to be feared, therefore, that the new rules will stabilise the present unsatisfactory state of Britain and other European countries which are faced with superior U.S. competitive power, and the determination of even poorer areas to industrialize themselves. Is there any reason to suppose that they will submit to this fate?

I doubt whether the reader will share Dr. Triffin's optimism (or the illusion of most of the British negotiators at the Bretton Woods Conference), that the Scarce Currency Clause would provide protection for countries which maintain full employment in the face of a depression in an important country. It would take some years before it ever came into operation. The ' liquidity ' approach to multilateral full employment[1] i.e. schemes which 'permit single countries to maintain full employment irrespective of the consequences of this policy on the balance of their international payments, by creating and placing at their disposal internationally acceptable means of payment' must be on a much vaster scale than the I.M.F., in all probability even vaster than the original ' Clearing Union ' scheme of the late Lord Keynes. Even then there are grave drawbacks to such schemes. ' To allow depressed countries to run up export surpluses which would permit the maintenance of full employment policies everywhere, has the drawback that the cumulative debt balances would be distributed haphazardly. Unless they are periodically forgiven they would tend to force mature deficit countries to adopt deflationary policies, as such countries will not in the long run tolerate a growing indebtedness, however vague the obligation to " repay " these " cyclical liquidity " debts '.[2]

The Bretton Woods Act had to provide a remedy for the exhaustion of the stock of any currency in the Fund (due to a continuing excess of exports of the country concerned) because unlimited borrowing by deficit countries was excluded by the scheme. This was achieved by rationing that currency, i.e. introducing multilateral discrimination against that country's exports. But because of (a) the distortion of the world economy due to the fall in European and the increase in the U.S. productive capacity, and (b) to the arithmetic of the Fund, the time which might elapse during a period of acute shortage of the most important currency, the dollar, before it is declared ' scarce ' might be anything up to four years, unless 25 per cent per annum borrowing limits on quotas of the deficit countries, are waived. (It should be noted, however, that the voting power of creditors is cumulatively strengthened, that of the debtors weakened, when borrowing takes place.) During that time, the only methods by which other members can maintain the balance between the supply and demand for the potentially scarce currency are deflation and devaluation. Under these circumstances, the spread of the depression could not be prevented.

If, however, the ' surplus ' area (the U.S.) consented to lend or make direct investments, the scarcity of the currency might not arise at all. In that case the rest of the world could maintain full employment by domestic ' anti-cyclical ' measures. But it is doubtful whether these would maintain the demand for the products of the export industries thrown out of work. This might well involve serious frictional unemployment. The increasing debt to the U.S. might, moreover, involve the loss of financial independence by the debtors.

Further discriminatory measures by way of discriminating quanti-

[1] Cf. my essay ' The International Aspects of Full Employment '. Reprinted Section 2 No. 3 and Vol. II. Section 7. No. 23.
[2] Ibid.

tative regulation of imports are permitted by the I.T.O. Charter (but are outlawed so far as Britain is concerned by the Anglo-U.S. Financial Agreement). This expedient is also insufficient to protect countries who have to rely on industrial exports for their existence because *each* country can only take *unilateral* action. There is no reason to suppose that third countries will discriminate in favour of ' dear ' supplies from those countries which are not depressed. Reciprocity which would force them to do so, is still outlawed.

A word of caution seems necessary at this point. If the International Monetary Fund should attempt to sit in judgement over measures such as, for example, the quantitative control over exports or imports, which are specifically exempt from its jurisdiction, and force members to forego certain measures (such as quantitative import restrictions), though other international agreements, e.g. the Charter of the I.T.O., permit them, the existence of the Fund will be even shorter lived than one fears.

We must certainly continue the attempt to achieve international stability within a full multilateralism, but must at the same time guard against a possible failure.

Conclusions:

The grave danger in the present trend of official thought in this country is that it concentrates almost exclusively on *negative safeguards*. However *necessary* these may be they are certainly *not sufficient* to maintain stability.

Multilateral stability, it seems, will depend on the extension, to a considerable extent, of planned economy, if periodic breakdowns are not to occur. This is one of the arguments in favour of regional arrangements, such as the Sterling Area, which combine the advantages of multilateralism with some measure of direct control. Moreover— and this may be even more important—only preferential arrangements will restore equality of opportunity in a world in which the size of countries differs very much, and in which industrial development is based on mass production methods, i.e. in which increasing means play an ever increasing role.

The Editors of the *Review* must be congratulated on their timely decision to reprint Dr. Triffin's article in Britain. The danger of intellectual isolation leading to international misunderstandings and clashes in practical decisions can only be overcome by mutual patience and willingness to understand each other's point of view. It is to be hoped that their example will be speedily followed on the other side of the Atlantic where the need for a reasonable and thorough study of opinions held in this country and on the Continent seems hardly less urgent.

7.

EXCHANGE DEPRECIATION AND ECONOMIC READJUSTMENT

Dr. Polak's recent article on devaluation[1] presents a further important step towards the acceptance of the case pleaded consistently by the critics of Bretton Woods. He argues, convincingly, that, even if we assume complete equality between countries in terms of their national income and foreign trade, devaluation by a country undertaken to readjust a disequilibrium in her balance of payments might—indeed is not unlikely to—cause equal or greater disequilibrium in the balance of trade of one or more other countries. If we drop the hypothesis of equality and take into account not merely the inequality of the size of countries and of their foreign trade but also the highly concentrated nature of that trade due to the peculiarities of the tariff systems, his conclusion seems quite inescapable.

The easy-going acceptance of the contrary view can, as he conclusively shows, only be attributed to the time-honoured habit of treating foreign trade problems in the theoretical framework of two countries, one of which is taken to represent the world and must, therefore, be considered infinitely large in comparison to the other country (i.e. assuming each country to be perfectly competitive in a perfectly competitive world market). He concludes, therefore, that a policy of lowering real costs (by increased efficiency generally and not by deflation) combined with the acceptance of some negative balance of payments in the transition period (by using liquid reserves or foreign credits, including the credit facilities offered by the I.M.F.) and possibly selective import restrictions, is preferable to devaluation.[2]

Unfortunately, Dr. Polak did not pay any attention to the secondary income effects of the readjustments. He did not discuss cumulative 'induced' balances and their peculiar nature, a procedure which would be permissible only if we could assume that all deflationary and inflationary impact effects from abroad are, or can be, instantly neutralized at home. This is certainly not the case. If the disequilibrium were considerable, and the international monetary disturbance caused by its readjustment large, it does not seem probable *either* that the relevant propensities *or* that investment, i.e., income will remain constant. Hence cumulative movements are only too likely. Under normal circumstances—i.e. when pent-up investment and consumption demand is not excessively high—it is to be feared that the *deflationary* shock will prevail in the sytem as a whole.

[1] J. J. Polak, 'Exchange Depreciation and Monetary Stability', loc. cit. XXIX (1947), pp. 173–82.
[2] Ibid., p. 182.

Dr. Polak tries to exclude this problem by dealing with 'effective' depreciation only, i.e. with depreciation not offset by converse movement of 'prices'. He is so much oppressed by the current problems due to the general inflationary tension that he only discusses the contingency when the effects of devaluation of a certain currency are frustrated by a rise in wages and prices in the devaluing country. We should not, however, forget the opposite danger, the danger that a devaluation is compensated by a further deflation abroad, thus intensifying a world-wide process of shrinkage. Unfortunately his analytical device implicitly assumes that all cyclical phenomena can be compensated by depreciation, and therefore begs the question of whether devaluation is always 'effective' in conditions of a cumulative deflationary process, when the total income of the system is falling.

Furthermore, perhaps again too much under the influence of present-day problems, he believes it is possible to make a sharp distinction between cases of what he calls 'overvaluation' and 'structural' disequlibrium. Only with respect to the latter does he concede any validity to doubts about not so much the efficacy as the suitability of devaluation. In the case of 'overvaluation' he believes 'it is to the interest of that country and of *all other countries* (my italics) that equilibrium be re-established by the depreciation of that currency.[1]

Now it seems difficult if not impossible to make such a clear cut differentiation as Dr. Polak seems to believe, between disequilibria resulting from 'overvaluation' and from structural changes. Dr. Polak's four categories of 'overvaluation' are a mixed bag. They include (1) the result of budget inflation, and (2) appreciation of the currency after a period when costs had readjusted themselves to an earlier lower level. Both these types result from a mistake of the government of the country concerned. The next two categories (3) the fall in the exchange value of other currencies and (4) the fall in prices abroad, reflect foreign policies. Thus Dr. Polak continues in the traditional refusal to differentiate between balances due to the cyclical fluctuations and general under-employment on the one hand, and balances due to other causes, i.e., either to 'structural' changes or to longer term policies of single countries. This failure must vitiate policy recommendations. Devaluation will be effective only if the resultant disturbance in international economic relations which has made it necessary, has been of a short-term duration. Then, and in my opinion, only then, can we expect that the 'balances are shifted back to their original equilibrium position'—*provided such equilibrium position did exist originally*. It is regrettable that Dr. Polak did not make

---

[1] Ibid., p. 181. The repeated failure of France to restore 'equilibrium' by devaluation should serve as a warning example.

K

use of the analytical device of differentiating between induced balances, i.e. balances due to the failure to maintain full employment demand, and other causes which would cause disequilibrium even if all countries were fully employed. He would probably have come to the conclusion that induced balances, due to deflation in a powerful country, are unlikely to be cured by devaluation, and that devaluation in those cases would, in all probability, generalize the trouble in just the same way that he so ably analyzed for the case of structural disequilibria. What is needed under such circumstances is either domestic action by the offending country or its isolation by those not affected.

In the case of induced balances due to a temporary inflation in, or a sudden appreciation of the currency of one country—while others maintain employment—the cure is obviously by devaluation. It must not be forgotten, however, even in this case, that the full employment in the other countries might have been maintained by this inflationary process in the deficient country (or rather the consequent surpluses of the other countries). Thus, where it is proposed to cure the disequilibrium by devaluation, care must be taken that the resultant deflationary shock abroad does not start a spiral of contraction. The post-1920 troubles offer several examples of such ' cures ' which turned out worse than the evil.

This warning is the more important as such relatively simple cases of ' overvaluation ' causing induced balances of a *short* duration are relatively rare. In most cases ' overvaluation ' will arise not so much from absolute price (and wage) movements resulting in a relative over- or undervaluation of a currency, but from far subtler changes in the economic system, such as different rates of change in technical efficiency combined with a similar degree of trade union pressure for higher wages; rise of new sources of supply which necessitates increased efficiency or reduction of wages in the old supply centre; and so on. They will be slow in making their influence felt, especially if the stricken country has foreign assets or credit with which to maintain its position. Thus such cases of ' overvaluation ' fade gently into what I called ' autonomous ' balances, i.e. balances which would persist in a world economy of full employment, and which Dr. Polak seems to call structural disequilibria. Indeed orthodox economists would (in a certain sense rightly) call such structural disequilibria ' overvaluation ' as they would contend that they could be expressed in terms of price. And as Dr. Polak seems to accept the static view of economic readjustment, he should agree with this line of approach. The only difference between these categories of unbalance is in the area of the prevailing price disequilibrium. But even from this point of view, only a gentle transition rather than a drastic break can be discerned.

Indeed, the real difference is not between Dr. Polak's ' price ' and ' structural ' disequilibria (as he disregards what I should consider the most important of any probable future balance-of-payments disequilibria, i.e. induced balances resulting from depression), but between price disequilibria which have not lasted long, (which, therefore, have not caused readjustments in other countries), and those price and structural disequilibria which have. The former were discussed above and were found to be mainly ' induced ' in character, and only partly curable by depreciation. So far as the latter are concerned, Dr. Polak has not made out a case that long-lasting so-called price disequilibria will not cause far-reaching and unequal effects in third countries. If they do, they must be treated like ' structural ' disequilibria, i.e. without recourse to depreciation. This is especially the case if the country suffering from such a disequilibrium is a large one whose imports and exports are unequally distributed geographically, and if it is a serious potential competitor with other areas.

It is as astonishing as it is regrettable that even at this late date, and despite all experiences we have suffered, certain economists continue to confound temporary disequilibria of short duration due, for example, to divergent monetary, economic, or social policies of governments, and the deep-seated fundamental disequilibrium, due to the ravages of a long and especially devastating war which is plaguing most European countries.[1] The view which regards the European malaise as a mere consequence of ' inflation ', ' excess liquidity ', and the ' overvaluation ' of currencies disregards completely the disastrous political consequences of a policy based on such an analysis. Only by creating mass unemployment could we now hope to ' balance ' Europe's international payments on a basis of returning to ' sound ' finance and ' free-market ' economics. Nor could one talk of a ' maximisation ' of real income. The maldistribution of scarce supplies through grossly unequal distribution of income would add to the unnecessary loss through unemployment. Politically, such an attempt would certainly end all hopes for the maintenance of the private enterprise system in Europe.

To attempt to treat the present European malaise as a temporary short-lived departure from a putative ' equilibrium ' to which the return is easy, instead of as a historically unique harsh break with all

---

[1] E.g., F. A. Lutz, ' The Marshall Plan and European Economic Policy ', *Essays in International Finance*, No. 9, Spring 1948. Those economists who, having asserted that the postwar international economic agreements were amply sufficient to bring about orderly reconstruction, now try to hide their discomfiture by asserting that there is no problem of a dollar shortage, but merely of inflation outside the U.S., remind one of the fond mother who, looking at the victory parade proudly exclaimed, ' Look Papa, everyone is out of step except our Sammy '.

that has gone before, a fundamental structural crisis which has to be cured by a set of careful and discriminating policies, must lead to repeated breakdowns. The first requisite of a rational solution is an increase in European productive capacity, which also implies a restoration of its balance. Marginal investment, however, just because of this lack of balance of the productive equipment paralyzing parts of the existing stock of capital, should yield exceptionally high returns. The restoration of Europe also demands a rationalization of European production by making use of modern techniques based on mass-markets. The second and hardly less important condition of success is the creation by cautious and co-ordinated planning of a large-scale economic unit within which this productive capacity can be developed. 'Free' market economics cannot give a solution in conditions of extreme scarcity. The creation of a full Customs Union does not answer this problem. The premature imposition of non-discriminating multilateralism (burdened with the lopsided concessions made to 'underdeveloped' countries at the I.T.O. Conference at Havana) on the relations of Europe with complementary overseas economic area (e.g. the independent British Dominions and Colonies) will put an unnecessary strain on the delicate process of readjustment and might jeopardize it altogether. Once Europe, torn out of its former functions in the world economy, has been successfully reintegrated by harmonizing a greater internal economic unity with special ties to overseas and other (e.g. Eastern European) complementary areas, the time will have come when she can compete on an equal basis with the more fortunate areas of the world, when the classical tenets on the international division of labour can again be applied to the 'real' world. Otherwise, all the efforts will end in creating dependent client states.

8

Political Economy

Sir D. H. Robertson, *Britain in the World Economy*. George Allen and Unwin, London, 1954. 7s. 6d. net.

R. G. Hawtrey, *Towards the Rescue of Sterling*. Longmans, London, 1954. 12s. 6d. net.

L. S. Amery, *A Balanced Economy*. Hutchinson, London, 1954. 12s. 6d. net.

If *Wissensociologie* (sociology of science) or social psycho-analysis were conceivable in England (but who would dare to enquire into the motives of gentlemen?) its practitioners would have real fun with the turns and twists (if not cycles) of fashion in economic doctrine. There is hardly any economist who, under the Labour Government, has not poured scorn on the concept even of a dollar crisis. The cause of our recurrent balance of payments crises was the Welfare State. This made us live beyond our means. All those who thought that the dominance of America in the non-Soviet orbit raised problems of great complexity were just cranks or crooks. Their views were an elaborate subterfuge, a ' laboured ' excuse concocted to get at the pockets of the poor U.S. tax-payers. Devaluation and dear money would ' cure ' all. The objection that the resulting situation would be much worse for the poorer countries than the dollar shortage, i.e. a concerted discrimination against American exports, was dismissed as ' political '.

The unanimity of respectable economists completely captured the Conservatives, who were in any case restive under the controls. They had tolerated these in war-time. Their existence robbed them of their financial veto-power over Governments, a veto-power which they exercised with such effect in 1931 in Britain, and 1936 in France. What could be better than a ' scientific ' justification of their prejudice and interests?

Once the Conservatives achieved power they went after decontrol with all their might. Their surprise and chagrin in finding themselves suddenly deserted by all and sundry of their academic following must have been really intense. There are today in Britain in academic circles as few adherents of a dash to (financial) freedom as it had opponents in, say, 1946-7, when the British (and Western European) position was infinitely more precarious.

Sir Dennis Robertson is certainly not one of them. No-one was wittier (or more bitter) than he was at the expense of the (very tentative) strivings of the Labour Government towards a more stable and just economic system. In these lectures to an American audience he explains the problems created by the second World War and the accession of the U.S. to complete dominance in his inimitable manner. It is a pity that his conversion did not come earlier. He might have helped in resisting some of the measures of decontrol which were largely responsible under Labour for the recurrent difficulties in the balance of payments. But the accession to common sense is to be welcomed at any time.

Professor Hawtrey and Mr. Amery were never men of fashion and they have not changed. Professor Hawtrey, will perhaps a little unfairly, be best remembered as the back-room author of the famous Treasury Principle, flamboyantly enunciated by Mr. Churchill at the nadir of his career: ' It is the orthodox Treasury dogma, steadfastly held, that whatever might be the political or social advantages, very little additional employment and no permanent additional employment can, in fact, and as a general rule, be created by State borrowing and State expenditure .' Professor Hawtrey's colleagues at the Treasury and the Bank took this view as an excuse for doing nothing, as a mathematico-scientific figleaf to hide their intellectual and emotional bankruptcy. Professor Hawtrey was far too farsighted and sensitive to leave it at that. He re-created in an idealised picture, the nineteenth-century environment in which the great merchant firms instantly transmitted variations of the rate of interest to economic activity by altering the amount of their stocks. Thus by varying the Bank Rate absolute stability could be attained—in the idealized model.

Actually speculative movements are far too strong for such sensitive control and merchants far too weak to make much impression. Professor Hawtrey, however, has not yet given up hope of his model. It is not absolutely clear what sterling is to be rescued from. Professor Hawtrey still complains of overspending— but he wishes to revalue sterling. He wants to curtail consumption but wishes to expand investment. It is not clear how all this is to be accomplished, nor indeed how all these things are compatible. It is equally unclear how his acceptance of ' full employment ' is compatible with real full employment when it demands a policy of stability of wages, i.e. a fall in the price level. Moreover Professor Hawtrey wishes to attain full convertibility for the pound, i.e. not merely the acceptance of non-discrimination but also freedom for capital export. Unlike Sir Dennis, Professor Hawtrey's attention is still so absorbed by the monetary problem that he continues to be unaware of the fundamental causes of the unbalance in international economics.

Mr. Amery is very conscious of these fundamentals. He has, rightly, been one of the early advocates of closer co-operation with the Commonwealth. Unfortunately his advice was not heeded betimes: the Ottawa agreements were not followed up by positive investment co-ordination and expansion. Nor is it easy to see how market forces could have achieved Mr. Amery's aims then (or could now). Yet Mr. Amery is loath to draw the logical consequences of his position. He hopes that agriculture can be ' restored ' by further subsidies, by permitting the landlord to charge higher rents, and by giving him further tax concessions and grants. Surely this method has been tried to surfeit. Nor can one support his wish to give further and bigger doles to mineral production: why should Britain be considered as *the* unit in which balance is to be achieved? Mr. Amery, moreover, accepts unreservedly the myth assiduously spread by retired civil servants, that the capital equipment of the country is being destroyed by taxation. He is still unaware of the fact that private industry did not even use the

capital at its disposal. One can wholeheartedly agree with his demand
for larger productive investment. It is doubtful again whether his
aims can be accommodated by the political framework into which he
forced himself. This, unfortunately, also applies to his international
policy. He sees that it is necessary to find a ' permanent solution of the
present unbalance in the world economy resulting from the dispropor-
tion between the immense, highly geared self-sufficient economy of
the U.S. and a number of isolated, unorganised weaker units '. But
on a private enterprise basis it will hardly be possible to achieve it.
Moreover the *Commonwealth* in contrast to the *Sterling Area* and the
European Payments Union is a historical organism which has little
to do with the economics of today. Mr. Amery might think he knows
the Canadian mind better than they do, but he will hardly be believed
by the Canadians. Moreover he seems firmly to ignore the fact that it
was the Colonies which recently lent to the Mother Country, not the
other way round. Indeed his conception of the relations between the
colonies and Britain is still that of Lord Milner or Kipling. The first
lesson which we must learn in order to be able to advance at all, is
that pitifully insufficient attention was paid by British administrations
to the possibilities of a conscious advance in the territories under our
control. The old tribal economy was shattered by the impact of market
economics and large-scale exploitative enterprise and nothing substituted. ' Partnership ' looked very odd to the coloured ' partner ' in
Kenya or Rhodesia, not to say South Africa. A book on the problems
of the Commonwealth in which the colour-bar and apartheid are
brushed off in a few lines is hardly likely to lead to trustworthy conclusions. All this is a great pity, as Mr. Amery's intuition about the needs
of the moment is right, and there can be no doubt that (unlike his
professional colleagues) he has tackled the right question.

9

DOING THE COMMUNISTS' JOB

Per Jacobsson, *Some Monetary Problems International and National.*
Oxford University Press, 42s. net.

This is a book of outstanding political and human interest, due to
the status, the energy and success of Dr. Jacobsson. As economic
adviser to the Bank of International Settlements and more recently as
Managing Director of the International Monetary Fund (appointed with
the assiduous help of the Bank of England) Dr. Jacobsson more than
any other individual, is responsible (or perhaps rather represents the

forces making) for the contemporary Western drift to stagnation through monetary mystification and economic obfuscation. In this volume he adds an exceedingly interesting sketch of the economic and monetary history in an autobiographical framework to his collected writings, which mark the milestones of Europe's decline into depression and war, and, since 1945, of the Great Debate between the protagonists and opponents of Full Employment and High Investment.

The interest of the volume is enhanced by the fact that there was a time when Dr. Jacobsson was in the van of unconventional economic analysis. I well remember a scene in Geneva when Sir Arthur (now Lord) Salter wept announcing the abandonment of the Gold Standard in 1931. He was obviously terrified of the inevitable inflation and ruin. His fears were shared by Sir Otto Niemeyer and Mr. Loveday, the arch-Conservative-Liberal head of the Economic Section of the League of Nations. Dr. Jacobsson energetically, fearlessly (and quite unsuccessfully) supported me against general disapproval in maintaining that the danger was a wholesale deflation of the rest of the world and that reflationary steps were urgently required. (He tells a charmingly kind story about those days (p. 327) but now fully agrees with his erstwhile chiefs.) It was his violent reaction to the Keynesian revolution which determined his more recent attitude to economic policy and divided him from progressive thought.

After the war, now well entrenched on the extreme Right, he conducted a vigorous and victorious campaign for the restoration of monetary policy as the sole governor of economic life, for convertibility and the abandonment of all subtler, direct controls. He attacked full employment policies as inflationist when such views were still very unpopular: Dr. Jacobsson never lacked courage. By 1955 his views were dominant in all but the poorest areas of the non-Soviet world, and in 1958 at New Delhi he seems to have been successful in imposing them on these too—insofar, that is, as the Russian competitive bids for influence in the non-committed areas will not prevent the Anglo-American chevaliers of *laissez faire* to have their way.

This victory of Asquithian (if not Gladstonian) liberalism together with the obsession with armaments have gone some way in sealing the fate of the West. The steady and hopeful advance which, until 1955, embraced both the well-to-do and the underdeveloped countries of the non-Soviet orbit has come to an end. In the U.S. and Britain there has been virtual cessation of growth in the last few years and the Western European boom now also seems to be fading out. There has been a sharp fall in the price paid for primary products and with it a grave setback in the poor areas. The uneasy stagnation in the richer, and crises in the poorer, areas, so characteristic of the interwar period, has been faithfully reproduced by the victory of Dr. Jacobsson's views. His pathetic efforts to enlist Keynes' posthumous article to strengthen his case for monetary control and his faith in the automatism of the market shows how uneasy he really is in this new intellectual posture. In contrast to this handiwork of Dr. Jacobsson, and his backers, and disciples, the Soviet and China have made gigantic strides. They are within striking distance of making good their claim of catching up Europe, and then the U.S.

The tragedy of the extreme anti-Communists is that, objectively, they perform the work of their enemies. The Bretton Woods Conference, which established the eventual supremacy of money-capital in the West, was the first step in this direction. When it was over, and at the Savannah Conference, the gullible optimism of the supporters of the Fund, like Keynes or Harrod, had been shattered, the analysis of the motives of the American policy-makers, especially of Mr. Harry White, who were obviously ruining the weaker countries of Europe, was confused by the mounting wave of spy-hysteria in the U.S. No decent person could join in the Communist hunt. Yet, in spite of Senator MacCarthy, it might well be argued that intellectually the most charitable explanation of Mr. White's behaviour is that he deliberately wished to weaken the Capitalist World. In point of fact it is more than probable that he was insufficiently intelligent or wicked to do so. He merely believed in text-book economies. By insisting that money be restored to its position as the ultimate arbiter, by cutting down development plans in the poor, and creating unemployment in the rich areas of the world, Dr. Jacobsson, once more, and perhaps even less consciously, is voluntarily doing Mr. Khrushchev's and Mr. Mao's job for them. A pity.

POSTSCRIPT

The first essay, written in 1931 at the League of Nations, represents my groping after an integration of the real and monetary treatment of the problem of international readjustment in a period of crisis. It represents, therefore, an attempt to emerge from the classical framework. It was largely unsuccessful because, though it perceived the need for stopping liquidation through foreign exchange control (then violently condemned by the Financial Committee of the League), it did not see the need for reflation. It was nevertheless rejected by both the Director of the Economic Department of the League and by the Chairman of its Financial Committee. This is not to say that devaluation cannot be a palliative or might not be an essential part of a policy package restoring balance. Indeed the shock produced by devaluation might be needed to stimulate exports and give a breathing space for the other remedial measures to begin to work. But the fashionable view which regards devaluation as a remedy is based on the experience of Britain in 1931 which is impossible to recreate.

Devaluation is a static measure, however; it only registers (relative) decay by reducing real wages. If the basic dynamic weakness of a part of an international system is not remedied, the decline in relative competitive power is resumed, and the monetary problem reappears. A repeated devaluation, or a floating currency which is impelled downwards by the same basic dynamic forces, liberate anticipatory income claims and speculation, and thus destroy the currency without bringing about a cure. Keynes by emphasising the superficial, monetary causes of Britain's discomfiture after 1925 obscured the more fundamental causes of her debility, the over-extended claims that the financial machine makes for capital exports on our exiguous saving, and the complete insufficiency and lacking effectiveness of our domestic capital investment. They were fundamentally responsible for our inability to cope with the relatively minor monetary problem caused by the return to the pre-1914 gold parity. They are still with us.

The rest of this section is firmly based on a neo-Keynesian analysis which rejects the simple multiplier model and takes cognizance of the impact of instability on the ease of readjustment. Once a cumulative movement has started, the possibility of purely monetary readjustment is gravely impaired, for reasons which are set out in the contributions included into the next two sections. This truth has not penetrated to the orthodox, as the two reviews clearly show. But in the U.S., the Staff of the Joint Economic Committee has begun (1960) a new era in official publications, by re-discovering the grave price in terms of lost growth, that has recently been paid, as a result of the foolishness of listening to traditional wisdom. Mr. Kennedy's victory might usher in a new era of greater understanding.

A second important conclusion, that emerges, is that it is the character of the dominant centre which determines the problem of employment in, and growth of, international systems. Their size, instability and sensitiveness to change in their foreign balance (depending partly on the relative magnitude of their international reserves) will shape monetary readjustment if direct controls are disallowed.

In the third essay of this section (No. 7) (1948) I continued the advocacy—begun during the war (No. 4) (1943)—of forming a large and diversified European economic unit including the Commonwealth to face the U.S. on an equal basis. Unfortunately this has come about on a different basis, with Britain's role sharply reduced and the Sterling Commonwealth largely disintegrated.[1]

[1] Cf. Postscript to Section 2.

THE DYNAMICS OF ADJUSTMENT II

INVESTMENT, PRODUCTIVITY AND TRADE

10

THE DOLLAR CRISIS REVISITED

In this paper an attempt will be made to show that:

(*a*) the dollar problem is a complex one with varying causes and phases, each of which demands different treatment;

(*b*) that it cannot (at least in its present phase) be explained on the basis of a classical model by a simple foreign-trade bias in American economic progress;

(*c*) that a segregation—except for analytical purposes—of the ' monetary ' process from the ' underlying real basic equilibrium ' is impermissible, as they co-determine one another;

(*d*) that U.S. progress must be regarded as one involving unequal, but (up till now) unbiased improvement in productive efficiency;

(*e*) that such *random* impulses emanating from growth, though unbiased, must not be assumed to be *neutral*, and that it is equally impermissible to assume that the impact effect of growth is *uniformly* distributed over the rest of the world. Hence models embodying two countries only, eliminate most, if not all, problems under discussion. The most important aspect of our problem is the geographical distribution of benefits and losses due to the developments in the U.S., because this is the main determinant of the limits and thus also of the possibilities of British policy;

(*f*) That classical models based on constant costs and excluding technical progress (which affects the relative efficiency of factors of production) can not, even when generalized into a multi-country model, deal with the problem under review; and that the fact of cost variability must be an essential determinant of policy;

(*g*) that the impact of this progress on poorer countries is destructive of their own development, unless met by their combining in devising appropriate measures of which

> (i) discriminatory protection,
> (ii) increased investment, and
> (iii) close collaboration in investment policy, will all be essential
> ingredients;

(*b*) that, finally, the choice of policy, especially the choice of the proportions in which discrimination and investment should be used, would be decisively influenced by the willingness of non-American countries to forgo immediate advantages of trade with the U.S. for future progress of their own economic systems; the chances, in the short run, of Britain being able to obtain such collaboration (if it were to give a lead) are much greater than generally supposed.

I. THE THREE DOLLAR CRISES AND THE STERLING PROBLEM

We shall first of all survey the historical setting, and this will enable us to analyse the nature of U.S. technical progress. We shall then be able to work out a dynamic model of the changing features of the dollar problem, and try to establish the wider theoretical implications of our analysis.

1. *The Dollar Problem*

In the most general possible manner, and without assigning any specific cause, the dollar crisis might be described as a persistent, though periodically acute, tendency for U.S. exports to outrun U.S. imports. In the context of post-war relative orders of magnitude of the ' independent ' countries making up the non-Soviet orbit, of their gold reserves, and of the sensitivity of their economic systems to outside stimuli,[1] this tendency implied a need for adjustment mainly or solely *in the rest of the non-Soviet world*, which was far too vulnerable to sustain passively losses of reserves sufficient to reverse the movement— if such reversal was at all possible automatically or by U.S.action.

This tendency of the U.S. to denude the rest of the non-Soviet world of international reserves can be caused by a number of factors, some on the supply and others on the demand side, some mainly international in character (i.e. connected with changing comparative cost conditions), some purely domestic (e.g. the pressure to increase impediments to foreign exports into the U.S. whenever they threaten to grow). The loss of internal balance, the fall in demand leading to a violent increase in the potential supply of U.S. exports (and a fall in imports) is also of the latter variety.

---

[1] i.e. the relationship between national income, savings, and foreign trade.

This explains the fact that the dollar crisis seems to have persisted under varying conditions. The rest of the Western World suffered when the U.S. were fully employed—in 1947, and again in 1951. It was prostrate when she had a setback—even a minor one, as in 1949. Balance was not restored when the terms of trade of the manufacturing countries improved (1949), nor when they worsened (1947 and 1951). An explanation based on a single cause can hardly be blamed for all these shocks.

2. *The Historical Setting*

Before we analyse the problem of causation systematically we might begin with an historical survey. In the last decade or so we seem to have suffered from at *least three different types of dollar crises*. They are intertwined in a complex manner but, at any one time, one might attribute to the one, or to the other, the main impact:

i. The first, which was the most apparent in the immediate post-war period, was the result of the desperate shortages in the war-devastated and weakened areas. The strength of the demand for American products was overwhelming as no substitutes, or substitute sources of supply, were available. Open inflation in the U.S. following de-control in 1946, far from helping, seriously aggravated the problems of the rest of the non-Soviet world as demand for U.S. products was all but rigid.

This problem was the cause of the complete breakdown of the attempt to enforce the wartime agreements on the restoration of the sway of the ' free ' price mechanism in international economic relations. It was somewhat diminished by the efforts at reconstruction and intensive productive investment in western Europe and elsewhere, efforts which were supported by the American loans to Britain and other countries, and by Marshall Aid. Output (and productivity) in most areas has regained and surpassed pre-war levels. Thus the most desperate shortages caused by the war have been dealt with.

There remain, however, its indirect effects, the loss of trade connexions by Europe in third markets and the thrust of the U.S. into a secure hold in them. There remains also the effects of the unsurpassed industrial and agricultural development in the U.S. which created new processes and new products. This residual has merged with the third problem to be discussed below.

ii. The second of the dollar ' crises ' is what one might call the *short-term dollar problem*. This is the problem of U.S. instability and its consequences on the rest of the world. It was predominant in 1925, then again after 1929, 1937–8, and yet once more 1947, 1949 and 1951.[1] It is made more acute by the inevitable emergence in the U.S. of beggar-my-neighbour policies in these circumstances.

iii.   The third is the problem of the *periodic readjustment* enforced on the larger part of the rest of the non-Soviet world (both primary producing and manufacturing competitors of the United States)[2] by the *superior competitive efficiency* in the U.S. in the widest sense of the word. This will be discussed at greater length in the next section. It is this tendency, incidentally, which results in a natural self-sufficiency of the U.S. through the periodic unassisted displacement of non-U.S. exports (the latest example is sports cars) causing severe losses abroad. The self-sufficiency of the U.S. (and the problems of the rest of the Western world) are—even in relatively prosperous times—yet further increased artificially by various government measures of protection. This phenomenon might be termed the ' medium term dollar problem'. It tends to increase the solidarity of the non-dollar areas.

iv.   The fourth problem, the problem of active competition of the U.S. for scarce primary products, has not as yet emerged. It was given a spurious actuality by the U.S. re-stocking panic in 1950–1. In fact this restocking panic was accompanied in the U.S. by a rearmament boom which violently increased U.S. imports also of finished goods and services (e.g. steel) from Western Europe. This restocking boom, therefore, differs in essentials from the problem of the future when there is unlikely to be a dearth of manufacturing capacity in the U.S., when, therefore, the position of the manufacturing competitors might be more serious.

3.   *The Concept of Superior U.S. Competitiveness*

In order to resolve these difficulties let us therefore first analyse the exact meaning of the phrase ' cumulatively increasing U.S. competitiveness '. Most authors seem to treat this increased competitiveness exclusively as a question of a *relative fall in U.S. export prices*. This seems a dangerously misleading approach.

American progress seems multi-dimensional, and the capacity of cutting prices is not even its most important consequence.

For certain restricted analytical purposes there may be no harm in expressing its effects in terms of wage-price relationships. In advising

[1] In 1947 and 1951 the instability was almost entirely restricted to the instability of stocks, especially Sterling commodity stocks. That this was sufficient to cause a crisis shows the extent of the weakening of Europe.

[2] In 1949 the pressure on the primary producers was more marked than on the manufactures, and in 1953–4 it is again this pressure which will probably precede the latter.

on policy, however, the drastic simplification implicit in this procedure must be borne in mind. To be sure, there is likely to be a price at which British products will become ' competitive ' with the U.S., even if their displacement from foreign markets by the U.S. was not primarily the result of price-cuts (or absence of price increases). Thus there will always be a price-discount which will offset favourable terms of credit or quicker or more certain delivery dates, etc. Equally price-discounts can make up for the non-existence of servicing facilities or skill in advertising or ' prestige '.

But it is essential to keep these causes of increased U.S. competitiveness separate, in order to be able to choose successfully the *socially least costly* counter-measures.

a. Supply Factors. Turning to the supply side, the most important factors affecting U.S. competitiveness are the following:

i. The disproportionately high investment capacity (including investment in research) which currently seems to reach the astonishing level of three-quarters of the total investment in the whole of the non-Soviet world, with research expenditure reaching an even higher proportion.

This investment can be divided into

(1) refinements in the production of existing commodities and services, also produced by other countries:

(2) the discovery and development of new or radically improved products.

The former will enable a cut in prices at home and abroad; the influence of the second is more far-reaching: it will displace products, and thus might force either dangerously drastic price-cuts or wholesale structural changes on their former suppliers. This process can perhaps be most easily visualized as the continuous creation in other countries of ' inferiority ' among export goods or the reduction of other countries' exports to the status of ' inferior goods '.[1]

Apart from this cause of displacement of the exports of other countries (especially luxury and capital goods) into the U.S., and even into third markets well supplied with dollars, there is a further, and probably more manageable, cause of U.S. superiority. This cause originates in its success in adopting mass-production methods enabling substantial cost-reductions. This cause is *adventitious* in the sense that it is (mainly) the result of the two large upsurges of productivity due to the stimulus of two wars. Had America's competitors not been

---

[1] This ' inferiority ' must be sharply differentiated from either the Marshallian (price) inferiority or from the inferiority due to an increase in income. The second is nearer to it. Cf. below, p. 151.

paralysed by these wars they could also have adopted them with equally
favourable results (though not without large-scale reorganization and
investment). It should be noted that the advantages under this heading
have been experienced in primary production (including agriculture)
as well as in manufacture.

The resultant aggravated competition which the saving on production costs makes possible might take the form of:

(*a*) increased expenditure on advertising;

(*b*) maintenance of large sales and servicing organizations;

(*c*) advantageous delivery conditions through maintenance of
stocks or because of the relatively large scale of current output
to foreign sales; or

(*d*) finally (and probably least important) straight price-cuts.

ii.   The intense dynamism of the system: its vast scale relative to
the rest of the non-Soviet world secures further decided advantages to
U.S. in its competition with other (manufacturing) countries. Even if
no actual deflationary pressure arises through the exhaustion of internal
markets and investment opportunities, the necessary capacity will
always be available to secure sharply contested extra-American markets,
and beat competitors through prompt deliveries. A less expansive
system could only secure this flexibility through actual deflation and
the maintenance of a (more considerable) degree of under-employment.

Paradoxically enough, this tendency to excess capacity might well
have a *favourable* effect on the U.S. terms of trade: the foreign pru-
chasers of capital goods might well be more interested in early profitable
operation (because quasi-rents are notoriously risky and uncertain in
the longer run) than in the price, and prefer U.S. products, even if
dearer, to others, if the latter are only available with some delay.

iii.   The dynamism of the system and the vast increase in the size
of the productive unit with which it is associated is also likely to stimulate attempts by U.S. producers to ensure against U.S. instability by
diversifying their market through international expansion. As cost
accounting is very arbitrary in the case of large-scale enterprise
conducted on an oligopolistic basis, they can easily do this—even if
smaller (foreign) firms would not or could not compete. At the same
time the fact that export trade is only marginal enables American
producers to take these risks.

iv.   Added to this precautionary motive—and hardly less important
—is the high prestige value of a world-wide organization. There are
further important tax-saving-accountancy considerations which will
undoubtedly stimulate the managerial *élite* of the biggest corporations,

L

even when it does not exactly fit the shareholder (profit) motive to extend operations.

v. The increase in the relative size of U.S. corporations, and of the relative availability of capital (savings) increases the lending capacity of individual U.S. firms relative to their competitors. This is further enhanced by the establishment of public corporations to finance foreign trade and the facilitation of tied loans. In poor countries where investment is likely to yield high immediate returns credit facilities are often more important than price.

Disproportionate investment and technical progress represent cumulative forces in several senses: in the first place they will cause an ever-widening discrepancy in the productivity in and outside the U.S. So long as full employment in the U.S. is maintained by private investment expenditure (and not by increased defence of social expenditure financed either by loans or by taxes falling on savings) it is likely that national savings—including corporate savings—will rise further with productivity and income, and, with it, investment capacity.

In the second place, investment in research is a typically increasing returns activity: inventions from being accidents or sparks of genius are reduced to routine activity. At the same time the monopoly profits connected with them enable vast new expenditure; by reducing risks even in the U.S. the process cumulatively stimulates the large units. The *circulus vitiosus* is completed by the fact that these units have great latitude in their competitive (incl. price) policies. The monopoly positions created in this way continue until the technique is assimilated by foreign countries abroad (if assimilation is not blocked by patent laws not suited to this peculiarly lop-sided international position) or until protection forces the U.S. firms to carry their activity abroad.

In distinction, superior availability and credit facilities do not represent cumulative influences though they might be very powerful advantages. This distinction is important in deciding our policy.

b. Demand Factors. No less important are the factors working on the *demand side* towards a recurring tendency for U.S. exports and services to outrun purchases—though some of them (advertising) are made possible by superiority on the supply side.

i. Even those American products for which adequate and basically competitive foreign substitutes exist obtain a prestige value (not the least through U.S. films) which is out of proportion to their usefulness. A sort of complementarity due to consumption habits arises.

ii. Beyond and above this automatic effect of industrial leadership the powerful salesmanship developed in the U.S. represents a powerful incentive to spending. Now in the U.S. this constant temptation to spending, and against saving, might well represent a sociological boon and a necessity if the ' free enterprise system ' is to survive. In poorer areas it is suicidal to permit it, as it reduces the limits of investment. On the other hand, ignorance of certain American products might indeed be bliss if this means that saving is strengthened or that the pressure to sell abroad in order to pay for these goods is reduced by their exclusion. The impact effect on the terms of trade and on the distribution of income of the poor countries of a ' liberalization ' of imports from the U.S. might be highly deleterious.

iii.   This effect is reinforced by a factor which to some extent can be regarded as a mixture of the two previous ones—the Veblenesque ' conspicuous consumption ' effect: U.S. prestige and salesmanship can easily penetrate the small upper classes of the poor countries which are often as rich as, or richer than, the (much broader strata of) Americans for which these goods have been mass-produced. The snob-appeal emanating from the U.S. is then reinforced by a domestic force.

The preference for U.S. products created by these factors and which has lately been described by the innocuous words of ' demonstration effect ' is ' irrational ' only in the sense that the psychical losses caused by a *total* elimination of U.S. products would be less than corresponding to the actual preference manifested. It is not irrational in the sense that the preference would not be re-established if the buyers would be exposed once more to the salesmanship and snob-appeal.

Liberalization thus might under certain circumstances promote profligacy, decrease savings, and thus tend to intensify the problems of the areas which have to increase their rate of interest if they are to reduce the growing handicap in their trading and competitive relations with the U.S. Even from this point of view a sharp all-round control of imports from the U.S. seems required. This argument is *different from*, and might modify the degree and quality of restrictions imposed merely to improve the terms of trade irrespective of the collateral effect of the restrictions on domestic distribution.

Sharply to be distinguished from this increase in the (individual) propensity to consume is the effect of the growing awareness of the masses of their wretched condition in large parts of the world. This is due partly to the rise of democracy and the destruction of colonial power, partly to the threat of Communism and the impact of the success of planned investment. In many areas, including Europe, this desire to speed up progress creates a threat of open inflation—and, unless that is ' suppressed ', leads to either a collapse or the policy of a monetary crisis.

It should be added quite emphatically that U.S. progress opens up new genuine possibilities of enjoyment and a decrease of toil. Efforts to mitigate its destructive consequences on the producer interests abroad—efforts which are essential if a further, and politically disastrous, increase in the inequality in the international distribution of wealth is to be avoided—must therefore take the form not indeed of the protection of inefficient and stagnant vested interests but a consciously guided stimulus to our own dynamic development. Otherwise any gain for the producers of outside countries will be more than offset by the loss of consumers' satisfaction. It is the one-sided haphazard nature of progress concentrated in one region which is to be guarded against—not progress itself.

c. Short-term Instability. We have up to now discussed factors which are *quasi-permanent* in character. There remain considerations of short-run instability to the relations of the U.S. with the rest of the non-Soviet world and inflicts avoidable damage not so much through a worsening of the terms of trade as through intermittent monetary shocks and unemployment.[1]

i. The first significant fact in this respect is that the U.S. has become a large part—over 50 per cent—of the total non-Soviet economy. On the one hand, foreign trade plays a relatively small part in the U.S. economy. Thus variations in the foreign balance have little automatic effect (as they are of the second order of smalls) on the U.S. national income.[2] Conversely any change in U.S. demand might have an overwhelming influence in foreign countries.

ii. The probable indirect multiplier effect in the U.S. through the banking mechanism of changes in her reserves seems also negligible. The reserves of the U.S. are vast—constituting some two-thirds of the total reserves of the non-Soviet world. They are, moreover, large in relation to any variation of the U.S. balance of payments. Stabilization in the U.S. will depend on volitional acts of the U.S. administration, and not on automatic monetary forces. The ratio of gold reserves abroad to the value of foreign trade, however, has declined as a result of the U.S. refusal to agree to an all-round increase in the price of gold despite the multiple increase of foreign trade prices. Whether an increase in gold prices would be the best possible way of dealing with

---

[1] Theoretically speaking there might exist an exchange rate at which full employment could be maintained despite the deflationary shock. Apart from the extreme impoverishment which such a rate might well imply in practice through the worsening of the terms of trade, competitive devaluation or automatic counteraction by the creditors may vitiate its effects. Equally the cumulative factors might well have an employment effect. Nevertheless there is a valid distinction between effects which are due to U.S. unemployment and those which would operate even if the U.S. were fully employed throughout the period.

[2] Cf. *A Foreign Economic Policy for the U.S.* (ed. S. Harris), chap. 25, Table 2, p. 458.

the problem, however, is very much open to doubt. Thus foreign countries are in no position to accept with equanimity threats to their reserves.

iii. The consequences of instability in the U.S. are aggravated by two further factors both resulting in a multiplier effect on the foreign balance of a given variation in U.S. home demand.

(a) The first of these is the self-sufficiency of the U.S., the causes of which have been investigated. A relatively small change in demand might often lead therefore to a more than proportional change in the (marginal) demand for imports (or exportable goods). This result might well be reinforced in case of deflation by administrative or legislative protection of American domestic producers.

(b) The whiplash effect is enhanced by speculative anticipations and consequential changes in U.S. stocks of commodities. The well-known weakness of the reserves held by foreign countries aggravates this risk.

II. THEORETICAL IMPLICATIONS

We are now in a position to survey the more general implications of our analysis of the causes of the U.S. competitive superiority. We shall, first of all, discuss some of the general problems raised in the analysis of the ' real ' (barter) sphere and then deal with the questions raised by the monetary unbalance.

Two preliminary remarks may be in place.

(a) In the first place, some of the confusion has been caused by treating *random* events as necessarily *neutral*. If there is reason to think that progress is distributed in a random manner over parts of one country (i.e. part of the system as a whole), the effects of progress are dismissed as unimportant because it is implicitly assumed that random effects always offset and cancel each other, i.e. that they are equivalent to *an unbiased uniform* progress. Professor Frisch's analysis of business cycles should have warned authors that in a dynamic setting this procedure is not permissible, even in a closed system.

In the present context this assumption is made wholly illegitimate by the fact that there is *no randomness* in the relations of the *parts* (i.e. countries) of the system to one another. On the contrary, there is a complete *asymmetry* in the dynamic relations of the dominant country to the rest of the system. The former initiates shocks and reaps the main benefit. The periphery has to adapt itself as best it can to the new situation. As we shall see, the actual developments can only be accounted for satisfactorily by reference to this asymmetry.

(*b*) In the second place—and not unconnected with this general attitude—it is almost instinctively assumed that problems in international trade can always be successfully explained by models containing two countries only. If the impact effects of the dynamic evolution of any of the units were distributed evenly among the other countries, or were negligible, this procedure might be justified. The deeply ingrained habit of treating *cetera* as *paria*, and neglecting secondary repercussions and distributional problems, can be defended if the problem is one of perfect competition and optimum (or unchangeable factor endowment). But in this context the U.S. is an equivalent to the *whole* of the rest of the non-Soviet world; i.e. of a different order of magnitude than other countries. On the other hand, the specialization of other countries (due partly to the development of foreign trade, partly to U.S. investment) has vitiated the assumption of the even distribution of impact effects. Thus the probable incidence of gains and losses becomes one of, if not *the* central point of the analysis.

1.   *The ' Real ' Sphere*: *the Inevitable Benefits of Growth*

Economic opinion was all but agreed that growth and progress in any one country was not merely beneficial on balance to the country itself but to the ' rest ' of the world. In the country itself the harm done to the producers of displaced goods was visibly offset by the benefits gained not merely by the consumers but by the ' new ' producers.[1] The extension to the ' world ' of this doctrine of the essential harmony of interest seemed less plausible. The greater was the triumph of the classical school for having accomplished it: its proof was furnished by the improvement of the barter terms of trade of the outer-world with the ' progressing ' country. It is this proof which necessitates the assumption of a foreign-trade bias in U.S. progress to explain the non-monetary discomfiture of the outside world.

There is, however, at any rate since 1929, no evidence of such a simple bias in U.S. growth. It seems, therefore, that we must look in a different direction for the explanation of the non-monetary difficulties. The validity of the classical optimism is beyond question—on its own assumptions. It is the unreality of these assumptions that explains the contradiction between prediction and reality.

(*a*) *The uneven geographical incidence.* The first problem which arises in this context is the uneven distribution of the impact effects of progress in the dominant country on the ' rest of the world '. An adequate

---

[1] No one denied that *some* people were harmed.

representation of the problems raised from the point of view of Britain[1] necessitates a model containing at least four countries. There is first of all the United States. In the second and opposite pole we have the United Kingdom. In between these are ranged countries which can be divided into two groups, each of which will have to be represented by a ' country '. The first of these consists of countries which are liable to benefit directly from the U.S. progress; the second of those which do not. The first consist almost entirely of primary producing countries, situated—as we have seen—mainly in the western hemisphere. The second group while mainly manufacturing is by no means entirely so: it is the essence of the dollar problem that there are a number of countries which are complementary to one another, and yet also competitive with the U.S.—a result of the U.S. being exceptionally large and a naturally self-contained country.

Part of the ' rest ' of the world thus will undoubtedly benefit by ' progress ' in the U.S.: U.S. demand for its products will rise, and, if the production of these goods is subject to decreasing returns, the terms of trade will be shifted in its favour *more than by the (relative) cheapening of U.S. products.* This part of the world either belongs to the Dollar Area and suffers from no dollar problem, or could become a member, being held back by *political* rather than *economic* reasons.

In the second group there will be countries which though indirectly (and to a lesser extent) benefiting from U.S. progress (because the price of their products is being increased or the price of supplies is cut) cannot be regarded as parts of the Dollar Area because their direct sales to the U.S. (both absolutely and relatively to potential purchases) are insufficient to permit them a neglect of other customers: they are more affected by the discomfiture of the latter than benefited by U.S. progress.

Finally there are in this group also countries which, like the United Kingdom, are overwhelmingly competitive in character and which cannot hope to derive benefit at all.

The first group is not merely restricted at the moment to few countries, but, as we have seen, it may well be (and it is not even unlikely) that military and political reasons will also in future restrict the area thus benefited mainly or entirely to the western hemisphere. The abundance of cheap capital in the U.S., and the fact that much of the natural wealth of the western hemisphere is still untapped, facilitates this restriction of the ' Dollar Area '. In any case, insofar as development of the ' rest of the world ' took the form of high-yielding U.S. investment (and much of the capital goods and technical skill

---

[1] If the problem were to be viewed from the point of view of a Dollar Area country (e.g. Canada) a three-country model might be adequate.

required being physically obtained from the U.S.) even an extension of the Dollar Area might not help but aggravate the dollar problem of the (shrinking) non-dollar rest of the non-Soviet world, though this problem will differ fundamentally from the traditional problem of the terms of trade of the extra-U.S. manufacturing areas, as there will be relatively abundant supply of primary products.

As and when (if at all) dollar imports eventually increase because of the relative exhaustion of natural resources and this increase begins to offset the effect of superior U.S. technical progress, the Dollar Area will expand (the rise of uranium mining has, as it seems, extended it now to South Africa). Whenever the unfavourable effects of U.S. progress, or a sudden fall in U.S. demand, overtake these shortages and decrease U.S. imports, the membership of a (number of) country(ies) in the Dollar Area may become questionable.

The classical model seems to have misled writers into thinking of the area benefited by the progress of a single country as large, and that harmed as small. As each single country was thought of as insignificant relatively to the rest of the world, and therefore rather specialized in its (potential) exports, this was only too natural. The phenomenon of the U.S. (which is equivalent in economic power to the whole of the rest of the non-Soviet world) could not be accommodated by this model.

Yet it can be argued that (even when all this is admitted and the relative slenderness of the number of the beneficiaries realized) the classical optimism could be justified. In some sense (no longer admitted as sense by modern writers[1]) the 'large' gains of a few beneficiaries could be said to 'offset' or 'more than offset' the small losses of the majority of the rest of the world. Even if this were meaningful, it would hardly mean much from the point of view of those harmed (or not benefited), as they will not be 'bribed' or compensated for foregoing policies which might reduce their discomfiture (though at the cost of preventing 'greater' benefits for the privileged rich). But it is quite obvious from our survey that the story is not exhausted by the geographical unevenness of the favourable and unfavourable effects of U.S. progress.

(b) *The nature of the dynamism of progress.* Part of the answer is undoubtedly supplied by the complicated nature of U.S. progress and especially its consequences on factor utilization (and values) in a micro-economic sense. Our analysis of the nature of U.S. progress has unquestionably established the fact that the number of possible combinations of the various factors operating is far greater than has hitherto been supposed: we can divide the cases

[1] Cf. ' Welfare and Freer Trade '. [Reprinted Section 1, No. 2.]

(i) according to the character of the process through time;
(ii) according to the mainspring of the growth;
(iii) according to the nature of its impact on industries;
(iv) according to its influence on factor utilization;
(v) according to the relation of the impact on foreign trade.

(*a*) Time
1. Uniform
2. Periodic
3. Random

(*b*) Causation
1. Investment
2. Returns
3. Psychology
(snob appeal, etc.)

(*c*) Industry
1. Uniform
2. Non-uniform
(*a*) necessities
(*b*) luxuries

(*d*) Factor utilization
1. Neutral
2. Capital saving
3. Labour saving

(*e*) Foreign trade
1. Not biased
2. Biased

(*a*) uniform
(*b*) non-uniform
(*a*) exports
(*b*) imports

It should be noted that insofar as foreign trade is determined by relative factor endowments (and in some sense it always is—though that sense might not be very meaningful)[1] the old acquaintances in dynamic analysis, the 'neutral', 'labour', and 'capital' saving inventions, will in all probability introduce a foreign trade bias, though their effects will by no means be limited to foreign trade.

Anyone with an appropriate bent can construct quite a number of cases—perhaps even write a treatise—each of which might then be followed out on the basis of *a priori* assumptions. A more scientific procedure would be, perhaps, to choose the appropriate model on the basis of factual knowledge.

We shall first of all analyse the problems that arise out of the impact on factor utilization and foreign-trade bias ((*d*) and (*e*)), then turn to the nature of its causation (*b*), and—as a transition to the 'monetary' problem—to the consequence on demand (*c*), and the implications of its time-shape on risk and the rate of growth (*a*).

(*c*) *The problem of 'inferiority' and displacement.* Such historical evidence as is available suggests that at present (and in the recent past) American dynamism is (and was)

(i) not biased as between primary production (especially agriculture)[2] and manufacturing. If anything, relative progress in the former seems to have been more striking.

---

[1] Cf. Samuelson, 'International Trade and the Equalization of Factor Prices', *Economic Journal*, June 1948, pp. 181–3.
[2] There is some bias against raw-material production.

(ii) Among manufacturing industries there is no bias towards 'import-substitution' rather than 'export competition' with other manufacturing areas, such as Britain.

This is not surprising, but exceedingly disconcerting. It means that the American dynamism is dominated by the combined effects of capital investment and technical inventions. These are able to overcome (c.f., for example, the case of textiles or rice) the effects of (static) relative factor endowment. There is, in other words, no reason to be confident that inventions will not render processes capital-intensive[1] which are at present labour-intensive.

Indeed, inventions counteracting existing comparative advantages, and suppressing (or rather offsetting) them, are not unlikely. In the first place they will be stimulated in the high-wage capital-rich country by the fact that no new demand need be created when an attempt is made to displace foreign products now imported (i.e. in which the country suffers from a comparative disadvantage): the existence of a market is known and the entrepreneur is able to concentrate on solving a technical problem (e.g. the success of the sports-car model in the U.S. which was opened up by the success of British manufacturers). The comparative disadvantage is made to disappear.

Once this happens, superior marketing techniques and the other stimuli, which have been discussed above, may, in the end, transform the industry into an exporter. Exports in which the weaker country had comparative advantage will suddenly disappear. Lately changes in technique made their full effect felt even in agriculture. The mechanism analysed by Ohlin (insofar as its applicability has not been destroyed by other factors, e.g. complete specialization) will be decisively weakened. The equalization of factor remuneration through trade is postponed or altogether reversed.

More generally, and in the second place, the fact that in the rich dynamic country, the productive factor which is in greater abundance elsewhere, is relatively scarce and expensive will stimulate its saving, even if there is no ready market now occupied by foreign competitors. Thus in the nature of things research will tend to be concentrated on technical problems which—if solved—are bound to decrease the value of the productive factor available elsewhere, and thus national income. The fact that research expenditure tends to be cumulatively concentrated in the 'richest dynamic' country intensifies this bias.

In the context of international economics the assumption[2] that

---

[1] [For a striking factual collaboration of this surmise, cf. Leontief's article discussed in this Section No. 12.]

[2] On all these matters, cf. Mrs. Joan Robinson, *The Rate of Interest*, London, 1952, esp. pp. 40–43 and 52–53.

technical progress, on the average, will neither be labour- nor capital-saving is not justified. Technical progress is not evenly distributed over the world. Thus not merely the locus of (and the direct gain from) the innovation will tend to become concentrated, but the nature of the progress will also be influenced. The non-arbitrariness of the geographic incidence of progress, which not merely separates the dominant from the dominated but imparts a bias against the less developed (and less dynamic) countries, is of the utmost importance in the diagnosis of our malaise.

The character of invention is dominated by the labour-saving propensity of the relatively low rate of interest ruling in the dominant country. But once progress and the technical revolution has been accomplished there is no way back. The process has become irreversible: the change in technique cannot be resisted by a fall in wages without undue hardship. Thus the principle of comparative costs loses much of its meaning: it is not sensible to ask what the relative greatest advantage is when (at the margin at any rate) the rate of change of the relative advantage is large. The losses suffered at the margin through the enforcement of repeated readjustments may well be greater than any gains due to the corresponding marginal increase in the international division of labour. As invention of the type discussed, far from increasing specialization (and thus increasing gains and reducing the risk of losses), decreases it (thus reducing gains and increasing the risk of losses), the limitation of trade might be beneficial.

The relative cheapness of expensiveness of foreign products does not seem to have much influence on the substitution of U.S. products. In fact (and within reason) the more expensive goods are, the less likely they fit U.S. production methods and tempt U.S. producers to active technical innovation. Even in raw materials technical progress does not have any obvious relation to relative prices—though of course unavailability (i.e. infinitely high price) has a powerful effect (e.g. artificial rubber). But (as the case of rubber in the nineteen-twenties shows) more routine measures of saving in the use of the primary product are unquestionably stimulated by a rise in price.

Thus the contingency of decreased demand for certain (imported) goods despite an increase in income, which is traditionally treated as an exceptional and perverse case, not claiming serious attention, turns out to be a common occurrence of vital importance. It should be noted that ' dynamic ' recurrent ' inferiority ' depends on the continuance of the superiority in research: otherwise it can better be treated as a once-for-all displacement of competitive goods. The emergence of such new and coveted products might diminish demand for a wide circle of other commodities and not only of their immediate substitutes. It should be contrasted with the Marshallian concept of inferior goods which depend on the income-effects of price changes.

This abrupt substitution of U.S. products might well be ' irrational ' from a social point of view, and impelled by prestige, selling and service organization, etc., especially in the case of capital goods where U.S. products might be over-capital-intensive (automatic) for conditions elsewhere. But in many instances the use of these capital equipments will be economic even from a social point of view: their productivity might be out of proportion to the older instruments and their price might be kept relatively low through the mass-production of machines unknown elsewhere.

This is the basic reason why ' there is a relatively large volume of foreign trade trembling as it were on the margin of advantageousness, and liable to be blown to one side or the other of that margin by small changes in the world circumstances.'[1] The dynamism of a large dominant country *because* it is *not biased* between primary and manufacturing production but biased against the productive factors which less developed countries possess in abundance, might cause disproportionately grave repercussion to the latter. The ' growth ' of the U.S. instead of making her more complementary to the ' world ' is likely to render her more competitive. It lessens, in a haphazard way, the scope of profitable trade with a large part of it.

(*d*) *The Cause of the superiority.* The superior dynamism of the U.S. will in part be due to increased saving and investment and heavy expenditure on research. Only emulation or greater technical aptitude can equalize this factor. On the other hand, we have seen that a considerable part of the advantage of the U.S. orginates in the possibility of large-scale production (i.e. the shape of cost curves, rather than merely in the intensity of investment) due to the adventitious favourable conditions enjoyed in critical periods of U.S. growth. Thus (temporary) protection abroad—if followed up by positive measures of investment—would enable there a large-scale reorganization of industry which would in fact be equivalent to the rise of ' infant ' industries. Without protection the breathing-space needed to permit this development is unlikely to be vouchsafed. In practice, therefore, the enforcement of the most-favoured-nation clause means that the rest of the non-Soviet world is kept in small units and prevented from reaping the possible benefits from known techniques.

It is for these reasons essential to know the exact cause of the dynamic superiority of the dominant country if counter measures are to be devised at the smallest social cost to the poorer areas.

[1] Professor Robertson, ' The Future of International Trade '. Reprinted in *Readings in the Theory of International Trade*, Philadelphia, 1949, p. 505.

(e) *The time-sequence and its importance.* The exact nature of the time-pattern of the dynamism is equally vital for the diagnosis of the problems in front of us. It cannot be represented, without subsequent detailed empirical analysis, as a process of either *known* uniformity or of pre-determined and *known* periodic *discrete* jumps in productivity in one country with the other remaining stationary. It is the interaction of the two economic systems, or rather the influence of the dynamism of the dominant economy on the development of the satellite, which is at issue. The problem is how the productive pattern and capital accumulation, i.e. in the long run, the volume of the total resources of, and the degree of their employment in, the dependent economy will be affected by the progress in the dominant country.[1] The assumption that the interaction does not influence the growth of the weaker area reduces the problem into a pseudostatic one. It is not possible to escape from the constriction of a static system by taking *growth* rather than total resources as *given*. All evidence points to the conclusion that progress is not even, nor has it a regular periodicity.

The *random and unpredictable character* of the technical progress through shocks unevenly distributed among the industries of the dominant economy thus imposes a new risk on all other countries.

(i) It threatens, through its cumulative effects, *periodic* monetary upsets in the ' weaker countries '.

(ii) It exercises a *general* depressing influence through the added risk introduced into the dependent economy. Thus the incentive to invest (already terribly handicapped by the difficulties besetting a dependent country) is further reduced because the risk of finding markets suddenly vanishing is difficult to meet. The weaker countries do not have protected internal markets from which to forage far and wide, nor the capital required to make constant adjustments. The gains of a greater international division of labour are offset by the reduction of the rate of progress[2] due to ' technical ' risk.

(iii) This effect is distinct from and additive to the ' monetary ' risk of a U.S. recession and to the equally destructive but more *permanent deflationary* pressure emanating from the greater flexibility of a more dynamic system.[3]

---

[1] I have tried to express this idea—rather unclearly and certainly quite unsuccessfully—(' The Concept of a Dollar Shortage '. Reprinted Section 1, No. 1,) by saying that ' the concept of the eventual equilibrium position has no sense independently of the path taken. Its position will be co-determined by the path of readjustment '.

[2] The idea of *uniformity* of advance probably arises out of the monetary mechanism which is affected in the same way by a random and uniform progress.

[3] Cf. above, I. § 3.

(f) *The implications of demand changes.* The traditional approach to changes in productivity treated the matter as if a smooth substitution could be expected as a result of the fall in the (relative) prices of the progressive country. It is possible that (even if a violent displacement of products discussed under the phrase of dynamic inferiority does not take place) high marginal income (and even price)—"elasticities" will lead to increased expenditure on imports in under-developed countries. Alternative supplies might not be available at the price, and, even if they were, the prestige of American products might induce a disproportional increase in their demand. We are not justified in assuming that an improvement in the terms of trade excludes or even minimizes the possibility of monetary disturbance.

Indeed, one might suspect that, where a large part of the marginal income accrues to profits, and where luxuries are imported, the benefits of U.S. progress to the under-developed countries would increasingly appear in terms of (new or improved) consumption—goods which *only the relatively rich* in the less developed countries can afford. Thus the balance-of-payments upsets will be accompanied by an increase in the inequality of income distribution. In principle, suitable direct taxes and subsidies could deal with this distributional aspect of the problem. In fact there is no such possibility.

The likelihood of such upsets is increased if U.S. progresses through aggressive and 'uneconomic' sales campaigns, etc. But the essential complementarity of consumption by itself may well (together with social prestige of conspicuous consumption) result in violent displacement of demand towards the U.S. in consequence of the introduction of new or substantially improved U.S. products. While improvements in capital goods may well in the long run increase the possibilities of the progress of the under-developed areas, no such advantage need accrue from those in consumer goods. Thus, in order to be able to benefit from the socially desirable consequences of U.S. progress, measures may well have to be taken to restrict the consequences on imports of the less desirable ones.

2. *The Monetary Sphere*

There is little to be added to the traditional analysis of the *monetary* complications. The main point is whether money wages and costs can be expected to rise *pari passu* with the increase in productivity in the dominant country. It is not probable that the entrepreneur will offer a level of remuneration which would completely wipe out their benefit from technical progress. Nor will they need to do so. The dynamism of the 'advancing' country continually releases workers through mechanization.   This necessarily acts as a damper on trade-union claims.

Thus (unless the government acts, and either lends, or spends) a certain deflationary impact will be exercised on foreign countries. This impact need not be very acute if the U.S. wages *are* rising, and if productivity abroad is not stagnant, and progress is due to steady and slight improvements.   On the other hand, the repercussion might be extremely serious if the progress takes the form of reducing foreign products to inferior status, and thus causing *grosso modo* dislocation rather than mere marginal displacement.   The various propensities might then be violently changed and serious monetary strain experienced even if the ' improvement ' is ' export ' biased.[1]

In concrete cases it will depend on the orders of magnitude of these factors, on the intelligence of speculators, and on the strengh of government controls (if any), whether the problem will become acute. If it does not, the main (and not inconsiderable) consequence will be a growing inequality in wealth and income (probably made even more painful by business fluctuations which poorer countries are less able to bear without hardship).

If the relevant financiers become aware of these prospects, as is likely after some repetition, even in the case of phlegmatic speculators, the consequences would be extremely serious.   Whether the inferior country tried to escape the strangulation by a series of devaluations or by ' freeing ' the currency would make little difference. In both cases anticipatory speculation will be rife, and a continuous flight of capital will ensue, leading to an impoverishment of the country, and an aggravation of the basic cause of disequilibrium.

The persistent though non-cumulative influence of the ' non-price ' advantages, which can be matched only with difficulty by price-concessions, will reduce the likelihood of defensive success.   The continuity of a basic cause of unbalance will also render evasive action more difficult: a temporary undervaluation, which (under ' static ' conditions) would permit the launching of a counter-attack, would be undermined by the dynamic process which continuously reduces the ' equilibrium ' rate of exchange and thus prevents the ' catching ' of bears by forcing up the rate of exchange (assuming that the reaction of the balance is favourable to devaluation or depreciation).[2]

Thus in order to safeguard the currency (and also to deal with non-price-competition, especially quick deliveries) the inferior coun-

[1] Cf., above II, 1. (f).

[2] For reasons explained elsewhere this expression is preferable to ' elasticities ' which cannot be assumed to remain constant in an operation of so finite and all-embracing scope. Cf. P. P. Streeten and T. Balogh. ' What is Elasticity? ' [Reprinted Section 5, No. 13].

tries will be forced into active deflationary-dear money policy to create continuous rather than intermittent unemployment. This will reduce investment and intensify the problem and endanger the progress of the poorer areas. Thus the relative impoverishment might be transformed into an actual fall in the standard of life of the poor and Marx's prediction will be justified on the international plane.

Should the U.S. react to the deflationary pressure generated abroad through beggar-my-neighbour measures, this would further aggravate the position and render readjustment through an increase in foreign exports impossible. If the U.S. would (as she indubitably could on the basis of her vast gold reserves) pursue an expansionary full employment policy, equilibrium could, in principle, be restored in the rest of the world by export surpluses through a rise in the standard of life of the dominant area rather than a fall in that of the poor.[1] Though this amounts to a further increase in the inequality in income distribution, it might not be unbearable politically. But even in this, more favourable, case the question arises whether an avoidance of these periodic upsets would not be preferable.[2]

Unfortunately the expansiveness of the U.S. system might be so violent as to make the sustenance at home of a continued (slight) overall excess of demand impossible politically, especially as anticipatory speculation might create bottlenecks in the American domestic economy and thus lead to internal disturbances even before international monetary balance is reached. If the increase in ' productivity ' is due to technical change resulting in displacement of foreign products, this is *a fortiori* probable. Indeed, the monetary ' equilibrium ' might then not be reached without serious impoverishment abroad. The alternative of restricting trade and thus minimizing the worsening of the terms of trade under these conditions becomes plausible.[3]

We perceive that there is no reason to analyse separately the monetary impact effects according to the nature of the ' real ' disturbance.

We may conclude this survey of the monetary sphere by saying that no ' equilibrium ' in the real, classical sense might be possible: there may be a running disequilibrium. This would be ' offset ' or plastered over by movements of money wages or exchange rates. It

[1] A sufficient fall in the latter necessarily ' cures ' the crisis by strangulation: but the question is not whether deflation and strangulation ' work ' but whether equilibrium could not be restored with a smaller cut in the standard of life.

[2] Cf. below on the improbability of complete compensation of the depressive influence through stimulus to other industries.

[3] It is gratifying that the erstwhile supporters of I.T.O. no longer wish to induce (poorer) countries which were forced through the war-time losses to restrict imports, to grant unilateral favours to the richer countries by abolishing direct controls without counter-concessions in terms of tariffs or customs regulations. [This is precisely what happened after 1954.] [1960].

will depend on the degree and nature of the discrepancy, of the speed of the development of the various units, and the flexibility of real resources (as against monetary expedients) how far the actual position can approach ' equilibrium '.

III. CONCLUSIONS FOR POLICY

We can now gather up the various threads—historical and analytical —of our argument and attempt to draw some very tentative conclusions for policy.

We have established that the optimism of the traditional approach to the fundamental harmony of interest between the dominant and the peripheral countries is not altogether justified.

1. An increase in productivity in the former tends to improve the terms of trade of (and thus transmit part of the benefit gained) to the latter, provided the latter are complementary rather than competitive.

2. If the dominant country is as large and as well endowed with natural resources as the U.S. (in sharp contrast to the previous ' dominant' country, the U.K.) it is not unlikely that the incidence of the favourable effects might (and probably will) be geographically very uneven. If the area benefited has a tendency to develop strong demands for U.S. products it might well be that on the one hand the displacement of U.S. from these (Dollar Area) markets will be difficult, but that, on the other hand, the solidarity of a large (and complementary) area outside the charmed circle could be maintained.

3. Technical progress is not unlikely to be haphazard, both in timing and industrial incidence. If any bias can be detected it is towards the economizing of that productive factor which in relation to others is scarce and expensive in the dominant country. This means, if there are (as there undoubtedly are) appreciable differences in wealth (and thus the long-run level of the rate interest), that technical progress is, if anything, likely to retard a tendency to the equalization of factor remuneration, i.e. it is likely positively to harm the poorer countries.

4. The dominant country on the basis of its large markets (not unlikely to be protected), and high investment, is likely to monopolize the highest increasing returns industries. Historically this tendency has been much reinforced by the paralysis of the periphery during two wars when U.S. progress was most stimulated. Thus in a large area of economic activity the periphery's inferiority is due to historical accident rather than inherent, unalterable causes.

5. Apart from these two types of ' real ' harm there are four rather

M

more 'monetary' features in the progress of a dominant country which are likely to harm the peripheral, less-developed area:

(*a*) economic fluctuations initiated by the dominant country—the 'Keynesian' case—will tend to reduce the gains derived from international trade;

(*b*) as economic progress is haphazard and initiated by the dominant country, trade consequent upon that progress increases the level of risk in the peripheral area, i.e. slows down investment and progress;

(*c*) in addition it is likely that freer trade will lead in the peripheral area to an increase in the propensity not merely to import but also to consume. This leads to a maldistribution of income and further slows down progress. It might also cause social tension and (through political pressure) inflation;

(*d*) the 'non-price' competition of the dominant country, i.e. (mainly) quick delivery, necessitates the permanent maintenance of a higher rate of interest to match by under-employment the flexibility conferred by more intense dynamism. In addition there is a greater capacity to extend credits.

What the relations of the dominant to the inferior countries will be, how many of the latter will benefit, and how many will be harmed by trade will depend (*a*) on the relative size and the nature of the dominant economy, (*b*) its willingness for co-operation and sacrifice, (*c*) on the intensity of its progress, and (*d*) on the existing discrepancy in absolute factor endowments. Equally the solidarity of the 'non-dollar' area (apart from sentiment) will depend on the ease with which 'marginal' countries just outside the Dollar Area can sell to the U.S., and how much their income depends on the maintenance of prosperity in the non-dollar area as a whole.

Eventually it is not unlikely that the U.S. propensity to import will increase and the 'dollar' problem proper will give place to 'primary product shortage' problems, i.e. the problem of the terms of trade of other manufacturing areas. But the time is not yet, and all statistical evidence points to the conclusion that it might not come in this generation.

The most desirable solution to aim at would consist in redistributing deliberate non-Soviet world income in order to speed progress in the less favoured areas. This would, on the one hand, stabilize the level of economic activity in the dominant country, and enable an increase in investment and the reorganization of the structure of industry (in order to profit from the most modern methods of production) in the less developed areas. Incidentally, this solution would minimize the need for discrimination against the U.S. Programmes to this end have been elaborated in profusion,[1] and this contingency need not detain us in detail. It should be noted, however, that even if it were adopted there would be *economic* grounds for permitting discrimination against the U.S. in order to enable the weaker countries to make use of the possibilities of mass-production, and meet certain types of non-price competition.[2]

This type of solution has no chance of being adopted in the near future.[3] Thus the remedial measures will have to be developed in the weak countries.

Whether and how far these remedial measures should and can take mainly the form of a discriminating direct (or tariff) limitation of trade will depend on the nature of the advantage secured by the dominant country. If this is adventitious—historical, and based on mass-production—the advantage of protection (provided it is followed by positive measures increasing investment and productivity) is obvious. In the same way, if regulation can induce an increase of investment and savings its effects may well much more than offset the ' drawbacks ' of ' lessened specialization ' in a static sense.

In the case of ' cyclical ' unemployment, the ' Keynesian ' case, it is now generally accepted that protective measures, through maintaining output at a higher average level, could increase national income, i.e. the gain through increased employment might outweigh the loss through decreased ' efficiency '.

A fortiori the case of an inevitably recurrent disequilibrium must be accepted as even more intractable to cure by ' internationalist ' action on the part of the weaker area (though the importance of an internationalist solution supported by the 'rich' country is enhanced because of the risk of recurrence[4]). The recurrence of the trouble weakens the power of adaptation of the ' poor ' country, because of the growing risk of anticipations. Hence a permanent limitation of trade, if it permitted an escape from the permanent deflation or from the inevitably recurrent problem, might be justified.

We have seen that the functional reasons of U.S. productive superiority can be divided into four main groups:

[1] Cf. Kalecki, Schumacher, and Balogh, *New Plans for International Trade*, Institute of Statistics, Oxford, 1944, my *Dollar Crisis*, Oxford, 1949, and the U.N.O. *Report on National and International Measures for Full Employment*, New York, 1949.

[2] This (and the Bickerdike-Kahn argument) as well as the monetary considerations discussed decide the case against free, or even freer, trade and non-discrimination. The fact that free trade might result in a fall in the standard of life of a certain country is by itself not a sufficient reason to reject it (as the traditional approach implies): the free trade might ' minimize ' the fall even from the point of view of the country which suffers the deterioration—unless the other factors are present.

[3] Cf. for example, the so-called Randal Report published after this essay had been finished.

[4] Such 'internationalist' action might include low-interest lending or 'free' grants.

(*a*) superior investment, including research;

(*b*) larger scale of production; both lower costs and lower risk for marginal export experiments;

(*c*) non-price competitive advantages;

(*d*) snob or advertising appeal.

The advantages conferred by the first two are cumulative in the sense that they lead either to an ever-increasing discrepancy between the standard of life in the dominant country and the periphery, or to an ever-increasing unbalance in the international payments of the latter (or a need for an ever-increasing degree of discrimination against U.S. exports). The last two are permanent advantages of a non-cumulative character.

The first (and most important) cause of the present unbalance of the world cannot be ' met ' except by emulation; only a positive and identically dynamic factor could offset its effects.

In Europe, at any rate outside of Germany, political pressure will not permit high accumulation without resulting in a tendency towards wage inflation unless a fair distribution of incomes is safeguarded. Thus inequality of income (including tax-evasion or non-distribution of profits) cannot be relied upon to secure savings: the State will probably have to provide a large fraction of the capital supply if high profits are not to lead to wage-claims.

For the rest the advantages now enjoyed by the U.S. could be gradually eliminated by discriminating protection against dollar exports coupled with positive action to reorganize production. Discriminatory restriction (though in the nature of a once-for-all measure) will be able to meet these effects of U.S. growth even if not cumulatively increased (a policy which would be plainly impracticable):

(1) some U.S. advantages (e.g. short delivery periods and easy credit conditions) are not cumulative;

(2) restrictions enable the maintenance of a higher investment rate in poorer countries, i.e. decrease the discrepancy in growth rates, because the resultant consumption demand can be made innocuous;

(3) restrictions prevent the emergence of new demands and thus help to increase savings; they eliminate ' Veblenesque ' developments. In this respect ignorance *is* bliss;

(4) restrictions combined with the increase in savings and investment permit industrial organization and thus lead to a permanent cumulative acceleration in industrial efficiency capable of meeting the problem raised by the existence of the U.S.

It should not be forgotten that in the areas well supplied with dollars the increase in U.S. competitiveness with the rest represents genuine gains. Thus when it is sometimes dramatically asked, in the all-or-nothing method of exposition, whether the conclusion that certain areas should consciously limit their trade with the U.S. implies the obviously absurd assumption that the very *existence* of the U.S. has *unfavourable* consequences to the whole rest of the world, the answer, is, of course, in the negative. The disappearance of the *totality* of U.S. supplies would represent a catastrophic impoverishment of the world as a whole. The supply of certain primary commodities would sink to famine levels, some countries would lose their main markets, and technical progress receive a terrible blow.

What this view implies is that the explosive rise of the U.S. when most other parts of the world were in the throes of wars has presented the rest of the non-Soviet world with very awkward problems of adjustment at the *margin* in most areas: the instability and increased competitive power of the U.S. has made the *limitation* (but certainly not the cessation) of trade imperative in some areas, if their relative impoverishment is to be avoided. This does not mean that full (or rather U.S. tariff limited) trade with the U.S. would reduce the *rest of the Western world* as a whole below the standard which would obtain if there was *no trade at all*. It merely means that *full* trade would reduce the real income of many countries and their main suppliers below the level which they could attain if they were permitted to apply *discriminating direct restrictions* on (unessential) U.S. exports. It means that the traditional analysis based on a two-country model, one of which represents the U.S. and the other the whole of the rest of the world, eliminates the significant problems of the larger part of the non-Soviet world.

11

Productive Investment and the Balance of Payments: the British Case

Professor Nurkse in his interesting article on the ' Relation between Home Investment and External Balance in the Light of British Experience 1945–55 ',[1] tries patiently to unravel the multifarious interconnections linking investment and the foreign balance. Few elements, if any, escape his notice. Yet when he has assembled all the carefully catalogued pieces it is difficult not to feel that the Danish Prince somehow got left out of *Hamlet*.

[1] Loc. cit. (May 1956), pp. 121–54.

The dominant theme of the long essay is the ' recurrent conflict between the needs of internal capital development and external trade balance '.[1] Though references to the need of maintaining economic progress are not lacking, the overwhelming impression conveyed is well summed up in a striking sentence of his conclusion where he asserts that ' in the particular British case there is considerable advantage in the use of home investment as an absorber of shocks in the balance of payments '.[2]   And he finishes his essay by saying that ' British experience in the ten years reviewed provides a lesson in growth in international economics, a lesson of some general interest to any country determined not merely to live, but also to grow within its means '. I suggest that if there is any lesson to be learned of the British experience it is that a policy of permitting conditions to arise in which productive investment has to take the brunt of ' balance of payments shocks ' is suicidal.

Professor Nurkse's ambivalence in discussing the British experience is due to his failure clearly to distinguish between the short- and long-run problem. It is further aggravated by his peculiar definition of ' full employment ' and his reluctance to give up his belief, despite some recognition of the prevalence of countervailing forces, in the effectiveness of orthodox reactions in international economic relations to price and income changes.

In this note I shall argue that an adverse movement in the balance of payments can be due to a number of causes, of which an increase in domestic demand is only one. Moreover, the increase in investment is only one of the possible ways in which domestic demand might rise. Proposals to remedy balance of payments deficits by measures operating mainly through cutting investment is bound in most cases to be inefficient, as it does not necessarily tackle the immediate cause of the disequilibrium. In the longer run, moreover, a cut in investment is bound to aggravate the problem of the balance of international payments by weakening, ceteris paribus, the competitive position of the country.

I shall begin with the analysis of the short-run problem. In the short run, investment is obviously one, but only one, of the competing alternatives to exports. This fact alone, however, cannot support the policy recommendation that an unbalance must necessarily be righted by a cut in domestic demand rather than by measures acting on other factors that determine the balance of payments, and, more especially, by a cut in demand brought about by a cut in productive investment. While an abrupt increase in domestic demand, other things being

[1] Ibid., p. 121. Similar statements of the problem are repeated on 125, 142–44.
[2] Ibid., p. 154.

equal, undoubtedly tends to encroach on the resources available for exports and tends to increase imports, an indiscriminating cut in demand will not in all circumstances, where balance of payments difficulties arise, restore the position at the least cost. In other words, a general deflationary policy might well prove costly in the sense of necessitating a much larger cut in income than the orginal unbalance in international payments and which could be avoided by alternative policies.

A balance of payments crisis may be due to capital movements. This we shall leave out of account since it cannot, and should not, be met by measures affecting home demand, but by direct control. An adverse movement of the balance on *current account* might be due to:

(*a*) a fall in the foreign demand for exports;

(*b*) an autonomous increase in the propensity to import due to liberalization of imports or advertising, etc.:

(*c*) an increase in home expenditure[1]; which in turn can be caused by an increase of:

    i. stocks,

    ii. productive investment,

    iii. consumption-good investment, especially housing, and, on a national level, armaments,

    iv. consumption.

(*d*) an increase in expenditure (especially on consumption and consumers' durables) and a decrease in exports caused by money wages increasing faster relatively to productivity, than in competing countries.

Whatever the cause of the crisis a cut in expenditure, and especially of investment, has been the stereotyped answer to it. A cut in stocks, if the cause of their increase was speculative (an important case which Prof. Nurkse treats fully), has obviously much to commend it, but it is difficult to achieve by global measures other than import restriction. An increase in consumption and imports due to liberalization however, might surely not best be met by such measures. Only if there is an unsatisfied demand abroad for the same type of goods will a discouragement of investment expenditure at home make a direct and immediate contribution to the balance of trade. If there is an unsatisfied demand for consumption at home, which is not dealt with, even that will not provide an alleviation. If there is no direct switch into exports, relief

---

[1] Which might be connected with (b) if it is due to an increase in consumption brought about by a fall in savings itself caused by the availability of attractive consumers' goods.

to the balance of trade will only come from a general fall in income and decline in activity. This is an unnecessarily wasteful remedy as the cut in real income might have to be a multiple of the improvement in the balance. The decline in production in Britain, moreover, was mostly accompanied by a decline in output per head.

Now there can be little doubt that autonomous changes in consumption played the most important part in the British balance of payments crises. It was the so-called domestic and international ' liberalization ' policy, which Professor Nurkse does not even mention (including the abolition of controls over hire purchase) which was mainly responsible for this factor.

It is inappropriate when analyzing the balance of payments, to distinguish between consumption and investment rather than between non-durable and durable consumers' goods on the one hand—including consumption of housing and certain public construction—and productive investment on the other.[1]

Let us now turn to the problem of whether the resources released are likely to be readily exportable. There is little doubt that so far as metal goods were concerned, this is indeed the case. Now Professor Nurkse is quite right in saying (p. 125) that investment and exports account for the largest absolute volume of metal goods. But is this relevant? Surely it is the *change* in the demand and not the absolute volume of the demand which is decisive for the balance of payments. And it is the *change* in consumption which accounts for the largest part of the *change* in the domestic use of these goods since 1950. It is his quaint view of the state of full employment which explains the neglect of these *changes*: he assumes a rigid state of affairs where every change in the use of resources must be *preceded* by a freeing of resources. This view is surely false. Full employment is not a definite state but a sort of phase or zone in which considerable variation of output is possible through variation in shifts and overtime. Moreover, resources themselves cannot be regarded as given. They increase continuously and this increase in production permits far greater flexibility than Professor Nurkse allows for.

The insistent demands for the liberalization of imports, coupled with demands for the abolition of direct controls at home, necessarily represent an attack on investment, for no means was available to guide other forms of expenditure or prevent their impact on the balance of trade. When monetary policy was the only available instrument for the control of the economy, investment could not be encouraged

---

[1] This also weakens Prof. Nurkse's view that the creation of credit is particularly connected with investment. Selective credit restriction or direct controls could distinguish between various uses of funds. But discriminating direct controls do not seem to be considered in this connection.

without also encouraging consumption and imports. In the absence of direct controls only a discriminating form of taxation giving incentive to selected investment while repressing consumption, including housing, could increase investment at the expense of other elements of demand. It is characteristic of the school of thought now dominant in Britain, with which Professor Nurkse seems to sympathize, that both the selective use of taxation and even the discriminating use of credit control is rejected. All these objections are implicitly based on the assumption that the entrepreneur and the individual consumer can best decide the optimum distribution of the national income between investment and consumption. It is now many years since Keynes demonstrated the absurdity of this proposition.

Nor is this all. Professor Nurkse at some points acknowledges the possibility of heterodox reactions to devaluation and other orthodox policies due to induced changes of either investment or savings (pp. 138–39, 145–6). These changes, e.g. the fall of savings as a result (say) of devaluation, would frustrate orthodox policies. But having mentioned them Professor Nurkse seems to neglect their importance. The attempt to separate income and elasticity concepts, however, breaks down in the fact that ' elasticities ' of demand for imports and exports are *neither independent from one another*[1] *nor independent of the level of employment.* Two dimensional diagrams cannot cope with the complexity of these interrelations.[2]

This brings me to the dynamic and long-run aspect of the problem. Nurkse recognises that the growth of production and investment might have some implications for the balance of payments problem. But he concludes (p. 140) that ' greater productivity tends fundamentally to help rather than hinder a country in maintaining external balance ' and thus he dismisses it as a factor of decisive importance. I suggest that this conclusion is entirely at variance with post-war experience. Both the United States and the German cases show that a growth rate which is the result of innovating investment tends to create a surplus in the balance of payments. This is due partly to a perverse relationship (if any) between the increase in real productivity and money wages, partly to the displacement of foreign supplies by the innovating producers.[3]

This brings me to my final point. It is, in all probability, not the *absolute* rate of increase in productivity that counts but the rate of innovation *relative to other countries.* The crucial question is how those

[1] If the balance of payments is a ' mirror image of spending ' (146) it was rather a distorting one under the British circumstances.
[2] [Cf. Nos. 11 and 12 below.]
[3] Cf. Mrs. Robinson, *The Accumulation of Capital*, pp. 90 and 162.

countries with the greater rate of increase in productivity react on the increase of productivity. The income effect of their increased real product will lead them to import more, and perhaps export less to third markets: but will their new or cheaper products displace those of their more slowly growing competitors? Both Germany and America have shown what can be accomplished in this respect by a dynamic economy. This problem is not identical with, though it is closely related to, the problem of the impact of innovation or increase of productivity on (wage) costs and prices. This is not to say that wage increases sufficient to offset the increase in productivity are impossible in the leading economies of a world system—only that they are rather unlikely, and *even less likely* are wage increases *which will avoid changes in comparative costs*. Yet it is this effect of the concentration of innovation on the dynamic systems which causes recurrent losses and enforces— avoidable—changes in the productive structure of the less progressive economies which may not be justified in the longer run. From this point of view the continued sharp increases in both United States and German investment and especially investment in research,[1] while British investment projects are being sharply curtailed, is ominous. (No doubt when this policy produces its inevitable results we shall be enjoined to ' cut our coats according to our cloth! ')

I conclude that these considerations suggest that the British post-war balance of payments problem has been mainly due to the failure of the once-for-all effort required to achieve a higher level of investment, the result of which would have easily carried both the adjustments required in the balance of payments and provided for the increase in both consumption and investment.

Diagrammatic Appendix

For those who like oversimplified and thus inaccurate illustrations, my view on the relationship between accumulation, employment, and balance of payments could be made visual by the following family of curves.

It is suggested that, *ceteris paribus* (e.g. disregarding all effects abroad which is obviously illicit) the balance of payments gradually worsens as effective demand increases. As over-full employment is reached the worsening becomes abrupt. The absolute level of the curve showing movements in the balance depends on the rate of accumulation. As will be obvious this illustration also neglects the fact that the level of

---

[1] According to the McGraw-Hill Company's latest census, research expenditure at $5.4 billion in 1956 is about equivalent to the whole of United Kingdom fixed investment and roughly three times the investment in manufacturing industry. And research is a notoriously increasing return industry.

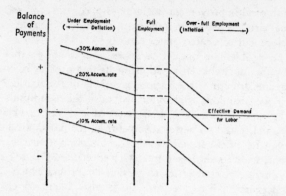

accumulation is not independent of the level of effective demand. But, in my view, it seems far superior to the diagrams purporting to express the supply and demand of foreign exchange which neglect all dynamic interrelations, of which Professor Nurkse's paper is a good example.

12

FACTOR INTENSITIES AND TECHNICAL PROGRESS

1. Both Professor Leontief[1] and his critics[2] agree in interpreting the results of his statistical investigation of the relative factor intensities of American exports and import substitutes on the basis of an impeccable orthodox framework of comparative statics. They all assume in the first place that equilibrium values rule at all times; secondly that the problem is of a once-for-all adaptation to a change in data. There is, of course, no justification whatever for these assumptions. The abrupt changes in the pattern of American exports, changes which have in no way been restricted to manufacturing, suggest that the rate

[1] 'Domestic Production and Foreign Trade; the American Capital Position Re-examined', *Proceedings of the American Philosophical Society*, 97 (September 1953), 332–49.

[2] Boris Swerling, 'Capital Shortage and Labor Surplus in the U.S.', *Review of Economics and Statistics*, XXXVI (Aug. 1954), 286–89; and P. T. Ellsworth 'The Structure of American Trade', ibid., 279–85, Professor Ellsworth bases his criticism of Professor Leontief on comparative labor intensities in the United States and abroad, but his paper also derives its main force from the argument put forward by Professor Swerling that foreign trade seems mainly determined by unequal supplies of 'natural resources', an argument which he restates at the end of his paper. The criticism boils down to a rejection of the use of a model with two factors of production, labor and capital only, for the explanation or analysis of American foreign trade.

of technological improvement (including improvement in relative sales technique) also has played an important, if not decisive role, in shaping the development of United States exports.[1]

2. The problem is one of *permanent disequilibrium*; this latter is caused by the inevitable lag in adjustments in a process of continuous and disparate growth of the various members of the world economy. Indeed if we abandon, as abandon we must, the assumption that the pattern in the evolution of United States exports can be explained by a static model, based on perfect competition, the paradoxical character of Professor Leontief's results vanishes, as their importance is enhanced.

3. Apart from its short-run monetary effects, tending to perpetuate its unfavourable consequences to weaker countries, which I tried to analyse elsewhere, disparate growth is also likely to change the composition of foreign trade through its effects on comparative costs.

Disparate growth will manifest itself either in the application of existing technical knowledge through larger scale investment than hitherto practicable or new technical invention, which itself is merely the result of large-scale investment in research, a typically increasing-return industry.

(*a*) The disparate increase in the supply of capital, which is likely to be accelerating, might itself result in a change in comparative costs, and it is by no means certain that such change will always increase comparative cost differences and thus the possible gains from trade (even apart from the case of infant industries and wrong specialization, now admitted to be vitally important). On the contrary, with the increase in the supply of capital its substitution for other factors of production in relatively short supply (that is, more abundant elsewhere) might become possible. The comparative cost differences are in these cases likely to be reduced and, with this reduction, *chance* of gains from trade decreases while the *risk* of losses increases.

(*b*) This tendency is likely to be accentuated by invention. Unless we assume that the labour market in the higher developed economy is perfect,[2] which would be patently absurd, entrepreneurs will have a strong incentive to develop techniques which result in cutting their demand for labour so as to keep wages from rising. Thus there is a strong presumption that research and development work in a country rich in capital will tend to be concentrated on technical problems, the solution of which is bound to decrease the demand for labour relative to capital. The fact that development and research expenditure is an

---

[1] Though unequal factor endowments undoubtedly play an important role in explaining both Professor Leontief's findings and a considerable fraction of total foreign trade.

[2] If the labour market is perfect a scarcity of labour might still provide a general stimulus for labour-saving.

increasing-return investment and that the capacity for undertaking it is increasingly concentrated in the richer countries cumulatively intensifies this trend. An environment in which interest rates are low and capital abundant will tend to foster inventions which are increasingly labour-saving.

Any of these inventions may ' overshoot ' the mark in either or both of two ways:

i. They may overshoot the mark by not merely overcoming labour-scarcity, but actually creating technological unemployment.

ii. They may overshoot the mark by being applicable to a hitherto very labour-intensive industry (for example, office machinery, calculators, textiles) far down the scale of previously comparatively advantageous items.

4. Technical improvement can occur whether through capital-deepening or invention itself: (a) in the refinement in the methods of production of existing commodities and services also (as hitherto) produced elsewhere; (b) in the creation of new or radically improved products.

The first will enable a cut in prices. The influence of the second might be even more far-reaching. It might displace older products (' dynamic inferiority '), and thus force either a very drastic cut in prices (and wages)—if the new technique cannot be adopted abroad—or the complete abandonment of the industry by the former suppliers.

This process is bound to depress the export prices or the volume of exports of the old suppliers through import substitution (for example, the loss of markets for Chilean guano and the increasing pressure on certain raw-material prices after the Korean boom caused by the increasing production of substitutes). Moreover the progressive country might well develop at the margin new exports which will tend to displace less progressive foreign producers. Thus even if *on the average* a product might appear labour-intensive in the progressive country, it does not by any means follow that this average labour intensity will express comparative advantage or disadvantage *at the margin* in a period of rapid change when new inventions are being introduced.[1] Thus the appearance of a paradoxical factor composition of exports is given; with the spread of utilization of the labour-saving invention, the average labour-intensity of the new export industries will be reduced. But in the meantime invention will turn to yet again different products and the process will repeat itself.

[1] If (as is probable) markets are imperfect, advanced firms might well find it advantageous to expand their markets abroad rather faster than at home. Lagging money wage adjustments intensify this effect by causing a sudden absolute fall in the price of exports.

5. The effects of this development are as far-reaching as they are disconcerting. Technical improvements (and/or investment) will be able to overcome the influence of the original factor-endowments on the international distribution of economic activity. Processes which were labour-intensive might suddenly be transformed into capital-intensive. Indeed the fact that labour-abundant poorer countries are engaged in production and supply of certain goods for export to the progressive country will tend to stimulate their displacement by the home production of the progressive country, for entrepreneurs in the latter in the search for new sales opportunities will know that they merely have to solve technical problems: the markets have already been created.[1]

Thus the comparative advantages and disadvantages are violently altered because differences between them have been narrowed, and random invention therefore can cause startling results as technical progress advances. It is this phenomenon which explains why, in Sir Denis Robertson's words, 'there is a relatively large volume of foreign trade, as it were, trembling on the margin of advantageousness, and liable to be blown to one side or the other of that margin'.[2] Far from increasing complementarity and thus increasing the scope of gains and decreasing the risk of losses from international trade, technical progress will tend to have the opposite effect.

6. Thus in a dynamic setting and with continuous technical improvements initiated mainly in the richest country, the classical mechanism described by Ohlin, which was supposed to diminish[3] the inequality in factor-rewards through trade, will work perversely. The inequality of factor rewards will not be decreased, or might even be increased, through trade: there will be a relative decline in the price of labour. If the displacement of export products or cut in costs of the goods hitherto exported by the less progressive economy is sufficiently large, an absolute fall in the wage level in that country might become necessary.

7. In the context of international economic relations between unequal partners, the traditional view, that the ' gains ' occasioned by technical progress will cancel the ' losses ' and that a net ' gain ' will be achieved, is devoid of meaning. Technical progress will not be evenly distributed

---

[1] In any case invention is likely to be concentrated in ' new ' industries, that is, in industries which have a high chance of capturing a large share of any increase in income. Thus the pioneer country is likely to have a low (if at all positive) marginal income elasticity for imports, while its exports will be in great demand abroad. Cf. P. Streeten, Oxford Institute of Statistics, *Bulletin* (February, 1955).

[2] Professor Robertson, ' The Future of International Trade ', reprinted in *Readings in International Trade* (Philidelphia, 1949), p. 505.

[3] And—under certain stringent (and in my opinion wholly unrealistic) assumptions, worked out by Professor Samuelson—fully to equalize factor remuneration.

over the world. The ' gain ' will be concentrated in certain areas, while in a large part of the rest of the world the indirect ' gains ' may not offset the direct ' losses '. The non-arbitrariness of the geographic incidence of progress will not merely separate the dominant and the dominated, but will severely differentiate between the complementary and competitive economies among the dominated. It will tend to impart a bias against the less developed, and less dynamic, competitive, or potentially competitive, areas. It is quite clear that the policy implications of this conclusion— the need not merely for protection, but for *discriminating preferential protection*[1]—would be most distasteful to most economists. This, perhaps, explains the consistent refusal to contemplate this case.

8. If technical progress in the United States is viewed in this dynamic setting, Professor Leontief's figures become startlingly plausible. Labour-saving inventions and techniques follow one another in so quick a succession that relative efficiency wages in America cannot become adapted to the new equilibrium level. Thus at the margin new exports emerge. The intensity and bias of technical progress in the United States have undoubtedly contributed to the fact that American exports appear to be relatively labour-intensive (though at the margin they may well be capital-intensive). In the same way the import substitutes must appear to be capital-intensive. It is the continuity of technical progress through investment and invention which creates new comparative advantages for American entrepreneurs in their unceasing struggle with competitors abroad.

---

[1] In the less progressive but complementary areas there might still be a case for simple protection on the plea of infant industries, or increasing returns.

POSTSCRIPT

The ' pure ' theory of international trade based on static or comparative static analysis is preoccupied with the problem of readjustment to the impact of a once-for-all or temporary change. Disparate growth, however, represents a continuous change on comparative cost positions. Professor Haberler, in a desperate effort to save the neo-classical theory,[1] tries to sustain the view that without a ' full blown and formalised dynamic model of growth ', analysis ' does not leave the realm of comparative statics '. This is entirely mistaken. Even if one does not share the enthusiasm of their authors either for the automatically serene or accidentally catastrophic type of mechanistic growth model, if the direction and character (bias) of the growth is defined, an entirely new problem arises. To the problem which was treated by Professor Samuelson and myself in a ' Foreign Economic Policy for the U.S.'[2] (i.e. the problem that a dominant country can undersell its weaker competitors all along the line and by creating a deficit impose unilateral deflationary readjustment), is added a further, and even graver probability of the process systematically recurring owing to the impact of the character of the technical progress of the dominant economy in its relations to the satellite. The dynamics of comparative costs explain the continuous increase in international inequality and suggest that the poorer areas will need to defend themselves by forming economic blocks.

The dynamic analysis of the effects of investment and technical progress on international trade, also suggests that the traditional view on the method of readjustment and its effectiveness need revision. Even the short run unfavourable effects of a cut in purchasing power, administered through methods which affect productive investment, might be so destructive to comparative competitive power as to worsen the balance of payments by a fall in exports. Models which treat these problems on the basis of fixed schedules represent a travesty of dynamics.

If, with the benefit of hindsight, I would like to modify what I have written, it would be to stress even more the immense importance of the self-abnegation of the U.S. in permitting discriminatory protection, in favour of each other, of the O.E.E.C. countries. I saw correctly that the inferiority of Western Europe was due to historical causes, and thus remediable by this sort of policy measures. I was, however, too sceptical about the time needed for the measures I advocated to

[1] 'Problems of Trade and Development', *The Review of Economics and Statistics*, Feb. 1960, p. 99.
[2] S. E. Harris, ed., 1948, pp. 447.

bring about recovery. Germany and France took the opportunity to increase investment behind the protective screen, while Britain did not. They achieved dynamism, Britain did not: 'liberalisation' was obviously not enough. My analysis of the impact on the balance of payments of a sluggish economy[1] of the dynamism of others has been fully borne out. The endless and rather boring repetition of British foreign exchange crises are an eloquent witness to the accuracy of the theory. My analysis of the resilience of the Sterling Area (Essay 10) has been vindicated in a backhanded way by the violence of the protest against its dissolution by Britain's proposed entry into the E.E.C.

The eclipse of the U.S. as the dynamic leader of the non-Soviet orbit might well be connected with the switch to the exclusive use of monetary controls which derisively slowed down her growth. The importance of innovation has also been demonstrated by the rise of European car exports to U.S., as has the effectivness of the U.S. eliminating foreign competitors once the danger of the attack had been realised.

The relevance of the analysis contained in the first essay (No. 10) has immensely increased so far as the vast underdeveloped regions and the multitudes of their populations are concerned. The Veblen-effects of liberalisation, together with the consequent increase in profits and rents, leads to the impoverishment of the masses, and the increase in imports. The consequences in Cuba are there for all to learn. Accelerated progress of those areas will depend on being able to use direct controls.

It will equally depend on being able to form large economic units,[2] on a preferential, discriminating basis. This is needed on the one hand to safeguard existing industries in each of the small instituent countries and, on the other, in order to be able to start new, large-scale units catering for the whole area (Africa or Latin America or South Asia). These units must be large in order to be, eventually, competitive in the world markets at tolerable wage-levels, despite the relative lack, for some time, of skill and knowledge. It is indispensable for the poor areas to achieve industrial competitiveness, as it will not be possible— unless Soviet trade policy changes (Vol. II. Section 9.)—for them to carry their development plans merely on the basis of exports of primary produce, the markets for which in the non-Soviet orbit do not seem sufficiently buoyant.

[1] It should not be forgotten, however, that the American losses of reserve have been mainly due to non-economic reasons, while here the balance of visible trade still remains unfavourable and presses heavily on ours.

[2] Cf. 'Economic policy and the price systems'. *Economic Bulletin for Latin America* (March 1961) and F.A.O., *Africa Survey* (Rome 1961), especially Part III, for which I was primarily responsible.

N

The rise of a vast self-sufficient dynamic economic unit in Western Europe with considerable protection of home production, by stimulating technical progress at home (not the least in agriculture and other primary products) would certainly tend to lessen the chances of rapid development in the poor countries, unless, following the example of the U.S., it permitted discriminating protection[1] in these areas and supported economic progress there by unilateral grants or low interest loans. It is to be feared that European orthodoxy is less prepared for this than the American was—except for the Eisenhower years; the menace of increasing Communist influence in these areas might, of course, stimulate decent behaviour by the rich non-Soviet countries.

The view that rapid growth tends to worsen the trade balance, which based on simplist Keynesian considerations—was generally held in the 1950's[2] and which was controverted in these articles has suffered a welcome, if far too belated, eclipse. Even *The Economist*[3] and conventional writers, formerly protagonists of the ' absorption approach' of deflation, now accept the view of the fundamental importance for the trade balance of rapid investment and innovation through the dynamic displacement of the products of less progressive economies.

[1] It seems that the African associated states of E.E.C. will be forced to negotiate individually with the Six on their association with the Common Market. This precludes successful industrialisation as they are too small and poor singly to support sufficiently efficient large-scale industry.

[2] Cf. e.g. the Symposium in the *Bulletin of the Oxford University Institute of Statistics*, 1955.

[3] Cf. R. C. Tress and J. M. Fleming, 'The importance of sustained growth', (*The Times*, May 23, 1962.). The conversion of *The Economist* dates sometime between the July 1961 crisis and its December 9, 1961 issue. By early 1962 its writers were convinced that they had ' always' been in favour of an ' expansionist solution' of Britain's economic difficulties.

DYNAMICS OF ADJUSTMENT III
STATIC AND DYNAMIC MODELS

13

WHAT IS ELASTICITY?

Recent disturbances in international economic relations have once more focussed attention on the analysis of the effects of changes in exchange rates on the balance of international payments. The method of analysing them by constructing functions of demand and supply of foreign exchange in terms of its price seems to have been generally accepted without further questioning. In an effort to come to determinate conclusions which might serve as a guide for policy, simple models have been constructed. The question whether the conclusions derived from them, indeed the concepts used, can be applied to real life is usually neglected. Income effects, if they are analysed at all, are brought in as a subsequent ' complication '. Occasionally the further assumption is made that the elasticity of supply of exports and imports underlying the function of the supply and demand of a currency is infinite. In all these manipulations the functions are considered to be smooth and continuous, independent of each other and reversible. Hence partial equilibrium analysis is applied to them without any qualms.

In this and a subsequent paper we shall contend that this approach to the problem is erroneous. In the analysis of international economic relations such concepts as ' elasticities '[1] and ' equilibrium ' rates of exchange are inappropriate in the first place because the commonly component ' elasticities ' are *interdependent*. Furthermore, *given* supply and demand functions or *given* ' elasticities ' cannot be used as guides to policy because the shape and positions (if the fiction of a ' function ' is maintained) of the ' functions ' or the amount of the ' elasticities ' will depend upon (1) changes in the market structure, (2) changes of the level of income, (3) changes of the level of empoyment, (4) changes in the distribution of income, (5) changes in the relevant prices themselves, (6) reactions in other countries. Some of these factors cannot be separated analytically from a proper examination ' of elascitity '

---

[1] ' Elasticities ' appears in the following in inverted commas to remind us that we are concerned with irreversible reaction to price changes and not with movements on independently given demand and supply curves.

reactions; others, though analytically separable, are separated at the cost of lack of realism and thus are useless for predictions or policy recommendations. In other words, statements of the type ' devaluation is indicated if the sum of the elasticities is . . . etc. ' have as little meaning as statements, so fashionable in pre-Keynesian days, like ' unemployment will decrease on wage-cuts if the elasticity of demand for labour is . . . etc.' There is no given demand schedule irrespective of the measure proposed. The very discussion in anticipation of measures, and those measures themselves, will alter the ' schedule '.

It is regrettable but inevitable that no single new method of analysis can be put into the place of the old approach. This limitation is imposed by the complexity of the problem which the customary method artificially, and mostly tacitly, assumes away. As far as policy is concerned, the arguments of this paper suggest the following conclusions. (1) Exchange rate adjustments *alone* are unsuitable remedies where international maladjustments are *large*. (2) They are also unsuitable if they would have to be used *repeatedly* and fairly frequently. (3) It is false to argue that appreciation of a currency is always a remedy when deficits cannot be eliminated by depreciation because ' elasticities ' are too low. (4) Even when and where exchange rate alterations promise to be suitable remedies, they are likely to be insufficient unless accompanied by *full employment* (or, often, ' over-full ' employment) *policies* in *creditor* countries; measures to counteract undesirable distributional effects or effects on internal monetary equilibrium; and possibly measures against certain oligopolistic or monopolistic reactions. Many policy recommendations in the past seem to have disregarded the overwhelming importance of employment policy and the level of employment for international economic adjustments.

Not only are the theoretical concepts and measures hitherto used in the analysis of foreign trade adjustments of doubtful value. Even more serious objections can be raised against attempts to establish statistically the order of magnitude of these ' elasticities '. Quite apart from the shortcomings of the data and of the statistical methods used,[1]

---

[1] Cf. e.g. recent papers by Orcutt, Machlup. These efforts to criticise the statistically calculated ' elasticities ' serve as arguments for the rehabilitation of devaluation (i.e. the price mechanism) as a suitable remedy for disequilibrium. They were meant to dispel the doubts that had risen as a result of the low ' elasticities ' discovered by the statisticians. But these very useful criticisms of crude statistical methods pay little attention to the objections analysed in this paper, which cast doubt on the possibility of establishing any trustworthy and useful functional relationship of that kind at all. It seems that even if it is true that the ' required elasticities ' are smaller than was thought, and that the 'actual elasticities' are larger than statisticians tell us, the definitions used by both the critics and the criticized are misleading. Forces which are ignored by their assumptions are likely to swamp the favourable effects of favourable ' elasticities '. The attempted rehabilitation of devaluation must, to that extent, fail.

not enough attention has been paid to certain logical flaws of the procedures adopted and the lack of realism of their assumptions. Both the attempt to use time series and correlate data of different periods for the same country, and the method of comparing the relationship of data of the same period of different countries, involve simplifications or neglect of inter-relationships which reduce the value of the results obtained. Indeed, the price and income ' elasticities ' and propensities thus obtained really amount to nothing more than mere historical descriptions and can yield no inference to causal relationship. In the absence of knowledge of the functional connection between the path of adjustment and its end position no predictions can be made. Any formal equations (e.g. on ' optimum tariffs ' or the criteria for successful devaluation) purporting to provide a basis for accurate extrapolation, really do not give more than descriptions derived from past data which are of small use for gauging future possibilities.

(1) THE INAPPROPRIATENESS OF PARTIAL EQUILIBRIUM ANALYSIS

The schedules of the demand and supply for foreign exchange, like the schedules of the demand and supply for labour, or for savings and investment, are aggregates to which the technique of demand and supply curves, with its implicit assumption of other things remaining equal, must be applied with great caution, even in the simple case of models of *comparative statics*.[1] When it comes to analysing actual situations the comparative static approach breaks down. Not only will the change in one of the variables result in a change *of the same order of magnitude* in the others, but *dynamic effects* will be set in motion which might *swamp the original cause of* the change.

[1] This objection on the plane of comparative static analysis is similar to Mr. Sraffa's criticism: ' This point of view (i.e. the particular equilibrium analysis) assumes that the conditions of production and the demand for a commodity can be considered in respect to small variations, as being practically independent, both in regard to each other and in relation to the supply and demand of all other commodities. It is well-known that such an assumption would not be illegitimate merely because the independence may not be absolutely perfect, as, in fact, it never can be: and a slight degree of interdependence may be overlooked without disadvantage if it applies to quantities of the second order of smalls, as would be the case if the effect (for example, an increase of cost) of a variation in the industry which we propose to isolate were to react partially on the price of the products of other industries, and this latter effect were to influence the demand for the product of the first industry. But, of course, it is a very different matter, and the assumption becomes illegitimate, when a variation in the quantity produced by the industry under consideration sets up a force which acts directly, not merely upon its own costs, but also upon the costs of other industries; in such a case the conditions of the ' particular equilibrium ' which it was intended to isolate are upset, and it is no longer possible without contradiction, to neglect collateral effects.' ' Laws of Returns Under Competitive Conditions ' Piero Sraffa, in *The Economic Journal*, 1926, p. 538–9.

Wherever foreign trade forms a more than negligible part of a country's national income, partial equilibrium analysis is no longer applicable. It is not legitimate to draw up a demand curve for imports on the assumption that all other prices remain the same. The demand for imports will not be independent of the change of prices of home-produced goods. That is to say, the conventional demand curve based on the assumption that other things remain the same, is subject to shifts. These shifts themselves are not simple, as some models try to envisage, but the result of an intricate network of relationships. Thus if, for example, we devalue our currency, demand for imports will depend:

(a) Upon the supply 'elasticity' of home-produced goods which are substitutes for imports, which in turn is affected by

(b) the home supply 'elasticity' of, and the foreign demand 'elasticity' for our exports. For the supply 'elasticity' of home substitutes for imports will be smaller, the greater the diversion of factors (and goods) used up in increasing exports. A substantial increase in exports leaves fewer factors available for substituting home goods for imports;

(c) the changes in income distribution accompanying the demand and supply changes which will alter the propensities to save, invest, and import.[1]

Similarly, the 'elasticity' of supply of imports is a function of the home 'elasticity' of supply of exports and of the foreign 'elasticity' of demand for our exports. If, after devaluation, foreigners spend more on *our* exports in terms of their own currency, goods and factors will be released abroad, which will make it more difficult for them to divert resources from *their* exports (our imports) to the home market, when the prices of their exports are reduced. A smaller total expenditure on our exports, on the other hand, will make this diversion easier and thus increase the 'elasticity' of supply of their exports (i.e. our imports). Both home demand and supply 'elasticities' depend upon the foreign demand and supply 'elasticities' and, by the same reasoning, the foreign 'elasticities' depend upon the home 'elasticities'. The 'elasticities' are therefore interdependent.

To apply to this type of relationship the term 'price elasticity' is therefore misleading. The reactions to price changes are lumped together into an elasticity concept as if they were similar to the reaction experienced in the case of a commodity the demand for which is an infinitely small fraction of total demand. In this latter case the repercussions can legitimately be neglected, whereas in our case, just as in

---

[1] This particular aspect, however, will be treated in a subsequent article.

the case of the general internal economic equilibrium, reactions are determined by shifts in other prices.[1]

Assume two countries, A and B. A exports textiles and B exports wheat, but both produce some wheat and some textiles themselves. A depreciates its currency. Textile producers in A will now have an inducement to export more, for the price of textiles in B will have risen in terms of A's currency. How great will be the increase in A's textile exports for a given rise in their price in B? *How great is the supply ' elasticity' of A's exports*? This will depend on a number of factors, but amongst them on A's demand ' elasticity ' for imported wheat. If its demand is ' inelastic ' factors will be released for the production of textile exports. If, on the other hand, its demand for wheat imports is ' elastic ', the increase in exports for any given rise in their price will be smaller. But A's demand ' elasticity ' for wheat imports is not given independently. It depends on a number of factors, amongst them on its supply ' elasticity ' of textile exports. The more textiles are exported for any given rise in their price (in B in terms of A's currency), the fewer factors are available to produce wheat at home, and, hence, the lower the demand ' elasticity ' for wheat imports. The answer to our original question, what determines the supply ' elasticity ' of A's exports is that it is partly that supply ' elasticity ' of exports itself. The same can be shown to hold for any other of the ' elasticities '.

This interdependence does not, of course, mean circularity. A determinate solution would result when the various ' elasticities ' are consistent with one another. But the important point is that a country's response to price changes is not simply a function of ' tastes ' and ' technical conditions ', but also a function of the changes in demand and supply abroad which will determine the availability of substitutes and factors to produce substitutes. It is well-known that e.g. the supply ' elasticity ' of exports is partly a function of the demand ' elasticity ' for imports. If the latter is low, a large amount of purchasing power will be absorbed by dearer imports, thus setting free domestic products for exports, and/or factors capable of producing exports. But one must remember that the demand ' elasticity ' for imports depends, in turn, on the supply ' elasticity ' of exports. For demand will be more elastic, the smaller the increase in the supply of exports which absorbs factors that could be used for producing import substitutes. And the two home ' elasticities ' will depend upon the foreign ' elasticities ', because the latter co-determine the changes in exports and imports. Thus, a low foreign supply ' elasticity ', for

[1] This explains the paradox that the formulae elaborated for the level of ' optimum ' tariffs is based seemingly on *foreign* ' elasticities ' alone: they implicitly contain a large element of the home ' elasticity ', being co-determined by them.

example, coupled with a low home demand ' elasticity ' will reduce the home supply ' elasticity '. For if home demand ' elasticity ' is less than unity, the value of imports will rise by less, the smaller is the foreign supply ' elasticity ' and thus fewer goods and factors will be released for export purposes than would have been available, had the foreign supply ' elasticity ' been greater.

The treatment of the effects of exchange depreciation in terms of four independent given demand and supply ' elasticities ' oversimplifies and falsifies the problem. A change in any one of them will inevitably affect the others, usually after a time. The assumption of the constancy of ' elasticities ' in time, even if we ignore changes of income, employment and distribution, is therefore hardly justified. An autonomous change in any one will have inevitable repercussions upon all others.

Determinate and independent demand elasticities could be assumed if supply were infinitely elastic. Since this is impossible in conditions of full employment, it would involve the assumption of unemployment and excess capacity. But this case, the one most favourable to an analysis in terms of given demand ' elasticities ', is least suited to a *policy recommendation* of exchange rate adjustments. Not only is demand likely to be highly ' inelastic' without any relief from low supply ' elasticities ' (as would be the case under full employment), but deficits arising in conditions of unemployment are not necessarily signs of disequilibria which should be cured by exchange rate adjustments.

(2) ASYMMETRICAL REACTIONS RESULTING FROM EMPLOYMENT EFFECTS

Many authors assume in their analysis of foreign exchange problems both independent and smooth demand and supply functions. In the last section it was argued that the functions are interpendent. In this section we shall consider certain reactions to changes in the value of the currency and consequential price changes which may lead to asymmetrical reactions of the type which is occasionally formalized in ' kinked ' curves. The view that functions tend to be smooth depends on coupling the assumption of full employment with that of high flexibility and absence of oligopoly. In actual fact imperfect flexibility and induced income variation will tend to produce different reactions to changes in the rate of exchange (different ' elasticities ') according to the *direction* of the change, and for two reasons. First because of oligopolistic relationships between firms. Second because of oligopolistic relationships between countries. Both are largely a function of the level of employed capital and manpower capacity.

The supply of exports at full employment will probably be ' inelastic' for a price rise and 'elastic' for a fall because home demand can easily absorb exportable goods. It is, as it were, the suction from a fully employed and relatively riskless home market which results in this asymmetry: goods are more easily absorbed than released in response to price alteration. A low supply 'elasticity' coupled with a low foreign demand 'elasticity' will mitigate the fall in foreign exchange receipts and, coupled with a high foreign demand 'elasticity' will reduce the increase in those receipts.

If, on the other hand, unemployment and excess capacity prevail, supply 'elasticities' for price rises may be high, approaching infinity, especially in industrial and plantation economies, and might be low for further price falls as the resistance of trade unions against wage cuts is undermined and bankruptcy forces (and enables) recapitalisation, even if the exchange rate of the country is held rigid in face of the depression. This however is not the full story.

The limitation of international reserves and the necessity to remain competitive would, in a world without commercial restrictions and without currency control have the same effects upon the policies of *countries* as excess capacity in oligopolistic conditions has on the policies of *firms*. It would make demand inelastic for downward and elastic for upward price movements. For a country which cannot afford to have its reserves further depleted would be forced to follow a devaluation or deflation abroad with much greater force than it would be inclined to follow an appreciation or inflation abroad. In other words, price cuts will be accompanied by price cuts of rival products but price rises will not. This effect will reinforce the asymmetry brought about by enterpreneurial reactions.[1]

The absence of a firm full employment policy will, beyond a certain point, have the same effect in a 'rich' country as the insufficiency of reserves in poor areas: the 'creditor' country will resist attempts by others to wipe out their deficit as the reduction of the favourable balance would create unemployment. On the other hand —e.g. Germany in the first half of 1950—they would gladly supply more exports and/or take fewer imports. Thus both small reserves

[1] If Prof. Duesenberry's assumption (in *Income, Saving and the Theory of Consumer Behaviour*', Harvard, 1949), that consumption is a function not merely of current, but of past peak income should prove correct, a further asymmetric influence would have to be expected. On the one hand downward readjustments will be difficult as import propensities will be higher when a (deficit) country tries to cut its imports than when it endeavours to expand them. On the other hand the shock imparted abroad by any one (surplus) country will be mitigated. If the unstable (surplus) country is an important (potential) competitor in capital goods industries the latter effect might not be sufficiently potent a stabilising influence to offset the difficulties encountered by the deficit countries as a result of the former. In that case the downward bias of the system is reinforced by this effect.

and the absence of full employment policies induces oligopolistic asymmetry of reaction.

A similar asymmetry will prevail on the demand side. In conditions of over-full employment the demand for imports becomes relatively ' inelastic ' for foreign prices rises (cf. the sale of Belgian steel to the U.S. at rising prices) and ' elastic ' for foreign price cuts. Price rises will not be as strong a deterrent, as price reductions are a stimulus to imports. This tendency will be reinforced if home producers of import substitutes—who are likely to be working at, or above, capacity— follow the price rises of imports but are unwilling to match price reductions. They follow rises because they can thus easily increase their profits; they refuse to follow reductions because they do not object to having the pressure of excess demand reduced by foreign supplies.

Conversely in conditions of heavy unemployment and excess capacity, demand for imports probably becomes ' inelastic ' for price cuts because domestic competitors try to match these cuts, refusing to allow their excess capacity to be increased further; and it will be highly ' elastic ' to price rises because over a wide range domestic supplies can be substituted without a rise in their prices. The downward inelasticity ' will be reinforced if losses have been suffered and financial reserves exhausted, while certain fixed costs have to be met.

This means devaluation as a remedy will be handicapped in boom conditions, when demand abroad might be expected to be ' elastic ', by the low supply ' elasticities ' of the devaluing country. Hence a *large* devaluation would be required in order to be effective and the objections to such a large devaluation arise out of its effects on real income and the home inflationary situation. Low supply ' elasticities ' which may be the result of technical limitations or, in the case of manufactured products, of monopolistic pricing policies which have the same effect as rapidly rising costs, will affect the terms of trade less unfavourably than higher supply ' elasticities '. The low demand ' elasticity ' for imports will not, on the other hand, be eased by a low foreign supply ' elasticity '.

In a depression, the hopes which might be aroused by high supply ' elasticities ' are dashed by low foreign demand ' elasticities '. It appears therefore that the attempts at rehabilitating devaluation as a suitable remedy, which are based on the fact that low supply ' elasticities' relieve difficulties created by low demand ' elasticities ', ignore the important fact that these ' elasticities ' must be related to employment and capacity levels. The situation then no longer looks so hopeful.

There is also another type of asymmetry, besides the price and output policies of *firms* in imperfectly competitive markets which is caused by the policies of *countries*. Unless there is rigid adherence to an international code of rules, any attempt to shortcut piecemeal adjustments by measures affecting the *whole* economy indiscriminately, e.g. tariffs, restrictions or devaluation, will be matched by competing countries. Whole countries will behave analogously to oligopolistically competing firms and their reactions cannot be neglected. Reactions to the generation of import surpluses will be for a number of reasons more rapid and more drastic than attempted cure of export surpluses, especially if the reserve position of the ' creditor ' countries is not comfortable. Even if it were, the employment effect might force retaliation (e.g. U.S. measures against the import of gloves, hats, watches, etc.).

One of the conclusions is that the maintenance of full employment, or perhaps even what is now termed ' over-full ' employment in surplus countries is a necessary (though not a sufficient) condition of success in any attempt to adjust international disequilibria through the price mechanism, i.e. by devaluation or appreciation as contrasted with direct controls. Low supply elasticities might be overcome in time by the depreciating country through fiscal policy. Retaliatory actions to price reductions either on the part of private firms or of whole countries are less probable if the creditors are in any case fully employed. If unemployment prevails in the surplus country, exchange rate adjustments will be unsuitable. International institutional safeguards against unemployment are therefore of the utmost importance if a restoration of the international price mechanism is to be attempted without results fatal to weaker countries. The habit of talking about ' elasticities ' without specifying the present and expected level of employment in all countries under consideration is highly misleading. The ' elasticities ' of demand and supply of exports and imports are largely determined by the level of employment: they are therefore highly unstable through time. ' World ' or ' national ' ' elasticities ' in the short run are far too dependent on short run factors. In the longer run (or on the average over business cycles), when employment no longer plays this overriding influence, conditions are so likely to change as to render the concept also largely meaningless.[1]

[1] Thus the experts' report submitted to U.N.O. on National and International Measures for Full Employment is to be warmly welcomed as it puts forward schemes to deal not only with this problem but also on the closely related problem of unequal technical progress.

The success of the 1949 devaluations supports rather than weakens our conclusion. The effects of devaluation were swamped by the U.S. revival. The price of the main U.S. imports from the devaluing area *rose in terms of dollars*. At the same time the fall of U.S. export prices was checked and U.S. delivery dates lengthened: the favourable effect of devaluation on the competitive position of the devaluing countries was not cancelled by further deflation in the U.S. Thus the superficial impression that the striking reduction in U.S. exports was due to high demand elasticities is largely misleading. The employment factor played the most important

(3) ASYMMETRICAL REACTIONS RESULTING FROM VARIABLES
OTHER THAN PRICE

Whenever competition is monopolistic or oligopolistic, and when changes in income are significant, the simplifying assumption that price is the chief variable is unsound. Frequently it is argued that although depreciation may make matters worse in the short run because demand will be inelastic, it is likely to improve the balance in the long run when ' elasticities ' will be higher. We shall argue below that, in the ' long-run ', multiplier and investment effects will have had time to work themselves out with the result that any price effects will be swamped. Let us disregard these effects for the time being, and accept the assumption that other things remain the same as far as income and employment are concerned. The argument then rests on the assumption that a readjustment of the productive structure and/or the overcoming of market imperfections will take time. But this ignores the fact that the interests to be displaced need also time to organise their defence, and that imperfections and low ' elasticities ' can also be built up by sellers in time. An attack on, say, the American market will have to meet a counter-attack as soon as it promises to be successful. The whole concept of a long-run demand schedule in conditions of uncertainty and oligopoly is of dubious value. If advertising is successful in capturing a market, it is likely to be no less successful when resistance or the struggle for recapture is organised[1].

In order to analyse the relationship between price changes and quantities demanded a number of variables besides shifts in demand due to advertising are relevant which are frequently ignored. Thus, demand is not only a function of price but also of a *change* of price. Price changes shake customers out of their rut and make them experiment. Strictly speaking, demand curves do not apply, for the amount demanded will depend upon the size and the speed of the preceding change in price. Steps on such a ' curve ' are not reversible and not

role. Moreover the price and wage increases in the rest of the world have only been delayed and are certain to come. In other countries the rise in the dollar price of exports helped to maintain stability, i.e. the situation was saved in spite of rather than because of devaluation. The reduction of dollar exports was decided upon and actually began prior to devaluation, and there has been some recovery in the volume of U.S. exports from the low point. As the reduction in the U.S. exports occurred when home demand in the U.S. was rising the competitive effort by U.S. business to retain foreign markets slackened. Any reversal of the trend in the U.S. would lead to renewed acute dollar crisis. Recent experience thus confirms completely the supreme importance of business activity in the dominant country, the U.S., for international economic readjustment.

[1] [This was strikingly illustrated by the success of the so-called ' compact ' car in the U.S.] [1961].

only point elasticities but also arc elasticities become meaningless. The ' equilibrium ' price, if any, is codetermined by the path by which it is reached.

Price is not the only important variable determining demand: the speed of delivery, available stocks, discounts and terms of payment are others. The existence of unemployment usually bestows advantages upon a country with respect to delivery dates and the availability of stocks of manufactured goods. It is a moot point whether and how much unemployment would spell greater all-round internal flexibility; but there is no doubt that excess capacity, plentiful stocks and a reservoir of labour will make for speedier deliveries of orders in exist-ing, and for capacity to undertake work in new, lines of production. The real cost of this type of competitive advantage is partly borne by the unemployed, and not expressed in lower costs and prices. In order to become more competitive, greater efficiency and price reduc-tions might be of little use in comparison with the creation of unem-ployment and excess capacity (however objectionable).

The advantages of free discounts and easy terms of payments are largely a function of the size of the firm. Large monopolistic concerns with more information about their customers have advantages in fore-going liquidity and shouldering risks which small firms, though possibly more efficient and offering lower prices, cannot emulate. Similar advantages accrue to countries with organised capital markets.

There are numerous other important factors amongst which only investment outlay on initial advertising can be mentioned here, where again the large firm has an advantage. Thus monopoly and unemploy-ment bestow advantages in factors determining demand which are often of greater significance than price variations. An analysis which pays only attention to price and quantity variations neglects these other variables which play a more important part in the oligopolistic armoury than price competition.

(4) SMALL *v.* LARGE DEPRECIATION

Sometimes it is argued that if a small depreciation is not effective, a large one must be, for demand must, at some price, become elastic. To this, there are two replies: first, it is now well recognized that price adjustments often fail to do their work where the changes are very large. A large depreciation may merely give rise to an additional bout of inflation and aggravate the foreign exchange difficulties.[1]

---

[1] It is curious for example, that Professor Smithies should argue that it is a point in favour of devaluation that import controls will be more easily administered after devaluation, without pointing out that the burden is merely shifted, and domestic anti-flationary controls are put under additional strain. (A. Smithies, *Review of Economics and Statistics*, 1950, and *Quarterly Journal of Economics*, 1950).

Thus the country may not succeed in curtailing imports and pushing exports. If it does succeed, on the other hand, by applying deflationary measures, the reduction of imports and the foregoing of exportable goods will necessitate a reduction in the standard of living. Now the same results in the correction of the foreign balance can be achieved with a smaller reduction in the standard of living if import reductions are *selective* and not indiscriminate. The change in the composition of imports can be more suitably geared to domestic social policies than if the work is left to the price mechanism.[1]

We conclude that depreciation may not be able to bring about the desired adjustment, or if it does succeed, it will be at a cost which may well be too high. Infinitesimally small changes in the exchange rate, to which the analytical and policy objections apply with less force, are likely to be ineffective. Large changes, on the other hand, cannot be analysed in terms of constant ' elasticities '. The fact that a large depreciation will make demand more ' elastic ' does not strengthen the case for devaluation if income and employment effects swamp the price effects, or if the reduction in real income is unnecessarily and undesirably severe.

(5) DEPRECIATION *v*. APPRECIATION

The argument that appreciation would improve the balance where depreciation fails because of low ' elasticities ' rests on very special assumptions. In order to refute it, it is not necessary to assume kinks in the curves, although the existence of certain kinks will strengthen the conclusions which can also be derived from smooth curves. It is quite sufficient to assume that elasticities change in a certain way with the movement in the exchange rate in order to show that it is not true that *some* change in foreign exchange rates will *always* bring about a restoration of equilibrium. Quite apart from dynamic complications to which we have referred and which we shall discuss again, it is perfectly possible that even in the case of smooth demand and supply functions both appreciation and depreciation will worsen the balance. We ignore here the problem that the curves representing demand and supply of foreign exchange beg the whole question of the four ' elasticities ' because each of them lumps together two, e.g. the demand for foreign currency expresses both the demand ' elasticity ' for imports and their supply ' elasticity '.

In Fig. (i) the demand for foreign exchange is represented by D and the supply of foreign exchange by S. The rate of £ per $ is plotted on the Y axis so that an upwards movement represents depreciation

[1] Sir Hubert Henderson, 'The Havana Charter', *American Economic Review*, 1950.

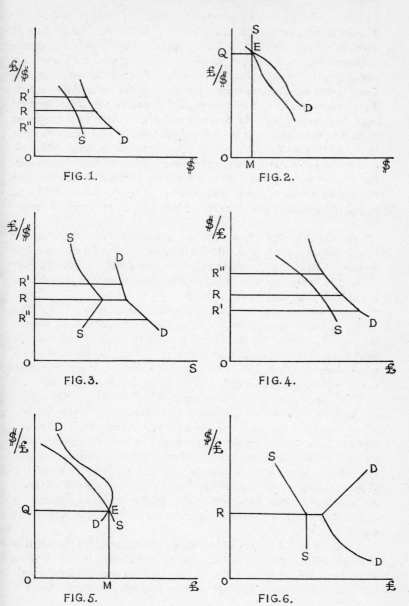

FIG. 1.

FIG. 2.

FIG. 3.

FIG. 4.

FIG. 5.

FIG. 6.

and the total receipts or expenditure in terms of $ are plotted on the X axis. If we start from a position of disequilibrium (D exceeding S) with an exchange rate of OR, both a depreciation to OR' or an appreciation to OR' will worsen the deficit. The shape of the curves is a perfectly possible one, at least over a range. The only limitation of their shape is that the D curve must slope down to the right (dollar expenditure on imports, with certain negligible exceptions, must decrease after depreciation), and the S curve, which may slope to the right or to the left, cannot slope to the left in such a way as to decrease the area of the rectangle OMEQ. (Fig. ii). This rectangle is the £ outlay on exports which cannot (with certain negligible exceptions) decrease. Hence at some point the S curve will cut the D curve from below and this will be a point of stable equilibrium E. (Fig. ii). But this may well be one of those cases where the invisible hand does its work by strangulation.

The difficulties of adjustment are aggravated if the curves at the ruling rate are kinked. (Fig. iii). We have argued that the change of the exchange rate itself will tend to make for such a kink so that whatever the exchange rate happens to be, in some conditions any alteration of it will lead to an increase in the deficit.

The position may be similarly represented in terms of £. The supply of dollars in terms of pounds constitutes the demand for pounds in terms of dollars. We trace the $ per £ rate on the Y axis and the total £ receipts and outlays on the X acis. Fig. (iv) shows the case where depreciation to OR' (which is now a downward movement on the Y axis) and appreciation to OR' both deteriorate the balance; (Fig. iv) shows the 'inevitable equilibrium' exchange rate which results from the fact that the total sterling expenditure must decrease at some point: hence the D curve must cut the S curve from above and this will be a point of stable 'equilibrium' E. Fig. (vi) shows kinked demand and supply curves, the kink depending on the actual exchange rate which has come to be established. Although the D curve can slope to the right or to the left, its slope to the right upon devaluation can in the worst case be a rectangular hyperbola, for the demand for dollars, expressed by the rectangle under the D curve, can at worst be constant.

Similar kinks in the schedules may also be the result of the fact that international competition is oligopolistic not merely in the sense of entrepreneurial reactions in the markets of most manufactured goods but also in the sense described at greater length elsewhere,[1] that the

[1] e.g. T. Balogh, 'The International Implications of Full Employment', in *The Economics of Full Employment*, Oxford University Institute of Statistics, Blackwell 1944. [Reprinted above, Section 2 No. 3.]

reactions of the competing national economies to policy changes in (powerful) economies are of an oligopolistic character. In their policy decisions they take note of the policy of the countries with which they compete.[1] To give an example, devaluation or deflation in a powerful country which has the impact effect of making all entrepreneurs in that country *more competitive* abroad, has usually been automatically followed by the competing economies as they would otherwise have been denuded of liquid reserves. Appreciation, on the other hand, need not be followed by an appreciation or inflation abroad. Indeed unless the rest of the world is already fully stretched the appreciation will lead to a loss of trade.[2] Hence a country contemplating a change in its exchange rate is in an analogous position to the oligopolistic entrepreneur whose behaviour has been represented by a kinked demand curve. The reactions need not be certain. The mere risk may be a sufficient reason to refrain from experiments if the country's international liquidity poisition is precarious.

14

EXCHANGE RATES AND NATIONAL INCOME

IN the previous paper certain difficulties were analysed which arise from the breakdown of partial equilibrium analysis and from the oligopolistic nature of the relationships. We have seen that the ' elasticities ' depend (1) upon each other (2) upon price reactions in oligopolistic markets, (3) upon employment levels, (4) upon the amount and the direction of price changes, (5) upon reactions in other trading countries.

We shall in the following discuss more fully (1) the effects of employment and income variations both in the short and long run; (2) the effects of changes in the distribution of income.

---

[1] This reduces the analytical value of efforts to circumvent the obvious and acknowledged difficulties of the time correlation analysis of elasticities by an analysis of simultaneously existing relations between the price and the quantity of foreign transactions of different countries. The fact that lower prices were associated with higher export figures does not permit us to conclude that, had the countries suffering from higher prices reduced their prices, their exports would have risen in the proportion indicated by the relation of price and exports between high and low countries. This difficulty is far more basic and ineradicable than the obvious statistical difficulty of measuring relative prices in a world where even certain raw materials, e.g. coal, were sold in highly imperfect markets.

[2] Under certain circumstances e.g. when the appreciating (or inflating) country is the main supplier of essential commodities its customers might gain if they followed suit (e.g. the U.S. in 1946–7).

(1) INCOME EFFECTS

An alteration in the exchange rate will affect income and employment in three ways of which only the first is usually analysed.

(*a*) There are income effects which arise from the change in the *volume of exports* and the *balance of trade*. These are supposed to be brought about by the interplay of the ' elasticities ' and have been fully analysed, notably by Mrs. Joan Robinson. They need not detain us further.

(*b*) There are effects which arise from changes in the *distribution* of income within the country. They are usually entirely neglected.

(*c*) There are finally changes in the *real income* of the country which result from changes in the *terms of trade*.

Now all these effects will alter saving, consumption and investment and hence the demand for imports and the supply of exports. Thus a deterioration in the terms of trade and the consequent reduction in real income is likely to reduce the demand for imports (although we have seen that it may give rise to inflationary movements in money wages which would have the opposite effect). It will also tend to reduce savings (which also has an inflationary effect). The concomitant shift to profits, however, is likely to raise savings and hence to reduce the demand for imports. The increased competitiveness of domestic business with foreign industry will provide new investment opportunities, etc., and, by raising incomes, raise demand for imports.

(2) SHORT RUN CHANGES IN INCOME

We shall consider the short-run effects on effective demand and monetary stability in this and the long-run effects on the growth of capital and income in a subsequent section. We shall discuss the question of how these changes affect the concept of ' price elasticities ' and of ' equilibrium rates of exchange '. The first concept is relevant to value theory, the second to welfare economics.

An alteration in the exchange rate is likely to alter the level of effective demand for the reasons given above. The customary treatment of initial price effects, to be measured by price ' elasticities ', and consequential income effects, to be measured by income ' elasticities ' and ' propensities ', is not satisfactory. Although the multiplier effects of changes in the balance of payments might conceivably be treated as ' secondary ', the effects on income of changes in the terms of trade and of distribution are simultaneous and *analytically inseparable* from the price changes. Exchange rate alterations are *ipso facto* income alterations. Moreover, if these income changes give rise to cumulative movements, the final reactions to price changes will be irreversible, for cumulative movements are not symmetrical for upward and downward changes.

A further asymmetry is introduced into the picture by the lack of perfect mobility of labour and the lags due to the time taken to adjust the capital structure of the country. The short-run effects of changes on investment depend on the direction and extent of the change. A reduction in net investment is perhaps most easily carried out. Even here strong complementarities might impede adjustments. An increase in net investment, though perhaps slower than a decrease, can be carried out more rapidly than an actual disinvestment of durable capital. The difference in lags however will tend to impart a deflationary bias into the system as a whole—which *can* of course be counteracted. Investment decisions are discontinuous in any case and their timing will also be affected by actual or anticipated shifts in any of the schedules due to changes in exchange rates. These, in their turn, will alter the relevant propensities to consume and to import.

Against this, it is frequently argued that one of the conditions of a workable ' equilibrium ' rate of exchange is the equation of aggregate supply to aggregate demand in the trading countries. Only if inflation and deflation or inflationary and deflationary pressures are avoided can the rate of exchange be expected to work.

This argument is based on the tacit assumption that the attempt to equate aggregate supply to aggregate demand does not itself alter the relevant propensities and schedules. Demand and supply functions, with respect to price and income are assumed to be given and policy does not affect them. If there are restrictions, demand is frustrated and presses against the walls of controls. But such assumptions are not always justified. Frequently, we are not dealing with comparable schedules in two situations, one of which contains restrictions, the other of which does not. Pressures of excess demand are often modified by the imposition or the lifting of restrictions.

It is very doubtful whether one can speak legitimately of the intensity of a *given* demand, exerting a *given* inflationary pressure against controls. Controls often work more like canals and drainage systems than like absolute dams, by diverting and reducing inflationary pressures, and thus altering the underlying situation. Thus recommendations that a currency should e.g. be devalued so as to make the restoration of ' equilibrium ' and the abandonment of controls possible, must face the following difficulties:

First, the rise in import prices and domestic prices resulting from depreciation and decontrol may itself aggravate the danger of inflation. Unless there is a substantial shift to non-invested profits in the export trades, a most unlikely contingency, consumption and investment demand will tend to exceed available supplies. If then additional deflationary measures are recommended in order to make the devaluation and decontrol ' effective ', it is by no means obvious that this would not involve a larger, more painful, and socially less desirable reduction in consumption and investment than that brought about by restrictions.

Second, the availability of imports, though at higher prices, may raise the *propensity* to import compared with the situation in which they were not available. Advertising, joint demand, habit formation and external diseconomies of consumption will play their part. The foreign exchange problem may thus be aggravated, and an even sharper dose of deflation at home might have to be used in order to restore ' equilibrium ' in the foreign exchange market. In short, restrictions on imports other than price restrictions often raise not only saving but the *propensity* to save (partly through favourable terms of trade which make money income stabilisation easier), and reduce not only imports but the *propensity* to import (by altering tastes and habits). There is no obvious reason why habits and tastes engendered by a free pricing system alone should be the ' right ' ones.

(3) EFFECTS OF CHANGES IN THE RATE OF EXCHANGE ON INCOME DISTRIBUTION

A finite devaluation of the currency *ipso facto* alters the distribution of income both within a country and between members of different countries and hence the propensities to consume, invest and import. It is therefore illegitimate to treat the problem as if it were a case of an infinitesimal variation whose consequences can be neglected.

The internal effect of a devaluation will benefit export trades and those producing substitutes for imports, while the consumers of imports and of substitutes for imports will suffer. Since wages must be assumed to be sticky there will be a redistribution in favour of profits. This will be aggravated if imports are largely necessities.

It is impossible to predict the net effect on savings but it is very probable that there will be a change. There are three possibilities; either there will be an inflationary impetus which might offset or more than offset any improvement in the balance from devaluation; or there may be a deflationary effect which would help the balance though possibly at a heavier price than is necessary, or finally internal monetary equilibrium is maintained but the amount of savings and imports is altered. In all three cases the movement in the exchange rate and the ensuing reactions are not likely to be reversible. Only in the case of zero net saving both before and after the change and absence of any monetary cumulative effects could one speak of determinate ' elasticities ', were it not for the difficulties mentioned in previous sections. In addition, one would have to take account of trade union reactions to changes in the cost of living, secondary income changes resulting from the change in the balance of trade (both on consumption and investment) and speculative movements in anticipation of price changes.

In multiplier analysis it is now generally recognised that changes in employment are not only a function of the aggregate marginal propensity to consume and changes in investment, but of the *composition* of these aggregates. Rarely are analogous qualifications introduced into the theory of demand and supply responses to exchange depreciation. Yet it is clear that the composition of the demand for imports and the supply of exports which depends on the changes in the distribution of income will affect the relevant ' elasticities '. Thus any given change in the exchange rate will have different effects upon supply and demand according to different consequential changes in income distribution.

These changes are not reversible and any given change in the terms of trade is always uniquely related to a change in income distribution. But it is well known that contractually fixed incomes are much more flexible upwards than downwards. A country whose workers have once benefited from an improvement in the terms of trade, and have grown used to a certain standard of living, may find it difficult to enforce the return to the old low real wage level if a deficit should demand such a readjustment. The worsening of the terms of trade might be brought about by unemployment, by a reduction in profits or in costs, but it is most unlikely that the movement will be parallel and symmetrical to the original upward shift. Hence ' elasticities ' will be different for upward or downward movements, according to the altered distribution of incomes. This is another reason for asymmetrical reactions.

Just as ' elasticities ' cannot be defined without provisos about changes in the income distribution *within* a country, so provisos have to be made concerning the distribution of income (per head) *between* countries. Changes in the distribution of income will affect demand and supply ' elasticities ' at least for three reasons: First, because they will change the composition of demand and supply. Secondly, because they will change the rates of growth of real income (by affecting saving and investment), and, thirdly, because they will affect the ease or difficulty of maintaining monetary equilibrium and preventing cumulative movements.

Hitherto we have discussed the difficulties that arise in the formulation of ' elasticity ' concepts if the distributed effects of price changes are irreversible. These ' elasticities ' are often used to recommend methods of achieving an ' equilibrium ' in the balance of payments through an ' equilibrium ' exchange rate. The concept of an ' equilibrium ' is often taken to stand for a desirable state of affairs. A few remarks may therefore be appropriate about the welfare implictions of an ' equilibrium ' rate of exchange.

Here again the two types of distributional effects must be considered: internal and international. The choice between foreign exchange and import restrictions of luxuries, combined with ' overvaluation ' on the one hand, and of an ' equilibrium ' rate through devaluation without restrictions on the other, is not one between a ' disequilibrium ' and an ' equilibrium ', but rather between two types of domestic policies of distribution. The concept of an ' equilibrium rate ' is meaningless for *welfare* theory.

The same is true of the effects upon the distribution of income between different countries. Again, restrictions coupled with ' overvaluation ' are not necessarily a sign of ' disequilibrium '. In so far as restrictions are used to prevent an undesirable deterioration in the terms of trade of a country whose standard of living is threatened, devaluation would not produce ' equilibrium ' in a sense in which it is something commendable. If the principle of the desirability of reducing extreme inequalities in international income distribution is accepted (analogous, though not necessarily identical, to that widely accepted for internal income distribution),[1] and if other means of income transfer (loans and grants) are impracticable, then the ' overvalued ' rate combined with restrictions is nearer to an ' equilibrium ' rate in a normative sense than the so-called ' equilibrium ' rate.[2]

(4) EQUILIBRIUM AND STATIC THEORY

The simple theory of exchange rate adjustments assumes a zero level of net investment and net saving. Without changes in the level of effective demand and without changes in capital equipment, a definite meaning might conceivably be given to an ' equilibrium rate

[1] Thus the principle that gross inequalities should be reduced might have to be qualified for international application for two reasons: First, external diseconomies of consumption are likely to play a smaller role internationally than internally, for people are more ignorant of standards in other countries. Secondly, it is divergencies from habitual consumption rather than the absolute level of consumption that make people (within limits) feel better or worse off. Thus the international principle would be as much the prevention of lapses from habitual living standards as the equalization of living standards. This is an important argument for Marshall Aid despite the fact that Africa and Asia are much poorer than Western Europe.

[2] Difficulties arise, of course, if the desirable *international* redistribution of income does not lead to a corresponding *internal* redistribution in the benefiting countries.

of exchange' with the qualifications discussed in previous sections. But positive saving and investment create a number of problems. In previous sections it was argued that the rate of saving and investment will be altered by exchange rate alterations in an irreversible manner, and that, even in the short run, the effects on real income, and on monetary stability must not be neglected. In the long run, when capital and real income must be assumed to grow, two additional problems arise for the definition of an ' equilibrium exchange rate '.

First, it will no longer be possible to construct a model with a positive rate of growth (' trend ') because that rate of growth itself cannot be assumed to be given. If it were independent of the fluctuations round it, a dynamic model might replace the static assumption of zero net investment. But the relative rates of growth of real income in different countries will give rise to disequilibria and the manner in which these disequilibria are adjusted will affect the rates of growth in real income. Thus a series of devaluations, even if they were practicable, might slow down the relative rate of income growth in the deficit country and aggravate the difficulties of adjustment in the future, while e.g. policies with less detrimental effects on the terms of trade and hence on (foreign trade) productivity might facilitate future adjustments by raising the relative growth of income and productivity in the deficit country. It is one of the difficulties of static equilibrium theory that it requires a dynamic theory of growth (domestic and foreign) before it can be applied to actual conditions, and that the dynamic changes are themselves a function of the adjustments envisaged by static equilibrium theory. The concept of an ' equilibrium rate of exchange ' is ambiguous because any one rate of exchange alters the conditions underlying the moving ' equilibrium '.

The second problem is this: if we assume that real income grows at different rates in different countries, a permanent cause of unbalance arises which impairs the application of such concepts as ' elasticities ' and ' equilibrium rates ' to long run problems. In the case of two countries, each expanding at a different rate, an equilibrium exchange rate is conceivable if either of two possibilities is realized: either the rapidly expanding country has a sufficiently high income ' elasticity ' of demand for imports to provide a market which expands at the same rate as its output, or a sufficiently high income ' elasticity ' of demand for its exportable goods to reduce the rate of growth of exports sufficiently to maintain balance; relative inequalities will then increase cumulatively, and cyclical instability will probably be aggravated, but there would be no secular pressure to deflate or devalue on the more slowly expanding country. Or else the rapidly expanding country must inflate its costs and prices (or the slowly growing country deflate its costs and prices) sufficiently fast to prevent unbalance. In this case, given favourable price ' elasticities ' a balance might be maintained, again, at the cost of cumulative inequality and possibly cyclical instability.

If either of these conditions is fulfilled the rapidly expanding country will not tend to generate export surpluses. Apart from the undesirability of these processes on grounds of equity and stability, the assumptions are not likely to be fulfilled. It is well-known that the income ' elasticities ' of demand for imports are likely to be low and that the pressure to inflate on a potential creditor country is weaker than the pressure to deflate on a potential debtor country. The monetary authorities in the potential creditor country may not want to inflate sufficiently, for distributional or internal stability reasons; even if they wanted, they may not succeed in expanding credit and raising prices sufficiently; even if they succeeded, the total expenditure on the country's exports may rise as its prices rise. Thus the brunt of the pressure would fall on the deficit country with the deplorable consequences of deflation.

The alternative would be a series of exchange depreciations. But clearly, the notion of an ' equilibrium rate of change ' of ' exchange rates ' is artificial. Anticipations alone would make it nugatory. Even if it were imperfectly foreseen, it would lead to a series of financial crises. Speculative forces would swamp the underlying ' real ' forces and expectations about the equilibrium rate of change of the exchange rate would produce grave disequilibrium. The well-known vicious spiral of inflation and devaluation would be at work, for internal price rises will also be anticipated and will aggravate the difficulties. Capital flight to the countries against which the currency is expected to be depreciated will be encouraged with very awkward effects on current account transactions. It appears that the concept of a constantly moving rate of exchange creates more difficulties than it solves.

Like the rate of interest, the ' equilibrium rate of exchange ' does not depend only on the level of effective demand but also on the rate of growth of real income. It will both affect this rate of growth (which, as we have seen above, is a function of productivity, an important determinant of which is the value productivity of the terms of trade) and be affected by it. This weakens the case of the ' elasticity optimists ' who argue that it is the long-run ' elasticity ' that matters if devaluation is considered, and that it is likely to be high. The longer the run, the more time will have passed for investment and real income effects to work themselves out, and swamp the price effects of devaluation. It is, of course, on the face of it, not obvious in which direction these effects will work in any particular case. But the concept of a long run ' elasticity ' of demand is unwarranted and the concept of a long-run equilibrium rate of change in the exchange rate is, quite exceptional circumstances apart, self-defeating.

CONCLUSIONS

The use of the concept of ' elasticity ' in the analysis of international economic problems has been shown to disregard complications of a sufficient order of magnitude to render the procedure inappropriate. The various functions, the ' elasticities ' of which are supposed to govern the reaction of the balance of payments to the variations of exchange rates, have been shown to be interrelated in such a way that the calculation of ' elasticities ' may involve indeterminacy as the functions are shifted and probably distorted.

Secondly, we found, as one would expect in the case of functions which represent macro-economic aggregates, that the state of employment in the constituent units has an important bearing on the reactions of the balance of payments to changes in the rate of foreign exchange and tends to render them irreversible and unique. Thirdly, the traditional analysis tends to neglect variables other than price/quantity relations, and thus gives an over-simplified view of these relationships. Fourthly, finite changes in the rate of exchange alter not merely the distribution of the national income but also the size of the real income. Thus not only the savings and investment schedules are changed, but with them cumulative movements are engendered quite apart from the secondary multiplier effects of the change in the balance which alone has received attention.

If all these factors are taken into account it would seem that the practical men who have always been disinclined to permit changes in foreign exchange rates once they were established, were more often right than economists.

Although some of our arguments point in the opposite direction, it appears that, on balance, they lead to the advocacy of a greater degree of exchange rate stability than is popular to-day. Though exchange rate alterations are suitable in *some* conditions, their value is doubtful if the necessary adjustments are *large*. And it is likely that in the literature the size of the required adjustments has been underestimated, and the effectiveness of devaluation in bringing about any given adjustment over-estimated. Hence slight adjustments may be ineffective and large changes may throw the whole international system into movements, the final consequences of which are exceedingly uncertain. Weaker countries who cannot take risks would seem likely to suffer most.

We have also seen that exchange rate alterations are unsuitable remedies if they would have to be used *repeatedly* at fairly short intervals. Finally, even where their application promises to be remedial, they ought always to be considered in conjunction with full employment and international distributional effects, and effects on internal monetary stability. Only if no excessive sacrifices of these alternative objectives are required can one advocate devaluation with a clear conscience. Orthodox theory based on the stability of partial equilibria and the variation method, suffers from the same deficiency as the theory used to justify certain wage policies: Far-reaching practical measures are prescribed on the basis of simple abstract models without consideration how to qualify and modify these models in order to adapt them to real life.

15

STATIC MODELS AND CURRENT PROBLEMS

Simplifying assumptions, and the construction on their basis of schematic models of the system to be investigated, as an aid to analysis, are necessary bases in all sciences. Economics, beset with all the complications in the nature of social studies, is certainly no exception to this rule. But authors availing themselves of such tools must remain conscious of exactly what they are doing, and must, in particular, be bound by the limitations of their models. To take an example from the natural sciences, it would be quite proper to construct a ' model ' by assuming that light acts as if it consisted of particles of colloid crystals. What might perhaps be considered as somewhat unscientific is to refuse to investigate closely whether this hypothesis can be verified, or claim (supposing that it were mathematically a ' simple ' case) that in order to save the determinateness of the solution, or the mathematical beauty of the structure elaborated, we should continue to work and prescribe further experiments on the basis of the colloid model, the facts of life notwithstanding.

These observations may seem trite. Yet how much of economic doctrine violates these simple canons! How much of the current disputes originate in the fact that protagonists conduct their case on different levels of abstraction while trying to advise on the same practical matter!

Of late the ' new look ' in economic models, attempts to construct economic models on the basis of statistical correlations and to predict future trends as a guide to policy, has come in for severe censure. The fact that interest in such explorations awakened mainly during the war, when the material, if available at all, was often unsuitable for the elaborate use made of it, has undoubtedly justified much of the criticism. Few objections were raised, however, to other, less explicit, less easily disproved, literary ' models ' which are utilized by ' pure ' theory. Yet it might seem that, however simple and wrong some of the econometric models have proved, they have infinite advantages over the beautiful gossamer structures of pure theory. Their assumptions are disclosed and the manipulations are patent. Moreover, they frankly try to build on the basis of scientific principles and are put forward for the purpose of testing. Even if the first few hundred attempts fail, they will have performed the useful function in elucidating the complicated interrelations in social development.

In contrast there is little attempt at even a perfunctory verification of the assumptions of the ' pure ' theoretical models. Indeed if they are subject to attack, a certain pride is shown in their uselessness; though this pride is usually not manifested when, in the absence of attacks, they are used as a basis of policy recommendations.

The present paper will discuss a model of this kind which is used by Professor Samuelson in his brilliant article on ' International Trade and Equalization of Factor Prices ' in the *Economic Journal* (June 1948). Professor Samuelson wishes to examine closely the theorem that commodity trade alone can only achieve a partial equalization of factor-rewards. He develops his argument on the basis of ' the simplifying assumptions most suited to the Ohlin analysis '.[1] Two perfectly immobile factors of production are assumed to be distributed in unequal proportions between two regions. It is further assumed that

(a) the same production functions exist in both countries, i.e. that the productive factors are identical and work in identical surroundings;

(b) the productivity of the region is not affected by the scale of operations, i.e. there are constant returns;

---

[1] Professor Samuelson might be thought slightly less than fair to Professor Ohlin in so far as the latter recognises the importance of increasing returns (chap. iii, pp. 52–8). Unfortunately there is no point of Professor Ohlin's statement at which a clear summary of his assumptions is made and a large part of the discussion is conducted on assumptions which exclude increasing returns as ' not compatible with long-run equilibrium '. In some ways the limitations of Ohlin's method are shown by his belief that foreign trade will ' reduce the disadvantages ' caused by indivisibility. He completely fails to see that his treatment does not differentiate between labour and other factors of production from a welfare point of view, and disregards the grave danger of ' free trade ' tending to perpetuate the disadvantageous original distribution of factor endowments in cases of increasing returns. The supply of child labour, for example, cannot be taken as a datum when judging economic policy. Moreover, as we shall demonstrate, endowment with ' capital ' is, at least partly, a function of the policies pursued.

(c) the productivity of factors is only affected by changing their proportions, i.e. they are completely homogeneous.

Professor Samuelson contends that if these assumptions are granted, Professor Ohlin has not gone nearly far enough in claiming that 'free mobility of commodities in international trade can serve as a partial substitute for factor mobility, and will lead to a partial equalization of relative (and absolute) factor prices'. He demonstrates that the equalization would be complete.

The proof of the theorem consists in comparing the two production-possibility curves of the two regions. These are assumed to be continuous. Equilibrium will be reached when the point of common slope on the two curves is reached. The ratio curves are constructed for the two industries, one axis being the ratio of the quantities of the two factors used, the other of their real incomes or physical marginal productivities. These curves are again continuous and *identical* for *both* countries, as the technical production functions are identical. They are contrasted with each other, and with a curve constructed showing the relation of the ratio of factor rewards to the ratio of the prices of the two products. At the point of equilibrium in both countries identical ratios are achieved: the proof is unanswerable.

Professor Samuelson sums up his conclusions as follows:

'(1) So long as there is partial specialisation, with each country producing something of both goods, factor prices will be equalised, absolutely and relatively, by free international trade.

'(2) Unless initial factor endowments are too unequal, commodity mobility will always be a perfect substitute for factor mobility.

'(3) Regardless of initial factor endowment, even if factors were mobile they would, at worst, have to migrate only up to a certain degree, after which commodity mobility would be sufficient for full price equlisation.

'(4) To the extent that commodity movements are effective substitutes for factor movements, world productivity is, in a certain sense, optimal; but at the same time, the imputed real returns of labour in one country and of land in the other will necessarily be lower, not only relatively but also absolutely, than under autarky.'

He adds specifically:

'Factor-price equalisation is not only possible and probable, but in a wide variety of circumstances it is inevitable.'

These are indeed surprising theorems.

Professor Samuelson concedes that he has proved too much and turns back accordingly to the assumptions on which his analysis has been conducted, in order to explain by their imperfections the discrepancy between his logical conclusions and the very different reality. He finds the most serious imperfections in the assumptions which underlie the limitations of ' factor-proportions analysis '. It is the great merit of his article that it has brought these to light by formulating them systematically and clearly.

Yet perhaps Professor Samuelson is open to the charge which he brings against Professor Ohlin of not pushing his reasoning far enough. His article is tantamount to a damaging *reductio ad absurdam* of the assumptions which underlie modern developments of international trade theory: and remembering some of his earlier exploits, I thought at first that this might have been his object in writing it. But this interpretation will not survive a careful scrutiny. Professor Samuelson, it is manifest, retains considerable tenderness for the assumptions which lead to such strange conclusions: nor do the conclusions seem so strange to him as they do to others. Indeed he treats them as sufficiently reasonable to provide the basis for a practical moral as to the dubious wisdom of large-scale emigration from Great Britain. This moral is sensible enough in itself; but it can derive no real support from an analysis based on assumptions as artificial as those of this model.

The defects of these assumptions are much greater and more fundamental than Professor Samuelson brings out.

1. The problem of defining identical productive factors in the two regions involves even greater difficulties than Professor Samuelson suggests: homogeneity in this sense would rule out the most important observable cause of increasing cost: the less than perfect substitutability for one another of different doses of the same ' factor '. If this is admitted the assumption that identical production functions will exist in the two regions must be dropped. It is so highly improbable that precisely the same pattern of imperfections in substitutability should be encountered in both regions that this contingency can be dismissed. With it goes the proof and the theorem.[1]

2. The assumption of constant returns to scale rules out most

---

[1] Moreover, it is illicit to assume that the opening of commodity trade will not affect the proportions in which productive factors exist, stimulating or obstructing their development or change. If, for example, in an underdeveloped area there is no possibility of acquiring industrial skill, and thus total specialisation seems indicated by the respective ' curves ', this condition will be perpetuated by trade with a more developed country, however advantageous it would be for that area to acquire skill.

foreign trade problems historically encountered. An attempt to ' assimilate ' indivisibilites by regarding each of the indivisible units of a factor as a separate factor would—like the assumption of homogeneity of factors and its consequences—reduce the ' explanation ' to a farce. For once we admit that indivisibilities within broad factor categories exist, then the historical size of the market becomes of paramount importance for the *further* development of the economy. Once an advantage of this kind is captured by a *country* it will have an automatic tendency to grow cumulatively. Even those checks which are held to prevent a too easy and complete victory of a *firm* which has snatched a superior position from its rivals—the growing difficulty of effective organisation and supervision beyond a certain point, and the increasing rigidity in entrepreneurial decisions—will not operate in the comparative position between countries even to the limited extent that they are observable in industry.

Such indivisibilities might be internal to firms in the regions. The effective limit of these will depend on the size of markets. The uniformity of tastes and customs which characterize a community will have a decisive influence in determining the possibility of utilizing them. Nor will there be, in *international* relations, the same mitigating elements of cost, i.e. sales cost, which are encountered by *firms* when they try to establish a special market for their own products. In international relations these ' sales ' costs are mostly borne by the community: the common schooling and tradition creates the cohesion of the market. These costs are not lower for smaller and poorer, than for richer, communities. Moreover, the ' prestige ' value of ' tastes ' and habits in the leading communities will represent a protection in the home and a preference in foreign markets. The imperfections of the international market are therefore much stronger and wider in scope than those of single industries usually treated. It is a pity that Professor Allyn Young's suggestive article[1] had so small an effect in its application to the theory of international trade.

The problem of international trade and its effects on the evolution of individual member countries of a world economy—much more even than the problem of economic evolution in a given community—involves the interaction of societies on widely *differing levels of development*. This is a totally different situation from the mutually beneficial exchange of commodities between traders of equal standing, subject to similar dynamic processes in their potential development, to which the considerations applicable to simple barter could be extended. Open relations viewed from this angle might be held to jeopardize, for

---

[1] 'Increasing Returns and Economic Progress ', *Economic Journal*, Dec. 1928.

the immediate gain from trade, the eventual achievement of equal opportunities by the more primitive or smaller community.[1]

The story only begins here. The size and wealth of the community itself create increasing returns over a wide range of activity. The rise of specialized firms, the extension and cheapening of services might be mentioned.[2] The growth of income thus engendered results in a more than proportional increase in capital as investment habits become adapted and shares can be placed. Far more important, however, is the cumulative increase of opportunity and also of the facilities to train or create special indivisible ' factors of production '. The growing pull of the dominant economy for the best productive factors, especially entreprenurial and technical ability of *other* regions, is hardly less important. Thus the discrepancy in indivisible factor endowment is further intensified. To neglect these essential features of economic growth is to neglect the most significant factors in the development of first England, then Germany, and, in our day, of the United States, and thus the real determinants of the pattern of international trade.

It has been objected that the size and wealth, at any rate of the greater, western countries is large enough to permit the organisation of optimal units in almost any branch of industry. Moreover, by engaging in international trade, it is said, the limits of *national* markets can be overcome.[3] These objections also fall into an illicit simplification of the conditions under which international trading takes place, and particularly the element of differential risk attached to foreign trade. Secondly, they disregard the importance of historical development in the evolution of patterns of industrial organization which cannot be explained by mechanical reference to maximisation of profit.

In modern conditions the existence of a large market possessing certain definite tastes and habits confers a substantial advantage to producers in that area (especially if it is protected). There is first the possibility of unfavourable regulations of sovereign governments over which producers outside the area have no direct influence, which renders foreign trade more hazardous than domestic trade. Secondly, adaptation to varying habits will necessarily lose the exporter some

---

[1] Graphically this would correspond to cost curves with several inflection points. The ' backward ' community cannot overcome the barrier before the second, etc., range showing increasing returns is reached and has to trade on the basis of the least favourable relationship. Education takes time. Social services are equally important.

[2] Including the supply of capital. Risk is reduced by low gearing based on a well-developed capital market. The financial strength of the government plays an equally important role.

[3] In this connection it is sometimes pointed out that Britain is the third or fourth manufacturing nation, with population eighth in size in the world. But the problem is not whether there are smaller countries but that the two wars enormously enhanced the power of two *supra-national* continental entities which differ in basic economic character from the rest of *national* economic organisations.

advantages enjoyed by the producers working mainly for a standard market. This is the sound core of the argument against the proposals to introduce mass-production methods into British export industries, though it is usually overstated, in so far as it neglects the influence lower prices might have in overcoming ' tastes '.

It would be possible by imposing standardization and concentration to overcome some of the disabilities attached to smaller markets. But it would be rash to expect that entrepreneurs acting on their own initiative would be inclined to such reorganisation. First and foremost common prudence counsels that they should distribute and limit their risk among a variety of products. Secondly, they are committed to a certain pattern and would be unwilling to start a mortal combat to eliminate their competitors. The so-called kinked demand curve is merely a picture of a frame of mind, yet it is a reality with which we must reckon. Thirdly, they will be afraid of the political repercussions of an attempt to reduce to a very few the number of firms in existence. These ' imperfections ' are so important that no realistic discussion of foreign trade problems should disregard them. Their existence certainly rules out in practice such reorganisation of industry as would permit a smaller country to equal the productivity of larger markets.[1] If State ownership of the industries is to be avoided, and it must be remembered that the protagonists of the price mechanism are hostile to nationalisation, the creation of a large market is the only way in which differences of productivity can be overcome. But even publicly owned export enterprise (i.e. one not subject to bankruptcy and annihilation) might be difficult to start in the absence of some certainty of success after a transition period which will in any case be difficult.

These considerations would seem to indicate that models which *a limine* exclude the possibility of increasing returns must be ruled out for the illumination of problems of international trade.

3. A further and connected problem arises in respect to the treatment of capital as a productive factor. In a static model it is quite justifiable to assume that quantity of capital is ' given '. The production pattern of the economy is then also ' given '. If then commodity trade takes place between these two static communities—and if we disregard all that has been discussed in the preceding paragraphs— some sense might be attached to problems of ' optimum ' distribution of factors.

Unfortunately for this view the supply of capital is to a large extent a function of investment possibilities. This includes the degree of

[1] ' Underdeveloped ' countries are at some advantage in escaping this cul-de-sac; for a new industry would be either organized on the most modern lines or not at all (e.g. the industrialization of Canada). But older industrial *exporters* are not in this position.

uncertainty which itself is not unrelated to the scope of foreign trade. In a less-developed country, faced with potential competition of a more developed, it will be influenced by that threat.[1] It also includes the cumulative processes enforced in the poorer country by the readjustment, which it will be less capable of sustaining unscathed. The eventual position of equilibrium will then be shifted to its disadvantage. The influence of the other factors making for increasing returns is thus further strengthened. The greater the accumulation of capital, the easier further accumulation, and the more smooth the equation of supply and demand through appropriate institutions (the existence of which depends on a certain availability of capital).

Indeed, if we take all these highly potent forces into account, one must wonder why trees do not grow into the sky, killing by their shadow all other plants which were left behind. The tendency to sharper cyclical reactions, the financial defaults on foreign debt which effect a potent redistribution of income, the pressure of protection; these are perhaps the main headings under which an explanation has to be sought.

4. This leads us to the last point.

The concept of ' equilibrium ' is highly unrealistic when employed to judge economic development in any one country, *i.e.* in comparing positions *through time*. And it loses all pretence at realism when it comes to an analysis of the *interaction of societies* which differ in economic development and social habits. Foreign trade then represents the sudden bringing together and continued coexistence of economies at different points of development through time. New wants and new products disrupt the structure of indifference curves. Complementary sets of wants, determined by social background, the transition between which is non-continuous, render impossible analysis by simple yet highly abstract hypotheses about the general behaviour of consumers. Nor is there any determinate *a priori* answer to be found about the likely shape of the path towards equilibrium.

If the optimum of general theory is scarcely applicable to the analysis of consumers' wants in a developing economy, the analysis of production possibilities is even less legitimate, even if we did not encounter those difficulties of a conceptual character which have been discussed above. Such an analysis implies an infinite number of production combinations, the transition from one to another of which is smooth and costless. Nothing is farther from the truth. The linkage in production-lines is intimate, and in the overwhelming majority of instances

---

[1] More positively these considerations necessitate a complete revision of the concept of ' infant ' industry and its extension to whole countries and regions. Cf. my paper on ' Some Theoretical Problems of Post-War Foreign Investment Policy, [Reprinted Section 6, No. 17].

P

the private cost of starting any new line of development is dependent on the parallel increase in other lines (if for no other reason because of the uncertainty of markets).[1] Social and private costs differ widely.

The combination of productive factors, especially of capital is not possible in infinite variety. Only a limited number of definite patterns are technically feasible. The transformation of one combination into another takes time and gives rise to formidable social costs which cannot be *imputed through the market mechanism*. If, however, the indivisibilities are large relative to marginal changes, the whole approach which tries to concentrate on the analysis of the latter is vitiated. We do not know *what are* the possible points in the production-possibility map, and we cannot say anything about the slopes, i.e. the ratios, at these unknown points. The stability of these relations and the path of readjustment are equally in doubt. The analysis yields no determinate answer.

Professor Samuelson's brilliant paper should earn him the deep gratitude of economists. By clearly setting out the basis of the most modern variant of the ' pure ' theory of international trade he has at last cleared the way for a new dynamic approach to this essentially dynamic problem.[2]

16

SURREALISM IN INTERNATIONAL ECONOMIC POLICY

TWO REVIEWS

I

Jacob Viner, *International Trade and Economic Development*. Oxford, Clarendon Press, 1953. pp. 121. Price 12s. 6d.

This booklet contains six lectures given by Professor Viner at the National University of Brazil on the most burning question facing that country and other poor areas. If the reader (and listeners) expected a new analysis of the problems of the causes of growth and development, of investment and the acquisition of technical knowledge they will be disappointed. Professor Viner, perhaps the foremost of the contemporary representatives of the classical school of the theory of foreign trade, seems to have thought that a defence of that theory was the

[1] Cf. ' Post-War Foreign Investment ', op. cit. on the differences between current private and future social costs.

[2] [After the completion of this paper Professor Samuelson published a further article on his theorem (*Economic Journal*, 1949). It further strengthens the mathematical proof of the ' theorem ' discussed in this paper without investigating the implications of its assumptions. Thus there is no cause for modifying or amplifying the present analysis: Professor Samuelson seems to have been even more strongly captivated by mathematical beauty than is assumed in this paper.]

most urgent of his tasks. His attack on over-simplified ' models ' of
the economic system, the analysis of which then is used illegitimately
to draw conclusions for the real world is as salutary as it is timely.
So is his scathing criticism of the Keynesian ' Liberals '. He demonstrates that devaluation is not nearly as effective in maintaining or
increasing exports as has recently been thought. Thus the wrong-
headedness of those who in this country cheerfully wanted to do away
with direct controls and return to convertibility is shown up by an
expert who is an ardent liberal himself.

It is when it comes to his positive thesis that the shortcomings of
Professor Viner's Ricardian approach show themselves. If the ' liberal-
Keynesian ' ' models ' of our economic problems are misleading, how
much more so is his own: it is based on perfect competition, and full
employment, and disregards the possibility of reducing costs through
mass-production. In the whole of the 120 pages there is no reference
to agricultural underemployment which (much more than overt
unemployment) is responsible for the dreadful conditions of most poor
countries even in South America. In a book on Economic Development the effects of new inventions, technological progress and the
movement of labour and capital on productivity are entirely disregarded. He then obtains a ' universal law of increasing costs ', a
' law ' which its first author, Mrs. Joan Robinson in her charmingly
characteristic manner described as ' frankly escapist ' and having ' no
relevance to any problem of importance in the real world '. Italy and
Spain are shown up as deterrent examples against industrialisation—
without contrasting the fate of their scanty but relatively prosperous
industrial, with the abject distress of their agricultural, areas, a contrast
which would certainly tend to lead to the opposite conclusion from
that which Professor Viner wishes to sustain[1].

We are then treated to the consideration of various vital questions
such as the need for an industrial elite, the problem of shifting rural
workers into industry, the dangers of inflation and so on. Professor
Viner has much of interest to say under each of these headings. But
the conclusions are not worked into his final argument. We are thus

[1] [It would be difficult to argue the case against the protection of the planned
industrial development of Northern Italy in 1961.]

[One is reminded of the amusing description of Prof. Viner's impact on President
Roosevelt by Mr. Ickes:

' With great unction Morgenthau then started to read a statement prepared by
Jacob Viner, one of his experts and a former professor of economics at Chicago.
He had not gotten very far before the President began to laugh and I could not help
joining him. I don't pretend to be an economist, but the argument presented was so
ridiculous as to be absurd. The President so viewed it, and at this stage Louis Howe
came in and the President greeted him with a hilarious statement, referring to the
Viner document in highly jocular tones. Morgenthau was willing to desist, but the
President told him to go ahead as he wanted to hear what Viner had written.']

left under the impression that all would be well if only entrepreneurs would be left with a suitable system of incentives, that the classical system of adjustments through deflation and income changes has worked satisfactorily and that the poverty of the largest part of the world is somehow due to Governments. It all is better left to the ' decisions of capitalists, entrepreneurs and workers '. It is not clear what powers of decision the latter have or how the entrepreneurs (if any) in these countries can overcome the handicaps imposed by the absence of industries or research facilities. No single entrepreneur can undertake the risk of starting a new industry. Yet a comprehensive plan would reduce the risks of each. But Professor Viner has at one point or another touched on the problem of infant industries and he can argue that he has ' dealt ' with the problem.

In the meantime the whole weight of his authority is thrown behind those forces which try to reverse the efforts of U.N.O. to give help to countries like Brazil in the form of free grants, loans and technical advice. Professor Viner seems to think that the fact that no-one has found an elegant, accurate and simple definition for what ought to be regarded an ' underdeveloped ' country is sufficient to ridicule experts who think that underdeveloped countries exist and demand help. Has anyone defined internal poverty more accurately? Yet if we had not dealt with it through appropriate positive domestic social policies, Marx's prediction of increasing misery would have been justified with disastrous consequences to democracy. It is possible that in the much more dangerous international relations the obscurantism of Western economists and politicians might bring about the victory of extremism. We have left far behind us the post-war high point of enlightened self interest which found its expression in President Truman's Fourth Point and the U.N.O. Experts' Report on Under-developed Areas. The performance of the new ' realists ' is as aesthetically disconcerting as it is politically dangerous. In Brazil where Fascism and Communism meet in attacking ' Yankee imperialism ' Professor Viner's sceptical discouragement of all hopes for a better future must have provided a welcome aid to the enemies of the Western democracy.

II

THE LEAGUE OF NATIONS ON POST-WAR FOREIGN TRADE PROBLEMS

Mr. Loveday and the skeleton staff of the League of Nations Secretariat[1] must be congratulated on their success in maintaining,

[1] *Quantitative Trade Controls. Their Cause and Nature.* League of Nations, 1943. (Professor G. Harberler in collaboration with Mr. Hill.) Pp. 78. Price 2s. 6d. *Trade Relations between Free Market and Controlled Economies.* League of Nations, 1943. (Professor J. Viner.) Pp. 92. Price 4s. 6d.

and even extending, the scope of international economic recording and research in spite of the manifold difficulties they are bound to experience. They must also be congratulated on having obtained the active collaboration of eminent outside experts in tackling urgent and thorny questions of international economic policy. There is no field of economic theory in which it would be more important to apply the knowledge which modern economic thought has placed at our disposal since Lord Keynes published his *General Theory*. Classical precepts on policy were based on assumptions which have become unrealistic as the result of the two world wars. There has been little systematic exploration of the problem whether quantitive differences in the readjustments required, as the results of the two-fold interruption by hostilities of the continuous process of economic change, do not alter qualititively the solution of the problems tackled by the classical school. In the field of international economics, moreover, the persistence of the labour value theory has contributed to the prevalent confusion of thought. If modern economists have tried to reformulate the classical precepts in terms of opportunity costs, their attempt, though formally successful, remained barren; when dealing with practical issues, they continued to think of comparative costs very much on classical lines, and to regard them as stable, or only slowly changing. Simultaneous and abrupt alteration of comparative costs, or of mutual indebtedness over a considerable field, with resultant repercussions on the structure of industry, and thus on social costs, was a contingency which was not seriously envisaged, or its implications analysed. The persistence and, spread of those ' mal-practices ' in the field of foreign trade policy which were universally condemned by ' experts ', should have resulted, but did not, in a reconsideration of the basic assumptions of the theory. Thus there is urgent need, before the executive organs are swamped by the day-to-day routine of demobilisation, for an independent international body to elaborate a minimum programme of action to prevent a repetition of the vicious circle of restrictionism of the last decade.

When we come to review the last two contributions of the League to the solution of this critical problem, the congratulations of a European economist must stop.

Apart from the historical descriptive chapters in these two reports, which succinctly re-tell the tale of the relevant aspects of commercial relations in the last decade or so, our knowledge is not materially increased by them. Indeed, it might be suggested without unfairness that, under the guise of complete impartiality, a misleading picture of the true inter-relations is given. Perhaps it is unreasonable to expect either Professor Haberler or Professor Viner, both of whom have made notable contributions to the older type of analysis, to make more than a cursory reference to the necessity of securing a world-wide agreement on domestic economic policies to ensure full employment, or to state unequivocally that the benefits of multi-lateralism depend on full employment and not vice versa.

The result is in any case disconcerting. Obiter dicta such as are produced by Professor Haberler (p. 20):

> 'We may characterise [quantitative trade controls] as a 'non-conformable' type of interference, a foreign substance, as it were, in the body of the free economy which necessarily leads to dangerous ulcerations and suppurations and threatens to weaken or undermine the individualist economy altogether. On the other hand, *Customs tariffs, even high ones*,[1] (are) . . . 'conformable' interferences which do not destroy the price mechanism on the functioning of which a private enterprise economy must depend.'

when wholly unsupported by analysis, are out of place in an objective report.

Again, Professor Viner inserts on pp. 82–3 a few sentences completely reversing all the conclusions reached in a long report:

> 'It should be made clear however, that if the mechanisms of the competitive market have broken down or are working badly, if the markets are pervaded by private monopoly, if private trade would be subjected to high tariff barriers which state monopolies can evade if they wish, the practice of bilateral government monopoly may prove less injurious to the participants than would passive adaptation to the badly-operating, monopoly ridden, tariff-bound processes of the market place. With respect to government trade monopolies, as with respect to exchange controls and the quota system, the case against them is strong only on the assumption that there is available as an alternative a smoothly working competitive market process, not subject to substantial interference by private monopolies and not restricted by tariff barriers more oppressive to trade and more discriminatory than the government monopolies themselves.'

This may formally safeguard the author. But they cannot sustain the claim for impartiality, when in the rest of the 92 pages the basic wickedness and economic inappropriateness of direct controls are painted on the basis of unrealistic assumptions which are never made explicit. On page 49, Professor Viner admits that the differences between the bargaining methods of the United States and other countries are not due to differences in ethical attitude. They are due to the fact that the cumulative application of commercial policies (which Professor Haberler has characterised as 'conformable' to 'free

[1] My italics.

enterprise ') created a special problem for the United States and the world. In spite of this, the whole of Professor Viner's study is a justification, on the basis of an incomplete presentation of evidence, of a system of 'absolute morality' in international economic relations which in effect would enable the United States to have its cake and eat it, retain its export surplus on current account for purely internal economic reasons (to stimulate employment without domestic reform) and nevertheless retain its commercial bargaining power.

The incompleteness of the evidence is best shown by the fact that Professor Viner, in spite of the wholly explicit title of his essay, refuses to consider the problem of trade relations between the U.S.S.R. and individualistic economic systems—surely the most urgent of the problems before us, as exchange control enables even individualistic countries to organise their economic system on a quasi-collectivist basis. To him, exchange control means exploitation and preparation for war exclusively. The planning of the international exchange of goods is considered as an attempt to impose better terms of trade than a ' moral norm ' which is (again implicitly) taken as that which would result from perfect competition. Whether perfect competition ever existed or not; whether, given the commercial and monetary policies of the United States and the prevalence of unemployment, his precepts would not in fact result in the prevention rather than the promotion of foreign trade; whether his ' morality ' is not a rationalisation of the attitude of the dog in the manger, never even occurs to him. In his view, exchange control inevitably results in a narrowing of the scope of international trade. Yet even in the case of Nazi Germany, which was unquestionably intent on war, and consequently tried to drive as hard a bargain as possible with smaller countries, there can be no doubt that benefits flowed from the clearing agreements to the Balkan countries. Goods were produced and exchanged between those countries and Germany which would otherwise have never been produced at all; German imports (and exports) in real terms increased more than United States imports in the period from 1933 up to the outbreak of the war. It is surely illegitimate to assume that a sale by the United States against dollars—which cannot be procured—is equivalent to an exchange of goods, unless we assume also that full employment and optimum capital accumulation obtains, not merely in the whole world economic system but in each single unit. If this is borne in mind, one inevitably begins to wonder whether this was the case before 1939, or even before 1914, or whether it is likely to be the case if the precepts of these experts are followed.

One of the most urgent post-war problems in the field of international economics is whether the social and political requirements—

including the maintenance of full employment—do not (at any rate in Europe, Asia, Africa, Australia and South America) necessitate the retention, in a modified form, of many war-time direct controls if economic individualism is to survive at all in these areas. If there is to be no world-wide agreement to institute international direct controls with appropriate executive agencies, this would seem to require the formation of regional blocs willing to elaborate common plans which would then have to control their international economic relations directly and quantitatively. This contingency, and its consequences to States which are determined to restore *laissez-faire*, is not even mentioned in either of the two studies. Economic theories and *a priori* economic policies which fit conditions in the United States and, at most, Canada only, should surely not receive authoritative backing by the Secretariat of the League of *Nations*.

Finally, a word must be said about that intriguing but very indefinite concept ' discrimination ' which is the *leit-motif* of Professor Viner's pamphlet—and Mr. Hull's policy. What is one to make of so convenient a piece of rationalisation as—at least implicitly—legitimizes export subsidies on agricultural goods and primary products, but condemns measures such as clearing agreements having identical results in the manufacturing field; which permits the cut of imports by tariffs and unemployment, but rules out measures by which the same effect can be obtained without unemployment? Bilateral bullying of weak commercial partners by way of reciprocal tariff bargains appears to be permissible; the conclusion of reciprocal agreements permitting the exchange of goods, which in the absence of the agreements would never have been produced, is condemned as exploitation. How is one to reconcile the M.F.N. clause and similar paraphernalia with the professed aims of ' liberalism ' when, in the last few years before the war, they were almost exclusively used to prevent a sane organisation of the international exchange of goods.

The importance of these documents is not limited to their contribution to the academic understanding of international commercial policy. The Economic and Financial Committee of the League, on which this country is represented, has accepted resolutions endorsing their conclusions. International agreements concluded on the lines suggested would, in my view, wholly prejudice internal reconstruction, and, through their inevitable breakdown, international amity.

POSTSCRIPT

The assumption of increasing costs has been general. Its logical consequence—*ad absurdum*—was Prof. Samuelson's ' proof ' of the equivalence of trade and factor mobility for the equalisation of remuneration. Yet Prof. Young's essay appeared in 1928 and Dr. Rosenstein's in 1943. My own analysis of the dollar shortage and the lopsided economic development was mainly based on the realisation that increasing returns and economies both internal and external are endemic and, indeed, affect not merely industries but whole countries and even groups of countries. At the same time economic union without elaborate institutional safeguards between countries at different stages of development, and unequal historical heritage and background can only lead to grave injury. Monetary manipulation, devaluation in ' floating ' exchanges can under certain circumstances and if accompanied by other measures bring about readjustment (especially if the system as a whole is at full employment). In isolation it is unlikely to yield satisfactory results. The application of the theory of Games (Essay 13) and the notion of asymmetric reaction yielded fruitful results.

The two essays written by Mr. Streeten and myself in collaboration, explore the neo-classical view of readjustment based partly on a price-demand schedules ('elasticity '), on the income propensity and foreign trade multiplier. We found that the abundant use of simple concepts, such as elasticity, was illegitimate, except perhaps to a tautological description of past events. Our essays had no success. Without confuting us, authors cheerfully continue their meaningless manipulation of useless concepts, and advocate highly controversial (and almost invariable anti-egalitarian policies on the basis of a conceptual framework which excludes essential aspects of the problem they pretend to investigate.

Nothing shows the complete change in conventional wisdom more than the general and uncritical acceptance of the tremendous benefits of being part of a large (Common) Market. The need for reorganising industry, to get rid of the oligopolistic integumen on efficiency is now largely neglected, or it is hoped that entry into a larger market will automatically accomplish it and also break the power of the Trade Unions to exact high efficiency wages.[1] If these imperfections are eliminated the case in favour of joining a large unit is considerably weakened, especially if its ' rules of the game ' prevent a planned acceleration of growth in any single unit.

[1] Cf. Vol. II. Introduction.

INTERNATIONAL INVESTMENT

17

Post-War Foreign Investment Policy

THE importance of a successful solution of the problem of foreign investment for post-war reconstruction is obvious. It must form part of any comprehensive attempt to ensure full employment on an international scale, and at the same time, be used to diminish the gross, and politically dangerous, discrepancy between the amounts of capital equipment available per head in the fully industrialized countries on the one hand, and in the under-developed countries on the other. The difference in real income between these areas would thereby be mitigated.

The present paper has restricted aims. We shall attempt to apply certain general principles, which have come to be widely accepted, to the field of foreign investment—a field where older misconceptions still threaten to influence the policy of the great Powers.

A. We shall inquire whether the freedom of private capital movements can be expected to lead to optimum distribution of resources. This problem will be dealt with under two headings. We shall first determine whether discrepancies between the gross and net private return do not vitiate the traditional view. Secondly, we shall bear in mind that the classical theory is based on the assumptions (*a*) that full employment is maintained; (*b*) that the rate of accumulation is governed solely by the decisions of individuals; (*c*) that the structure and quantity of capital equipment, as well as the skill of the population, is a given datum (i.e. independent of the employment and investment policy of the Government). Whenever these (implicit) assumptions are not fulfilled the ' classical ' conclusions are called into doubt.

B. We shall try to show that capital autarky does not necessarily involve intolerable sacrifices of the standard of life of poorer countries, provided an appropriate policy with regard to the distribution of national income is pursued.

1. The first approximation to a theory of foreign investment is simple. The yield of capital investment, it is said, is—as any other price—the index of its scarcity. Capitalists try to invest in areas and outlets where the return is highest, and it is taken for granted that, if

this condition is fulfilled, the real productivity of capital will also be at its maximum. Therefore, it is argued, interference with the free flow of capital would not only hinder economic progress in backward areas, but the rich countries would also be acting against their own interests, since such interference would mean that they would have to be content with a small return on their investment.

Even during the period of continuous upward trend—which cyclical fluctuations interrupted only temporarily—of the nineteenth and the beginning of the twentieth century, when internal and international political risks were limited and the economic system of the world was homogeneously individualistic (though at very varied stages of economic maturity), this picture was far from being accurate.

The process of foreign investment was not, as orthodox theory would have it, a gradual equalization of returns on capital in a static system, operating through contrary movements of prices (and incomes) in the lending and borrowing countries. It operated even then through dynamically determined waves of investment opportunities resulting in an increase of investment at the (lending) centre and the (borrowing) peripheries. The opening-up of new areas through foreign investment intensified the booms and shortened the depression and thus co-determined the upward trend of the period. But this stimulated and did not retard progress in the lending countries.

The relative backwardness, moreover, of over-populated but under-developed countries tended to be stabilized by this free interplay of economic forces.[1] The *relative* advantages gained by the industrial countries were cumulative. Attention was focussed on the case of the opening up of under-populated and potentially rich areas.

2. The present state of affairs, at any rate, is essentially different. In international economic matters, we are confronted with an almost complete disintegration of the world economy. The opposing belligerent camps are more or less hermetically sealed against one another. Even between Allied nations, the blockade, counter-blockade, and shortage of the means of transport has reduced inter-communication to a minimum strictly regulated on the basis of military necessity. During their enforced autarky—which has necessarily induced far-reaching changes of the productive structure not merely of the belligerents, but also of the neutrals—the enemy countries had to mobilize their economic system for war; and this resulted in further structural alterations which renders the re-intergration of their economic structure

[1] Internationalism of the *laissez-faire* type, therefore was always a questionable policy for these territories. They were kept in economic dependence, not by brute force as the European countries under Hitler's new order, but by the ' rules of the game ', which, though historically established by force, became in due course of time, elevated to the status of ' the rule of the law '.

into a united world economic system more difficult.[1] Technical progress has been very rapid throughout this period, but has been, necessarily, extremely uneven geographically.

The present rise and development of autarkic units contrasts sharply with the interdependence of economic progress before the last war, in spite of the fact that industrial and agricultural protectionism had become sharp in many parts of the world after 1880.

Given these changes—however regrettable their cause—the reversal of the trend can only come gradually and will, probably, even if enlightened policies are followed, not lead to the position which would have come about if the double interruption of international economic development had not taken place. Technical progress enforced by the blockades has produced ' Ersatz ' materials which have come to stay in their own rights. Marketing connections and creditor-debtor connections have been broken and liquidated. Their re-establishment will be difficult and may prove costly. The ' natural ' relative advantages will be less because of the rise of ' substitute ' products, the increasing importance of technique in determining productivity, and finally, because intimate business connections once broken, the natural inertia (i.e. imperfections) of markets work against the old, and in favour of the new, suppliers.

3. Technical progress has had a further and equally important consequence. In the last century, industrialization and the intensification of agriculture depended on the extent of the supply of entrepreneurial ability and capacity to invest as well as of highly skilled labour. This limited the area and the rate of potential industrialization in many parts of the world where, unlike England and the United States, the income distribution favoured classes who were incapable of productive enterprise or unwilling to engage in it. There was also no alternative to private enterprise, however inefficient, as practical experience of the working of a different system was lacking, and administrative capacity was not available for large-scale public enterprise in the countries which needed it most. But now large-scale enterprise using labour of little skill is possible.

At present, the pace of industrial progress in poorer areas depends primarily on the systematic large-scale application of up-to-date knowledge through the establishment by the State of a few mass-production units managed by a small number of technical experts and utilizing a labour force which can be easily trained (even in primitive areas) to the required semi-skilled standard. The raising of the standard

---

[1] These autarkic units began to form, not in 1939, but at least as early as 1929. In certain areas, such as Central Europe, the centrifugal development away from international interdependence has been uninterrupted since 1914.

of life depends therefore on the conscious and co-ordinated planning of industrial development by public agencies (for the risk and the initial cost of establishing such units can hardly be borne by private investors), and not on the chance of possessing energetic entrepreneurial social classes. We cannot, for these reasons, accept without analysis the traditional views on foreign investment as a guide for post-war reconstruction policy.

A. PRIVATE INVESTMENT AND PROGRESS

(a) The Freedom of Capital Movements.

Entrepreneurs who have a free choice between different investment opportunities in different national areas will act on the basis of *pure net return*. This must be sharply distinguished from the *gross overall return*, i.e. the observable return of the investment on the basis of the market price of the asset and the income stream it yields. The gross overall return includes (a) the risk premium, (b) direct taxation falling on the income stream which is payable after the (nominal) income has materialized. We shall call pure gross return the yield which remains after the deduction of the risk premium but before paying tax. Thus we have three yields: (a) gross overall, (b) pure gross, and (c) pure net. In the case of foreign investment the problem of double taxation complicates the matter and stands in the way of the equalization of pure gross returns internationally, as entrepreneurs can escape double taxation by not investing abroad. To this extent the foreign direct tax acts as a duty on capital import.

The classical theory assumes that pure net returns (which are taken to be equal to pure gross returns) depend on relative capital intensity of production and tend to be equalized by competition.

In the past thirty or forty years, however, the internal rigidity of the economic system increased substantially. Competition, moreover, became more imperfect. In consequence the return from investment can no longer be regarded as an index of the scarcity and productivity of capital; it is influenced much more by the degree of monopoly in industry. Economic and social policy which prevents monopolistic exploitation or attempts the re-distribution of the national income consciously in favour of the poorer classes (e.g. by control of prices),[1] or controls the rate of interest, will reduce the gross overall return on capital as contrasted with areas where such regulation does not obtain.

The investors' behaviour depends not simply on the overall return, but also the riskiness of the investment. If such measures safeguard full employment, they will reduce the objective riskiness of

[1] Possibly as a measure facilitating the maintenance of full employment.

investment. It is unlikely, however, that the fall in the risk premium in respect of areas which follow progressive policies will offset the enforced decline of overall return. The reason for this is not far to seek. The confidence of private investors, rightly or wrongly, is not usually heightened by progressive social policies. Indeed, if capitalists fear political changes thought to be inimical to their interests, even a high gross overall return on capital will not tempt them to invest. The risk premium rises. Pure gross return falls. The same applies to policies (such as, e.g. full employment policy pursued through deficit spending) which would leave gross overall returns unchanged or even increase them. An outward flow of capital might set in which might, in the end, defeat the attempted progressive economic policies.

Nor is this all. It is not the pure gross, but the pure net return on capital (net of taxation) which determines the actions of the investor who has not committed himself. The difference between these yields varies widely in different parts of the world. In sharp contrast with the past state of affairs, direct taxation of income now reduces net returns very substantially below gross. The reduction will be heaviest in the most progressive economic systems. If private investors were permitted to equalize net returns internationally, the pressure on progressive economic systems would be overwhelming.

We conclude, therefore, that private net return on capital after taxation does not provide a valid index of its scarcity or productivity. Hence the freedom of capital movement will not necessarily lead to an optimum social distribution of capital between countries. Countries which wish to pursue progressive economic policies are, on all counts, not merely justified in maintaining the strictest control over capital movements, but are forced to do so.[1]

(b) Foreign Investment and Private Profit Expectation.

The second axiom of classical theory is that maximization of world output would automatically be brought about by private enterprise on the basis of profit expectations. This belief is based on the assumption that the current return on private capital investment—or rather the even less perfect criterion of current expectation by fallible investors of the total private return on present investment over a long period—provides a sufficient index of the desirability of the international capital investment from the point of view both of the lending, and of the borrowing country.

[1] In the United States, with its vast liquid reserves, a control over the export of capital might not be a *conditio sine qua non* of progressive economic policy. In Europe, including Britain, it certainly is an essential measure and will remain so in any future which it seems fruitful to contemplate. The attempt of the Blum Government to prevent sabotage of its radical internal policy by frightened investors through the export of their capital was defeated by appealing to the ' liberty ' of the individual.

This view presupposes that social and private net returns are proportionate, if not identical, in the short, and in the long run. It therefore presupposes that private investors foresee all adjustments which have to be made and developments which occur in the lending and in the borrowing country as a result of the investment. It assumes that the consequences of the lending and of the servicing and repayment of the loans are either known or if not known are irrelevant from the point of view of the *communities concerned*.

But private investors cannot, in the nature of things, form an opinion about the indirect effects of their decisions. We shall therefore discuss some of the most important cases in which total social and expected private net returns might be expected to differ significantly from one another.[1]

(i) *Current and future private yields* on capital investment might differ considerably. The flow of foreign investment does not in real life take place in an equilibrium situation of full employment. If that were the case, new capital investment would increase the capital equipment per head and result in a gradual fall of the yield. Wages would increase and labour would be transferred from less to more productive uses. This process would gradually equalize the marginal efficiencies of capital in different countries.

In actual fact additional private investment tends, in a position of less than full employment to increase the yield of capital and start an upward spiral. This spiral is simultaneous or nearly simultaneous in both the lending and the borrowing countries. It will stimulate investment both in the borrowing and in the lending country, thus providing its own justification for the duration of the boom. Whether and in what direction gold movements will take place will depend on the magnitude of the multipliers and the income and price elasticities of demand and supply in the borrowing and lending countries respectively.[2]

(ii) *Current and future private returns* might differ substantially in *new industries*. (This case is to be distinguished from the preceding one by the fact that it concerns the problem of varying returns to scale: the case under (i) could apply in principle with constant costs). This is one aspect of the difference between (current) private and (future) social cost, the aspect which concerns the private investor. The general case will be discussed below under (iv). In this context we need to mention

[1] Cf. e.g. M. Kalecki, *Review of Economic Studies*, February 1937; and N. Kaldor, *Economic Journal*, 1938.
[2] The German import of capital in the period 1924–8 provides a good example for the case in point. Its abrupt end when the speculative boom in the U.S. suddenly raised the private expectation of profit in that country, is equally illustrative of the problem under discussion.

merely that differences of this type, described by Marshall, will arise
when the increase in the scale of production decreases cost either for
individual firms within the industry which is expanding or in other
industries which supply the materials and services. The risk of starting
industry on a sufficiently large scale, however, is prohibitive unless the
programme of industrial expansion is consciously planned and co-
ordinated (cf. below (iv)). The classic 'infant industry' argument,
which covers these cases, applies to a far greater range of industries
than generally supposed. Indeed, if correctly interpreted, it can be
applied to the (under-developed) economic system as a whole. In
many cases tariff protection might equalize the difference and thus
resolve the contradiction between private unprofitability and public
desirability. It would seem, however, more efficient to direct investment activity by the grant of a subsidy (*a*) because the budgetary
charge which thus becomes necessary renders the burden visible and
it can be properly allocated, and (*b*) because the subsidized industry is
more amenable to public control, and therefore steps can be taken
more easily to safeguard efficiency and prevent protection from giving
rise to an increased degree of monopoly in the protected industry and
thus either to monopoly profits or the continuance of inefficiency. As
we shall see below, however, the most important cases of constructive
planning cannot easily be accomplished by relying entirely on private
enterprise however modified by public intervention and assistance.[1]

(iii) the most important of the divergencies which have to be taken
into account, is that which may arise between *current social* and *current
private* cost. A special aspect of this case has been dealt with under (i).
The most important cause of this is the under-employment of an
economic system. If there is unemployment the social cost of additional production (for home and foreign markets) is obviously less
than the net private cost of the additional output to the employer
increasing his scale of operations. The community must directly or
indirectly maintain the unemployed. Their capacity to work if kept in
idleness over a prolonged period of time will, moreover, deteriorate
thus further increasing and extending the incidence in time of the
social loss. It might be argued, therefore, that the State could justifiably
stimulate exports or home production competing with imports.
Attempts to attain full employment by increasing the foreign balance
by increasing exports—by depreciation or export subsidies—would
be to create balance of payment problems abroad and are likely to be

---

[1] Most *laissez-faire* attacks on protective policies assume implicitly that the State
will rely entirely on the price mechanism to bring about the desired change and
would not use direct controls. This explains the identification of protection with
the support of inefficiency and monopoly.

countered by the foreign countries which are affected. The lasting favourable results of such a policy are likely to be negligible. The harm done by retaliation is likely to be considerable. The policy of stimulating export surpluses would, moreover, tend to limit the increase of the real income consequent on the increase of employment, partly because it would divert productive effort into directions in which the country has no natural advantage, partly because the forcing of exports would tend to turn the terms of trade against the country.[1] A country suffering from unemployment as a result of a slump abroad would, however, be justified in protecting its balance of payments if it at the same time takes steps to increase home demand and thus regains full employment. Without protection its balance of payments would worsen.[2]

It would, however, be open for a strong country suffering from unemployment to stimulate its business activity by granting long-term loans on favourable terms on condition that those loans are spent exclusively on its products. In contrast to the method just described, this policy is not open to the objection that it depresses business activity elsewhere. Nor would it necessarily worsen the terms of trade of the lender as it would create additional demand abroad for its products. Indeed, under favourable circumstances, e.g. if the loan gave rise to a general expansion of activity and given a high income elasticity of demand for imports in the borrowing country the loan might turn the terms of trade in favour of the lending country. This tendency would be strengthened if the investment increased the productivity in industries which supply the lender with primary products. But if the lender itself is not merely a mature industrial country but also a large-scale producer of primary commodities even the fact that the loan is used for the purpose of industrialization need not have the normal effect (as in the case of purely industrial lending countries) of tending to worsen the terms of trade of the lender. In any case the ' automatic ' effect of an increased demand in the borrowing countries on the terms of trade could be increased (and, if unfavourable, consciously altered) if the loans were used to bring about more intimate connections between the lending and the borrowing country and thus to increase the imperfections of the markets of the borrowing country in favour of the industries of the lending country.

[1] Similar ' over-export ' takes place if labour in the industries affected by unemployment accepts exceptionally low wages. The export subsidy is then borne by the workers. Tariff protection (and most forms of control of imports) has the relative advantage of turning the terms of trade in favour of the protectionist country.
[2] Or rather to restore the balance to its previous state if the slump abroad had the impact effect of worsening it. (Cf. *The Economics of Full Employment*, Oxford University Institute of Statistics, Blackwell 1943).

Q

This, in fact, would happen if the management, running and servicing of the new capital installations, financed by the foreign loan, created in the borrowing country a special demand for the skilled man-power of the lender, or if the commercial and other connections established would ease the difficulties of export.[1] The impact effect of these foreign loans on the lending countries' economic system will depend on a number of factors. If the lending country suffered from unemployment an additional investment would increase employment and consumption. Hence its social cost would be negative, whether the investment was home or foreign. If the increase in effective demand was entirely due to foreign investment this would not increase domestic capital intensity as much as would home investment,[2] though, in contrast to the continuation of unemployment, it would not, of course, retard it. Thus foreign investment may retard the relative improvement of the share of wages in the national income. Total national real income, however, would increase more than it would have done through an exclusively home investment because of the relative improvement in the terms of trade. If the increase in employment would otherwise have increased the difficulties of balancing current international payments, e.g. because the foreign elasticity of demand was very low, this relative improvement might be important if not essential. This might well be the case if other countries pursued a forward foreign investment policy. Otherwise the choice between home and foreign investment will depend on political considerations, including home social policy pursued (e.g. the possibility of distributing the improvement in the national real income fairly.)[3] In the long run the lending country must adapt itself to having a demand for imports greater than originally corresponding to full employment, so as to permit the servicing of its foreign investments without deflation or default.

The consequences of this policy to an industrial country, which was unable to compete in lending with a more fortunate rival, and thus unable also to maintain its own markets and connections, might be

[1] These imperfections should be distinguished from a decrease in the cost of home export due to increasing turnover and the increasing perfection of the knowledge of the borrower's market by the lender (and *vice versa*) which will turn the terms of trade against the lender without decreasing his real income. 'Tied' loans enforce imperfection in favour of the lender.

[2] If the alternative to foreign investment consisted of ' pure ' i.e. unremunerative, public works, the choice is between the ' communal ' enjoyment of the works created and the increase in real income.

[3] The phenomenal increase in British foreign investments, in the nineteenth century, despite heavy losses suffered as a result of over-speculation and frauds, simultaneously with an increase in the standard of life of a rapidly growing population could in all probability be attributed to some such development. Given an efficient organization the United States could parallel the British example in this century on a vastly greater scale.

serious. Its terms of trade would, in all likelihood, deteriorate. The industrialization of backward or primary producing areas would tend to decrease the supply of primary products, partly because the absolute volume of supply may fall as a result of the transfer of productive factors from primary to secondary or tertiary industries,[1] and partly because the increase in the standard of life in the backward areas will increase their demand for primary products in competition with the mature industrial countries. The import prices of the industrial country will tend to rise. If the industrial country does not create any new demands for its services and producers' goods, and the market for these is very imperfect, depending on the grant of loans, its export prices may fall seriously. The consequent worsening of the terms of trade might prejudice its material progress.

(iv) Finally we must consider some cases in which the *current private* and *future social* returns differ significantly.[2] The future social return must be interpreted as embracing gains accruing to the community (direct and indirect) through the changes made possible by the new development. Investment of this type will be desirable from the long run point of view of the community as a whole, though no private entrepreneur could undertake it at his own risk because the return directly accruing to him would be insufficient to cover the cost incurred and the risks borne (or vice versa).

(*a*) The planned creation of new industries would lessen the risk borne by each part of an industrialization plan if it were attempted singly by individual entrepreneurs. The latter could, therefore, not undertake investments except if tempted by exorbitant rates of profit or interest to cover their risks. The publicly financed and coherently planned industrialization, however, would eliminate the risk of the new undertaking being unable to find profitable markets, by concomitantly and generally raising the purchasing power of a country or a region as a whole.[3] Thus Government agencies in the lending and in the borrowing country, by co-operating with one another, could, even without financial loss, promote an investment programme at much lower rates of return than would be acceptable to single investors financing individual ventures abroad. The further reduction in the lenders' risks and thus a fall in the gross rate of interest or return (i.e. the burden on the borrower) would accrue from the fact that

---

[1] This effect need not exert itself in the case of over-populated areas. Cf. A. J. Brown (*Industrialization and Trade*, Royal Institute of International Affairs, 1943).

[2] From a logical point of view this category embraces the previous groups. In this context we shall only discuss the cases which do not fall easily into the narrower classes already analysed.

[3] On this and related points cf. the interesting article by P. N. Rosenstein-Rodan (*Economic Journal*, 1943).

public agencies need not take into account the liquidity of the assets acquired in the course of the investment programme. Public agencies could always obtain finance. The private investor, on the contrary, would encounter the additional risk of not being able, in emergencies, to liquidate his asset.

(b) The cost structures of any single investor (excluding the cost of bearing risk dealt with above) is not independent of general economic progress. It will be affected—increased or decreased— by the rise of other industries, the development of transport and other communication facilities (cf. above). The training of man-power is especially a cost which no single entrepreneur can incur, as the benefit does not necessarily accrue to him unless the movement of labour is restricted. The same applies to the cost of transport, which decreases with increasing turnover. The competitive position is thereby cumulatively strengthened. The cost of providing such facilities must be borne by the community as a whole. Government agencies by their taxation policy could effectively impute general costs and recover windfall capital gains accruing in the system as a whole, and thus not merely regulate economic incentive, but also safeguard a satisfactory distribution of the national income. Without adequate central planning and control of the execution of development plans, monetary instability, speculative excesses, and a misdirection of productive resources might result from that competitive scramble for man-power and supplies, which occurs regularly in booms with consequent losses to the community.

(c) Industries which depend for efficiency on mass-production methods are unlikely to be started in small economic areas. The establishment of such industries depends on large amounts of capital equipment. They are subject to very high risk, as in a small economic area their internal market in an unplanned system, is uncertain, and their possible outlets by exports at least precarious, on account of the potential retaliatory measures abroad. Foreign investors will, moreover, be apprehensive that the governments in those areas will intervene against the establishment of one or a few large-scale concerns even if the country could support them, not merely because of the threat of monopolistic exploitation once the foreign-owned large-scale concerns eliminated the small and inefficient native producers, but also because the process of elimination will inevitably result in distress to the small producers and cause political agitation. It is, therefore, improbable that private enterprise will lead to the establishment of optimum scale units of production in smaller national economies. Publicly owned, or publicly guaranteed and controlled industry, whose markets are assured by the general industrialization plans and the consequent increase in consuming power would make possible far more rapid economic progress in many areas of the world than would reliance on private initiative. The waste of productive opportunities could be ended without having to fear monopoly exploitation and the dissipation of (at least part of) the gain in excess capacity.

We might conclude that in view of the existence of significant differences between the social and private returns on capital investment, unregulated foreign investment could not secure optimum production and maximum progress, either in the backward areas or in the lending countries. The difference between ' objective ' (social) and ' subjective ' (private) risk is considerable enough to prevent a substantial and, in certain circumstances, overwhelming, portion of investment programmes which would be technically practicable and economically profitable under a planned system of industrial development. Returns which are substantial enough to tempt foreign investors would be so high as to reduce substantially, if not nullify, the benefit of the development concerned to the borrowing country.[1] If these developments are financed by means of fixed interest loans contracted in periods of expansion, which seemingly justified the commitments, the position of the debtor might be seriously worsened as a result of the borrowing.

The most important task of foreign investment in future will be to aid the industrialization of backward areas. To accomplish this task, however, industrialization must be planned and executed through the co-operation and initiative of the governments of the lending and borrowing countries in some suitable way, through an International Investment Board.

This conclusion is considerably strengthened if the problem of repayment is envisaged. The fact that this problem did not arise in the nineteenth century and did not form part of the classical discussion of the subject was due to a fortunate coincidence of economic development in the west of Europe and overseas. Foreign investment in that period was mainly undertaken to open up empty overseas areas for primary production. Repayment proceeded smoothly except in the case of palpable frauds and speculation, because at the same time the population of the creditor countries increased rapidly and with it the demand for the commodities the production of which they had financed. If effective demand in the lending countries in the long run is not increased to a level corresponding to over-full employment,[2] a stable

---

[1] The portion of the national output of some colonies taken in the shape of profits of private companies in those areas, amounts to a more considerable part of the output than the rate of current saving even in the richest areas.

[2] i.e. to a level of demand which in a closed economic system would lead to inflation, in an open economic system to an import surplus. This could be done, for example, by a systematic reduction of working hours while maintaining wages if the terms of trade cannot be turned in favour of the paying country.

position cannot be maintained. Foreign investment can only solve the problem of surplus in the balance of payments in the medium long run. In the shorter period deflationary crises in the lending countries could be prevented from spreading and thus causing international complications and general bankruptcy by appropriate currency agreements. Without such agreements on home and international economic policy the ' capacity to pay ' of a country cannot be guaranteed however ' sound ' the purpose for which the foreign loan or investment was at the time of lending.

B.   FOREIGN INVESTMENTS AND PRIVATE CAPITAL

It is largely assumed in discussing problems of international reconstruction that capital development, within each country and internationally, depends entirely on voluntary saving. If this were immutable, poorer areas could hardly hope to achieve an ordered industrialization programme without the help of richer countries. In addition a rapid industrialization would seem to require the continuance of a considerable inequality of income, for in those areas the working classes cannot save. Even so, they could not under all circumstances rely on the wealthy saving and investing a sufficient portion of their disproportionately high incomes. Indeed, it might not be possible even in richer, more mature countries affected by the war, e.g. Britain and France, to pursue at one and the same time physical and social reconstruction on this basis.

Physical reconstruction in those circumstances would depend on the encouragement of entrepreneurs, i.e. on increasing the inequality of income. But an increase in the income of the richer classes might (while increasing saving) also increase the demand for foreign goods and services the procuring of which will be especially difficult in the post-war period.[1] Social reforms, on the other hand, would increase the income of the poor and consumption in general and so encroach upon the volume of practicable investment. The dilemma cannot be solved by exclusive reliance on private initiative.

Fortunately the assumption that the rate of investment depends on the rate of voluntary saving (at full employment) is incorrect and the conclusion therefore invalid. It would be possible to render economic progress independent of the voluntary decisions of individuals by financing investment out of communal or enforced savings. Invest-

[1] e.g. foreign travel. The South American millionaires were notorious absentees in Europe and spent there a considerable portion of their income, which, had it been to increase capital equipment at home by purchasing foreign machinery, would have considerably accelerated economic progress. The position was the similar in Central Europe.

ment finance institutions could be established by using revenue obtained from progressive direct taxation, and/or private savings, enforced by a strict control of consumption, could be canalized for the purpose of domestic and foreign investment and controlled by an Investment Board.

A simple re-distribution of income might have little effect in mitigating poverty.[1] The proposed method of tackling the problem, however, opens up wholly new prospects. Economic and social progress would no longer be alternatives tending to be mutually exclusive. At least partial capital autarky can be established by government investment policy without hardship in poor areas.[2]

The maintenance of full employment and the abolition of disguised unemployment would represent a far greater gain than the help received by backward areas through foreign loans for their capital development in the pre-1939 period, a large part of which was, moreover, wasted. If measures are taken, moreover, to enforce efficiency in production and prevent the investment being dissipated in imperfectly competing excess capacity, the cumulative increase in productivity, even in poorer areas, would establish a firm basis for a rapid advance in the standard of life.

International agreements which would make possible the international maintenance of full employment by using any deficiency in effective demand in the mature countries to further the development of the under-developed areas would be welcome. But, in view of the foregoing they must safeguard the independence of the debtor to pursue internal policies which it deems desirable. The basic programme of industrialization must be domestically financed. If, in addition, the aid of mature countries can be secured it would hasten reconstruction while aiding the lending countries in the management of their economic affairs. If such satisfactory and equitable international solutions should prove impracticable, poorer countries—especially if they establish close

---

[1] Though its indirect effects in maintaining effective demand might be considerable; with this aspect of the matter we are not concerned in this context. Estimates such as those by Mr. Colin Clark (*The Conditions of Economic Progress*) which have been recently used to show the Utopian character of hopes for rapid economic progress, are based on the assumption that capital accumulation is exclusively financed by voluntary savings. They have no relevance to economies in which industrialization and investment are planned such as the U.S.S.R., Nazi Germany and war-time Britain.

[2] The Government, of course, need not restrict its finance to public, but could also stimulate private, enterprise by its investment funds. The suffering of the people of the U.S.S.R. was due not so much to capital autarky but partly to the sudden worsening of the terms of trade of the U.S.S.R. with the outside world, due to deflation, and economic nationalism, partly to the social revolution carried concomitantly, and finally to the forced pace of industrialization due to the justified fear of outside military attack.

co-operation with one another and so make possible a wide regional division of labour—need not despair of the future even in the absence of foreign loans from mature countries.

C. CONCLUSIONS

Our considerations indicate that, in order to secure optimum progress:

(1) most countries must maintain rigid control over foreign payments if they wish to pursue progressive economic policies.[1]

(2) No reliance can be placed on private profit expectations as a guide and criterion for international investment.[2] International investment must be planned and undertaken by some international agency in conjunction with an international currency agreement.

(3) Failing such agreement and the establishment of an international Investment Board, poorer countries can rely on communal saving by way of taxation or rationing, plus investment control for their planned and speedy economic development without having to enforce intolerable hardship on the poorer classes of their population. Exchange controls will give them all powers necessary to prevent the increased taxation or restraint on the entrepreneurial classes from exerting a deterrent effect on capital investment. The gains which can be derived from planned investment and maintenance of full employment are in all probability, far greater than any advantage which could be derived from the aid of unstable mature countries unwilling to enter into satisfactory international agreements.

18

THE NEW PLAN FOR AN INTERNATIONAL INVESTMENT BOARD

The U.S. plan concerning the organisation of international long-term lending after the war has now been published. The limitation of means is not one of the drawbacks from which the new scheme suffers,

[1] This conclusion has been accepted by the more thoughtful of American official experts (*The United States in the World Economy*, p. 20).

[2] ' The fundamental requirement is that investment programmes be formulated on a comprehensive and long-range basis and executed at a reasonably regular rate and in a manner that will both strengthen the economic and social structure of the borrowing country and provide reasonable returns and adequate safeguards to the investor. The responsibility for developing such programmes will doubtless be borne chiefly by the governments concerned, and much of the capital may have to be provided through official agencies. Certainly the methods of foreign-bound flotation employed in the ' twenties would be both unacceptable to the individual investor and undesirable in the interest of international stability, (*The United States in the World Economy*, p. 19.)

though it could, if suitably employed, usefully supplement the currency stabilisation scheme whose provisions were announced earlier.

A long-term international investment scheme should fulfill two aims. It must first enable member countries to pursue a policy of full employment and deal in a suitable manner with surpluses and deficiencies in the balance of payments of member countries arising solely out of the depression of any one of the major participating countries. It must secondly enable the orderly industrialisation of areas poor in capital equipment, so as to permit a general increase in the standard of life of the world as a whole.

(1) In our Supplement No. 5 on the New Plans for International Trade we have tried to outline a scheme which, by a suitable close interlinking between a currency equilisation or clearing scheme and a long-term lending scheme, would permit the maintenance of full employment in any participating country irrespective of the policy pursued abroad. This task was to be accomplished by arranging loans to backward areas sufficiently large to wipe out the international trading surpluses and deficits of the participating countries. These loans were to be used to obtain commodities from the deficit countries to help them in readjusting their balance without forcing them in their turn to deflate or to pursue an autarkic commercial policy. This scheme did not render superfluous a readjustment in those countries whose deficit arose out of reasons other than the depression abroad, but even these readjustments would be helped by the proposed mechanism as it would eliminate the danger of a generally deflationary spiral consequent upon the readjustment.

The new scheme does not provide for such a close interlinking between the currency and long-term lending schemes, an interlinking which in the nineteenth century was, with occasional jerks, achieved by the domination of London over the international gold standard due to its monopoly position in short-term finance of international trade linked with continuous foreign lending. Certain paragraphs of the memorandum indeed which caution against long-term lending to countries pursuing unwise budgetary policies, suggest that the authors of the plan would be opposed to the use of foreign loans coupled with budget deficits to promote world-wide full employment, a method which would lessen the need for national recovery projects involving protectionism merely for the sake of maintaining the balance of payments. The scheme should therefore be further elaborated and reassurance ought to be sought that the bank's ample means will be used for the right purpose.

(2) International help in industrialising backward areas ought not to be made exclusively dependent on the function of the Bank as a

stabiliser of world employment, i.e. in part on the depression of big industrial countries. This aspect of long-term investment schemes should only be a *balancing factor* in a programme of industrialisation, or, in other words, whenever a large mature country is depressed, that depression can be made an occasion for *speeding* up the industrialisation by using the idle capacity of the depressed country directly or indirectly for that beneficient purpose. The basic programme of industrialisation, however, must be based on a *deliberate temporary foregoing* by the *richest countries* of the fruits of their own high productivity in favour of backward areas.[1] This can be done by a consistent and steady lending which is not interrupted whenever any of the mature countries nears full employment. The success of such a long-term industrialisation programme depends, however, on the replanning of the economic structure of whole areas (not even of single countries) and such programmes should not be restricted to giving occasional loans to individual public or private projects. The reason for this condition of success is that a coherently planned industrialisation scheme will give far higher real returns than individual ' projects '. This does not necessarily mean that private ventures should be excluded, but any such ventures must be co-ordinated with the plans elaborated for those areas as a whole.

The scheme as outlined does not envisage such coherent planning, unless indeed the proviso that the investment banks should only extend credit when normal private channels fail can be interpreted in this way. It stands to reason that no single individual firm could either replan a borrowing area or, contrariwise, mobilise in the lending country sufficient funds to help in the execution of that plan. It would be necessary therefore to amplify the provisions under which the new investment bank is prepared to grant credits.

(3) A further point is of some importance, though logically it is implicit in both earlier points. It would be essential when granting these loans to determine in advance the general lines on which the servicing and repaying of the loans is to be effected. Otherwise the repayment may well initiate a general deflationary spiral which must frustrate the attempt. If the industrialisation plans of whole regions are worked out on the basis of the best technical information available, and with due regard to the probable developments in the lending countries; if, moreover, the problem of currency stabilisation is solved in the way indicated above; the problem need not arise. The maintenance of full employment all round by the mechanism described in

---

[1] If full employment in these areas is maintained by ' useless ' public works (or arms expenditure) then the international help in industrialisation of poorer areas would not involve a fall in the consumption of the richer areas.

(1) would in any case sustain world demand. Care can then be taken that demand in the creditor countries should be increased even further so as to cause an excess of imports. Special measures, e.g. the use of the products of the newly industrialized areas for social services, or for further internal and international investment programmes of the 'lending' country might be considered. This indeed happened accidentally during the nineteenth century, but unless some attention is paid to the qualitative, apart from the quantitative, aspect of the problem, the coincidence facilitating smooth transfer need not repeat itself in the coming decades.[1]

On all these three points, further amplification of the United States scheme is urgently required, without which it cannot by its mere amplitude of means provide a satisfactory solution of the problem of maintaining full employment internationally and obviate a further bout of acute economic nationalism.

19

DOMESTIC VERSUS FOREIGN INVESTMENT

Introduction

The problem of the relative merits of home and foreign investment from the point of view of a capital exporting country has once more been raised in a *Symposium* published in the *Bulletin of the Institute of Statistics* on the future of the Sterling Area, and by some comments made in *The Observer* by its Economic Editor.[2] Some of the arguments apply, *mutatis mutandis*, to capital importing countries.

We are, generally, in agreement with Sir Donald MacDougall's paper. He has, however, confined himself to a rigorous analysis based on rather restrictive assumptions, and he is mainly concerned with a country receiving capital from abroad. A discussion of some of the wider issues, also from the viewpoint of a capital exporting country, may therefore be in order.

Some of the differences of opinion arise from the fact that different authors discuss the problem on different levels of abstraction and on different assumptions. This is evident in Mr. Scott's recent analysis[2] of Mr. Shonfield's advocacy of a general discouragement (in contrast to selective control) of capital exports, and stimulus to domestic investment and capital imports.

[1] Cf. On the latter point, Dr. P. Rosenstein-Rodan, *Economic Journal*, September-December, 1943.

[2] *Bulletin of the Oxford University Institute of Statistics*, November 1959. *The Observer*, February 28th, 1960. See also A. Shonfield, *British Economic Policy Since the War*, 1st edition, p. 109, 2nd edition, p. 110.

Mr. Scott initially assumes perfect competition and infinitesimal changes. When he relaxes the assumption of perfect competition, he replaces it by marginal revenue equals marginal cost and full cost pricing. When he relaxes the assumption of infinitesimal changes he confines himself to indicating the diminishing marginal productivity of capital.

Mr. Shonfield overstates the case for home investment, confuses value added with the marginal productivity of capital and marginal with average yield, and derives policy conclusions from irrelevant statistics. But the kernel of truth in the thesis is that the geographic product in the country where higher investment occurs will tend to increase by more than the amount appropriated by the investor.

Whether a country should, from a national point of view, discourage capital exports and encourage capital imports will depend on the relation between the divergence of private profits and national gains at home and abroad. We first discuss some of the causes that give rise to such divergences under the headings of (i) external economies in disequilibrium, (ii) terms of trade, (iii) indirect effects of foreign investment on employment and income in conditions of non-Keynesian unemployment, underemployment and differential labour productivities, and (iv) the effects of certain policies, including taxation.

External Economies

We think that the essence of the case for curbing foreign and encouraging domestic investment can be stated quite simply. The later elaboration attempts to show the precise mechanism by which private profits will tend to diverge from national benefits.

It is obvious that this case can be based only on the assumption that the benefit from the act of investment is greater than the resultant increase in the income of the investor and that the locus of this benefit will be determined by the locus of the investment. Theoretically it must therefore be considered as an external economy.

Consider an act of investment which raises world product. If the whole increase resulting from this investment can be appropriated by the investor, social and private returns are equal. But normally he will have to share it with others, for the new investment will raise wages or lower prices, so that workers, other entrepreneurs and consumers generally will benefit. Some of these benefits will be offset by losses to other income groups. But in certain conditions, specified later, there is bound to be a *net* increase in production which does not accrue to the investor.[1]

---

[1] It is, of course, possible to envisage situations in which the investor is able to sweep up more than the increase in production; then private returns exceed social returns.

Granted the existence of such net external gains, the question arises whether the chances are not higher that they will accrue to nationals if the investment is domestic, and to foreigners if it is undertaken abroad. Tax considerations would certainly suggest an affirmative answer, terms of trade and employment considerations may, however, modify it.

We are here concerned not only with those external economies where the *output* of one producer is affected directly by the *output* of other producers, but also with those discussed by the writers on under-developed countries (e.g. Nurkse), which arise from *finite* additions to plant and equipment and from the *disturbance of equilibrium*.[1] They relate the incomes and profits of one group of people to the actions of other people. We are concerned with the wider concept of *pecuniary*, not only with the narrower concept of *technological* external economies. It is, however, not only in underdeveloped countries that these can be important, but also in advanced industrial countries.

Let us begin with a cost-reducing investment in a particular industry which leads to expansion of its capacity. The prices of its products will be lowered and the rewards of its factors will be raised. The lower product prices benefit the users of the product, the higher factor prices benefit the suppliers of the factors. It is, of course, true that the suppliers of rival products and the hirers of rival factors will suffer some losses. But the cost-reducing investment has raised the real national product as a whole, and in so far as this increase is not wholly appropriated by the investor there must be a *net* addition to some other incomes.

These benefits are partly Marshallian consumers' and producers' surpluses, partly the result of outward shifts of the production-possibility locus (upward shifts of the marginal productivity curve if index-number problems are solved), not wholly appropriated by those responsible for the shift. They depend on either (i) a finite addition to total production with equilibrium restored after the investment is

---

[1] The concept of 'external economies' here used was first elaborated by Allyn Young (*E.J.* 1928): 'Every important advance in the organisation of industry, regardless of whether it is based upon anything which, in a narrow and technical sense could be called a new 'invention', or involves a fresh application of the fruits of scientific progress to industry, alters the conditions of industrial activity and initiates responses elewhere in the industrial structure which in turn have a further unsettling effect' (p. 533). Allyn Young focused attention on external cost reduc-tion, Rosenstein-Rodan shifted the emphasis to external investment incentives which are due to demand-creation (*E.J.*1943). In both cases profits of others have risen. Balogh applied Rodan's concept to foreign investment policy (*O.E.P.* 1945). Nurkse and Hirschman further elaborated the concepts in the setting of underdeveloped countries. Scitovsky's distinction greatly clarified the discussions and one of the two present authors, Paul Streeten, has much benefited from it and used it in his contribution to this article. ('Two Concepts of External Economies', *Journal of Political Economy*, April 1954). Arndt, too, has helped in sorting out the different meanings. 'External Economies in Economic Growth' (*Economic Record*, 1955).

carried out, or (ii) a disturbance of equilibrium that sets other profit-seeking actions in train, which move the system away from the original equilibrium.

Disequilibrium

When the analysis proceeds on the assumption of marginal productivity of capital schedules, the rate of return on capital is the *rate of interest* that would prevail if all long-term adjustments were made and full equilibrium had been reached. *Profits*, however, are a sign of *disequilibrium*, and an incentive to its removal. The investment may then eliminate the profits as it restores equilibrium. But investment may also raise profits in other industries and thus income and savings. It then leads away from the original equilibrium position. Investment in steel makes steel cheaper. This means bigger profits in building, which uses steel. This leads to expansion in building. This in turn raises steel profits and leads to further expansion in steel. Equilibrium is reached only when successive doses of investment in all industries affected have eliminated profits everywhere. Only then is the socially desirable amount of investment also the profitable amount. This position need never be reached in principle, and, as we emphasised above, is never reached in fact. Thus initial profitability in each single industry understates social desirability not only by the whole of producers' and consumers' surpluses, but by more—*viz.* by the benefits from the series of consequential adjustments towards a steadily receding and changing ' equilibrium ' position.[1]

Investment in (say) steel may also give rise to profits in

(*a*) coal if coal is used in steel production;

(*b*) cement if steel and cement are complementary;

(*c*) oil if oil is a substitute for coal;

(*d*) consumption goods bought by the now better-off steel, coal, cement and oil workers.

Any losses in substitutes for steel products used in the production of these substitutes, complements with these substitutes, substitutes for the products used in the production of substitutes, and goods bought by factor-owners suffering these losses, must be on balance less than the gains, if the initial investment has shifted the production possibility locus outwards.

Investment that lowers the cost of producing a certain product is only

[1] The fact that investments are planned on the assumption that growth will continue and that demand will expand faster if price is lowered does not affect the argument. Since the expectations of the majority are bound to be less optimistic than those of the optimists, there must be external economies for the more cautious.

one instance of investment moving the system away from equilibrium by giving rise to higher incomes and profits in other sectors. Besides cost-reducing investment there is product-improving and product-innovating investment, and these, too, will initiate a series of consequential investments.

A policy guided by the national interest ought to consider all the various types of external economy. It cannot be expected that investors in one industry (say steel) should take into account the consequential benefits, not because they lie in the future and are uncertain, but because success depends on the investment decisions of others, based, in turn, on their expectations of investment in steel. Discrimination against investment abroad by itself will not guarantee that the chain reaction of domestic investments will be set off. But if the conditions for such a cumulative expansion are present, either because there is an alert entrepreneurial class, or because the government is ready to take positive action to coordinate investment plans, the withdrawal of capital from abroad can be an important source of capital.

Three questions may be raised at this stage. First, why need the capital that sparks off the growth process be drawn from abroad rather than from another domestic investment project? Secondly, would not the growth process attract capital from abroad, or capital that would otherwise have gone abroad, even in the absence of government restriction? Thirdly, could it not be that the cumulative process would yield higher returns to the investing country if it took place abroad than if it were ' artificially ' fostered at home?

The answer to the first question is that the sources of capital for the expansion triggered off by the initial intervention are indeed many. They are (1) the growth of incomes due to economies of scale and innovation, (2) the higher savings ratios called forth by (1) and by the newly-opened up investment opportunities, (3) the capital set free from projects now obsolescent, and (4) the diversion of capital that has gone abroad or might otherwise have gone abroad. Although the last is only one source, there is no reason why it should not be tapped.

The answer to the second question is that in our argument the marginal productivity schedule does not shift upwards autonomously but its shift is the result of the coordinated investment plans.[1] In the absence of such coordination, no such rise is to be expected and investment will not take place. In order to create the conditions of high

---

[1] This is analogous to the ' balanced growth ' argument in underdeveloped areas. The growth can, of course, be triggered off by an unbalance. The belief that other investment is being undertaken, creating markets, will induce imitation. Thus the existence of an overall plan might speed growth even in an economy not subject to central planning. The success of the so-called Vanoni Plan can be attributed to this fact.

domestic profits, the opportunities have first to be created. The fact that afterwards private investment will be attracted and will be diverted from foreign countries to the home country is an additional gain from the initial act of intervention.

The answer to the third question is more difficult. Clearly, the cumulative process may proceed more successfully abroad and the profits thus earned, as well as any improvement in the terms of trade (see next section), may benefit the investing country more than if the capital had been forced to stay at home. But it is probable that many of the ancillary activities clustering round the centre of growth will be conducted by foreigners abroad and benefit them if the investment is located there. Nevertheless, investing countries can substantially and cumulatively benefit from investment abroad, and host countries can become cumulatively dependent on foreign capital, with un-favourable net long-run consequences to themselves, as Canada and pre-1929 Germany have shown.

Bottlenecks and the Locus of Investment

A particular instance of cost-reducing investment is that which breaks a bottleneck. Although highly profitable for a time, it raises profits on all under-utilised productive capacity and in all those lines where the exploitation of economies of scale was restricted before. It is therefore misleading to assume, in this context, constant capital/output ratios for increments in investment. Once equilibrium is disturbed, the heterogeneity of the various pieces of capital equipment becomes crucial. Specific pieces are complementary with other pieces and with other resources. Investment is attracted into high-yielding lines, but high yield is an index of specific scarcity. By removing this scarcity, capital/output ratios in other lines are reduced and expansion is stimulated. But expansion creates new bottlenecks and new profit opportunities. This zigzagging path of the capital/output ratio is part of the process of expansion and affects the notional ' long-term equilibrium ratio ' towards which the process tends.

It is impossible to derive the capital/output ratio for a specific foreign project from prevailing capital/output ratios in the foreign country. This notion, once the long-term equilibrium path is left, has no significance. Investment will be biased towards high yielding projects. Profits may be high because competition is imperfect, because the industry is highly protected and domestic rivals inefficient, because the foreign firm has special advantages, such as advanced know-how or patents, or because an expanding world demand meets the inelastic supply of wells, mines or plantations. If profits are high and likely to remain so for any of these reasons, the prevailing marginal productivity of capital gives no clue to the profitability of single ventures. The marginal productivity curve is not a continuous function. If, on the other hand, investment is in a competitive industry, or if, though initially high, profits are soon competed or taxed away, profitability will be low and will fall short of total social productivity.[1]

A partial remedy for the inability of an investor to reap the whole product resulting from his investment is full integration of industry, so that pecuniary advantages accruing to any sector accrue to the whole. But even if the economy were organised as one giant firm, profits need not reflect the full benefit, for, as we have seen, some of the net increase in production is passed on in the form of higher wages.[2]

Terms of Trade

Foreign investment will increase the production of goods abroad above what it would otherwise have been, domestic investment will do the same at home. There is a presumption that external pecuniary economies discussed in previous sections will accrue to foreigners from the foreign investment, to nationals from the domestic investment. But this need not be so if we allow for changing terms of trade.

There are four sectors in which the divergence between national and private (or world) interest may be particularly important: domestic investment in exports and import substitutes and investment of domestic capital abroad in the investing country's imports and export substitutes. Investment that reduces directly or indirectly the costs of exports and foreign export substitutes generates pecuniary external economies abroad, whilst investment that reduces directly or indirectly the costs of imports and domestic import substitutes (though other countries' importers share this benefit) generates these at home. (For industries making complements to exports at home and complements to import substitutes abroad the opposite is true.)

Can one therefore say that British investment abroad that raises the production of goods Britain imports should be encouraged, while that which raises the production of products competitive with British exports should be discouraged? Unfortunately, no such simple conclusion is possible, for it depends, apart from all other complications

---

[1] It should, however, be noted that a substantial excess of domestic returns over interest or profits remitted abroad is not necessarily an argument for attracting foreign capital. The successful servicing of loans and equity investment does not depend only on the host country but also on the demand and supply pattern and on the policies pursued by the investor's country. Attempts to repay may be frustrated and deflation forced on the remitting country, as post-1929 experience has shown.

[2] The diffusion of gains and the necessity for privately unprofitable investments or of simultaneous action, discussed in the last two sections, represent inherent disadvantages of an economic system in which decision-taking is left to numerous independent individuals.

R

such as the transfer problem, also on what would have happened to exports had it not been for the investment abroad. If foreign countries are determined to produce substitutes for British exports, either themselves or by inviting American or European firms to establish subsidiaries, it is better for Britain to replace her own exports by putting up subsidiaries abroad, than to cling to a doomed position. Moreover, the firms producing substitutes for exports abroad will require components from Britain and will generally have closer trade links, and might thus salvage the investing country's terms of trade.

It follows that, in deciding upon the optimum policy for investment abroad from a national point of view, it is not sufficient to consider the direct and indirect effects of investment upon the terms of trade compared with the current situation. The autonomous trend of the terms of trade must also be taken into account.

The important effects of foreign investment on the terms of trade through the consequential international transfer problems are too complicated to be treated here. One would have to distinguish between

(i) the transfer on capital account and the transfer of interest and dividends on current account; on capital account one would have to distinguish between (a) autonomous foreign investment, which involves a transfer problem, and (b) trade-induced investment (credit is given in order to promote export sales, or to finance an existing export surplus) and investment-induced trade (tied loans, direct investment by subsidiaries), neither of which involves a transfer problem on capital account, and both of which may give rise to ' negative ' transfer problems, when the complementary demands of the foreign country exceed the loan;

(ii) the various *methods* of correcting an imbalance (whether they worsen or improve the terms of trade; how one country's action is met by others);

(iii) the *types* of foreign investment undertaken, i.e. whether financial (equity of fixed interest) or direct;

(iv) the various patterns of supply and demand that arise from the investment and determine the response to whatever methods of correction are chosen (i.e. income and price ' elasticities ').

It is plain that no presumption about the comparative movement in the terms of trade resulting from an act of foreign or domestic investment can be established. We cannot even say that the primary will be stronger than the secondary effects. Thus, on current account, a deterioration of the investing country's terms of trade from its investing abroad, in say, export substitutes can be more than offset by the improvement resulting from the remittance of profits, and an improvement from its investing abroad in imports can be more than offset by the deterioration resulting from foreign tariffs imposed in order to remit profits.

Investment and Employment

If there is general unemployment of men and machines, the national costs of a domestic investment project are substantially below the private costs. The social benefit is greater than profits by the additional wages (minus any unemployment relief) whereas investment abroad yields profits only. It is, of course, true that additional domestic investment in these conditions does not require a cut of foreign investment. Nevertheless, private profit considerations unaided by a full employment policy, may lead to socially excessive investment abroad. In conditions of Keynesian full employment the question arises whether the government is able to maintain full employment in all circumstances, or whether its ability depends upon (a) the provision of equipment (rigid techniques) or (b) the absorption of labour at ruling wage rates (rigid wage rates). Thus if there is an increase in the working population either through immigration or through natural population increase, or if more labour is set free by labour-saving inventions than can be re-employed by the rise in production, the maintenance of full employment may depend upon the provision of additional machines or upon reduction in wage rates. If in the absence of these provisions ' non-employment' (distinct from ' unemployment') would rise, national benefits from domestic investment exceed profits.

A special problem arises if the economy is divided into two sectors —one with rigid wages (downwards) and machines (industrial sector), the other with flexible incomes and no machines (rural sector). Full employment is always maintained, but productivity in the flexible income sector is below that in the rigid wage sector, and absorption of labour in the rigid wage sector is limited by available machines or merely by the relative dearness of labour.[1] Once again profits from investment in the rigid wage sector understate the national benefit. The wages received by the newly employed exceed their marginal productivity in the rural sector and this excess should be added to national gains.

This last case presents an extreme example of a more general phenomenon. A specific act of investment might raise the average productivity of labour in the economy as a whole for any *given* amount of capital, because it permits a move from low-to high-productivity occupations, because it shifts demand from low- to high-productivity

[1] Cf. MacDougall, p. 210.

goods, because it improves skills, because it makes workers more
' productivity-minded ', etc. In all these cases national gains will exceed
interests and profits.[1]

On the other hand, there are certain national advantages of direct
investment abroad. Thus a large firm may be able to reduce costs more
drastically when demand recedes by laying off workers and shutting
down factories abroad than at home, where the government may
exercise greater pressure and a sense of national responsibility may
temper the profit motive. There is evidence for this in U.S. investment
in Canada, and the same might happen here.

Policy Issues

There are certain advantages and disadvantages of investing abroad
which arise from the fact that it makes possible or necessary the pursuit
of policies that otherwise would not have been possible or necessary.
Thus foreign investment normally enables a country to exert pressures
of various kinds to promote sales of exports. This may be the result
of trade agreements, of tying sales to loans, of the psychological links
forged by credit, or of the more direct links of foreign subsidiaries with
their parent companies. Some hope and others fear that foreign investment may give the investing country political control.

On the other hand, if the foreign private investment (or, for that
matter, government aid) is unstable, it requires frequent adjustments
in the balance of payments of the receiving country. If this means that
this country must maintain larger holdings of liquid international
reserves than would otherwise be necessary, a loss of yield results.
However, if reserves were not reinforced under such conditions, while
devaluation is ruled out as ineffective or undesirable and balancing
loans are not available, deflation would have to be applied with a loss
of employment and production. Thus both holding additional reserves
and not reinforcing them have for the recipient country serious drawbacks, which reduce the favourable effects of capital imports. Exchange
rate variations are inappropriate for short-term adjustments and, even
if effective, have drawbacks of their own. It is true that these disadvantages result not from foreign investment as such but from its
instability. But foreign investment is notoriously unstable.

The disadvantages to recipient countries are most apparent when
lending abroad and borrowing from abroad are used as buffers to
absorb shocks on the domestic economy.[2] When other methods of

---

[1] The extent of improvement resulting from investment will depend also on the
intensity of research and the energy with which it is applied.

[2] This is particularly dangerous for short-term capital movements with which we
are not concerned here.

adjustment between domestic wage and price targets on the one hand
and savings and investment targets on the other are ruled out, foreign
capital movements could be used to maintain high employment levels
without inflation. Thus an excess of domestic attempted savings over
domestic investment at full employment can be steered abroad through
foreign loans, whilst a deficiency can be the occasion for borrowing
from abroad. On these assumptions, foreign investment or borrowing
abroad becomes the only means of maintaining full employment without inflation. The situation is analogous to that of regional adjustments
within countries, except that there is no unified international capital
market. If no international monetary and fiscal policies for stabilisation
are pursued, a country that has foresworn all other measures of adjustment can thus shift the burden of instability on to foreigners. But
borrowing from and lending to foreigners must not be advocated in
order to maintain employment and stability. It would become necessary
only because the policy makers in the country had ruled out all policy
alternatives other than global monetary controls and the latter had
failed to work. If this ' export of instability ' abroad is managed well
and in close cooperation with the countries which are recipients of the
excess of exports or suppliers of the imports, it might not be destructive
to balance abroad.[1]

In some cases government policy can reduce or remove what appear
to be high private costs of foreign investment. Foreign investors
probably systematically overestimate the risks of investment in capital-
poor countries. This may be the result of greater ignorance, fear of the
strange or of political events, or illiquidity. Profits before risk allow-
ances will tend to be high. Special tax concessions may increase them
further. Actual net private profits from such investments will tend to
exceed expected private profits after risk discount. If the investor's
government were to stimulate this kind of investment by providing
information, guarantees, participation, etc., profits, national gains and
gains for the host country may all go up.[2]

The present system of double taxation agreements yields taxes on
profits from overseas investment to the foreign country, and only the

[1] It was in fact advocated as a means of stabilising the world economy by plans
worked out at the Oxford University Institute of Statistics during the last war (*New
Plans for International Trade*, Oxford 1943).

[2] In many European countries, on the other hand, there are other and more
important obstacles to foreign investment than the comparison of private yields.
Apart from the deterrents of government regulations and different institutional
arrangements, many companies have taken action to prevent large blocks of shares
from falling into foreign hands. Intended to prevent take-over bids, these actions
also reduce passive participation of foreign investors in any other than the few top
companies. See article IX in the series of articles in *The Times*, ' Europe's Recovery ',
March 11th, 1960.

excess of domestic over foreign income or profits taxes to the home country. Domestic investment yields its full tax harvest to the home country. The overseas trade concessions introduced in 1957 have removed even this excess for the undistributed part of the profits of overseas trade corporations. Most advanced countries make similar concessions. When governments of underdeveloped countries attempt to attract capital by waiving taxation on foreign capital, the investor in these circumstances compares the yield *gross of taxation abroad* with *net* yield *after taxes at home*.

Conclusions

Once the assumptions of perfect competition, divisibility of factors and products, diminishing marginal productivity of capital, constant terms of trade and adjustment to equilibrium positions, are abandoned, it is impossible to say with certainty whether, from a national point of view, investing abroad is preferable to investing at home, or whether foreign capital should be attracted into or kept out of a country. Much depends on the industries and the conditions in which the investment takes place.

The traditional rules of the intellectual game, on which the traditional diagrammatical set-up is based, assume:

(*a*) decreasing returns and increasing costs throughout;

(*b*) existence of a long-term stable equilibrium which is seldom basically altered and which is disturbed mainly by once-for-all changes which do not necessarily change the eventual equilibrium position; and (possibly)

(*c*) shifts in these curves (with unaltered shape) as a result of improvement in technical knowledge.

In point of fact:

(i) The existence of decreasing returns is based upon a *cet. par.* assumption which is difficult to verify. All that is shown by experience is a process of improvement interrupted by periodic fluctuations.

(ii) The position at any given time is not one of ' equilibrium ' and none can in fact come about as changes are continual and adjustments take time. These changes alter the volume and composition of output. They also continually alter the ' position of eventual equilibrium ' (i.e. the position of balance which would be established if no further changes took place). Thus no position of ' eventual equilibrium ' will in actual fact ever be reached. The diagrammatical analysis understates, therefore, the importance in development of the locus of investment and the cumulative nature of certain strategic projects. The ' shift ' of the 'curves' (i.e. the movement from one point to another) may itself depend on coordinated investment plans for which capital that would otherwise have gone abroad, or can be repatriated from abroad, is needed.

The attractiveness of investing abroad for a capital exporting country will depend on whether it takes the form of direct investment, portfolio investment or fixed-interest lending, whether the investment is autonomous or trade-induced, and into what industries, and areas, it moves. Unless the direct and indirect yields of investment abroad are very high, there is some presumption that, from a national point of view, domestic investment is preferable at the margin.

In a fully developed country an increase in foreign-owned capital may have unfavourable effects, unless it occurs in a competitive industry, unless it raises the productivity of labour for a given amount of other resources, or unless technical knowledge and experience are diffused from foreign firms to the rest of the economy. It must, however be remembered that even the most favourable conditions for attracting capital from abroad can be more than offset by the difficulties created by transferring the ensuing profits or interest to the investing country. Unless this transfer is facilitated by the policies of both investing and receiving countries, attracting capital from abroad for purposes which do not directly or indirectly assist the transfer might detrimentally affect the balance and the terms of trade.

In underdeveloped areas where employment is limited by capital shortage, i.e. where there is non-employment or rural underemployment, the addition to national income will be larger than if the labour force were fixed or if productivity were equal in all lines. On the other hand, the increase in foreign profits might be dramatic. It is also possible that the cosmopolitan interest might be better served if the fully developed country invested at home, increased its rate of growth, taxed an (increasing) portion of the ensuing gain and redistributed it by free grants.

The presumption that domestic investment yields greater external economies to the investing country than investment abroad is insufficient to justify drastic curtailment of foreign investment or the general encouragement to the entry of foreign capital from abroad. It constitutes a case for control of capital exports (and, indeed, for both control and promotion of domestic investment projects) and of foreign participation in domestic investment. This control could be used to prevent excessive capital export in order to avoid a sharp deterioration of the terms of trade in a period of stress, and deflationary action at home. While all definite judgment in these matters seems dangerous, there is also a presumption that capital imports which are large in relation to domestic savings should be avoided as they might lead to a subsequent sharp deterioration of the balance of payments and the terms of trade.

None of the foregoing should be taken to imply that the national economic interest can be identified either with the national general interest or the social interest. Capital exports can be used for political or economic warfare,[1] and for philanthropy. To contribute towards the raising of the standard of living in poor countries is our specific duty as members of the British Commonwealth, and our general duty as members of the commonwealth of men.

[1] The fact that economic sacrifices can be used for political gains, and that economic gains can involve political losses, is illustrated by Nazi Germanv's economic policy in Eastern Europe.

POSTSCRIPT

The problem of foreign investment was as perplexing and teasing in inter-war Britain as any other. Keynes perceived at an early date that under the regime of general income tax and increasing organisation of labour the private profit motive did not automatically yield optimal results from a national point of view. Private and social returns from investment would not coincide. In the earlier essays (especially No. 17) I did not differentiate sharply enough between the traditional basis of equilibrium analysis, the marginal efficiency or productivity of capital, and the violent increase in profits as a result of disequilibria or monetary phenomena. The rate of profits in the highly developed areas has risen appreciably and endangers further the fate of the poorer territories. This has only partly been due to the maintenance of full employment in the former. While the importance of this condition was rightly stressed in the war-time papers, its unfavourable implications to the fate of the poor were not fully realised.

In the first of the Essays written in the middle of the war I tried to push this analysis further, and take into account increasing returns, variability of employment, and thus of monetary windfall profits. I developed here a form of the balanced growth approach, and came to the conclusion that some control over capital exports would prove inevitable if progressive economics were to reap maximum progress without undue foreign interference. This was the basis of our attack on the first American draft of the constitution of the International Bank (Essay 18), which failed to link the short term desideratum of monetary stability to the long term aim of gradually equilising capital supply per head. At this point the project-by-project approach, prohibiting lending for general development plans, and providing only for the *direct* foreign exchange costs of the project was the rule. Hence the indirect effect of the project on consumption and investment and on imports would not have been taken care of by the loan. On the various occasions this restrictive rule caused potential borrowers to refrain from making use of the Bank for fear of losing some of their scant gold reserves. Eventually this absurd restriction was abolished but no integration has as yet been achieved between the short and longer term goals of international economic cooperation.

The project approach still bedevils foreign aid and reduces its effectiveness. Its harm is increased by the year-to-year appropriation of aid.[1] The need for comprehensive planning and coordination between various specialised fields has nevertheless increasingly come to be accepted. Among international agencies the F.A.O. has been the

[1] Cf. F.A.O. *Interim Report;* Mediterranean Development Project.

pioneer of this approach. After the Eisenhower era the United States has come to accept the need for it, as shown by its sponsoring an overall plan for Latin America. Equally accepted—save by the lunatic fringe of laisser-faire—is the need for a collective endeavour, in under-developed countries, to increase savings and investment beyond the limits which would spontaneously be imposed by the low propensity to save (even of the rich) in these areas. Even if the fully industrialised countries contribute generously to the industrialisation of the poor, the main burden will have to be borne by the latter; sufficient saving to guarantee appreciable progress cannot be hoped for in those areas without enforced collective saving.

Many of the current issues concerned with British policy are dis-cussed below, Volume II. Nos. 23 and 24.

In the war-time essays the problem of full employment was stressed but the decisive importance of cumulative growth was not disregarded. It has come to be the decisive factor in the struggle for economic supremacy between the wholly planned economies and those who rely—to a considerable extent at least—on decentralised decisions.

The warning on the need for exchange control to free progressive governments from the extra-constitutional veto of financial interests has been fully vindicated. One of the main reasons if not *the* main reason for Britain's persistent post-war weakness, was the dogged determination of the Bank of England to use any improvement in the balance of payments to relax exchange control (cf. Volume II. Intro-duction, section 8)—instead of buttressing the competitive position of the country through increased productive investment; ' confidence ' in the pound, the veto of financial interests, the gnomes of Zurich have once more become *the* decisive factor in shaping policy. Thus a semi-deflationary atmosphere is retained at the cost of perpetuating productive inferiority.

The problem of exchange control has also arisen in the U.S. With the weakening of American industrial leadership the problem of securing the compliance of financial and industrial interests with the requirements of government policy to maintain employment and growth has been posed in the U.S. The sabotage by Wall Street of the Kennedy programme raises the question how long the artificial creation of panics through capital exports can be tolerated.

REFERENCES

The essays collected in this volume were first published as follows:

I   1   *Manchester School*, 1949.

     2   *Economic Journal*, March 1951.

II   3   *Essays in Full Employment* (Oxford University Institute of Statistics, Blackwell 1944).

     4   *Review of Economic Studies*, 1943.

III   5   Unpublished. (Written as Memorandum for the Financial and Economic Section of the League of Nations in 1931. It was refused by Keynes for the *Economic Journal* in 1932. The conclusions were amply vindicated. (1960).)

     6   *Review of Economic Studies*, 1946–7

     7   *Review of Economics and Statistics*, November, 1948.

     8   *New Statesman and Nation*, 1954.

     9   *New Statesman and Nation*, 1959.

IV 10   *Oxford Economic Papers*, June, 1953. (The purely statistical parts have been omitted.)

   11   *Review of Economics and Statistics*, 1957.

   12   *Review of Economics and Statistics*, 1955.

V 13   *Bulletin of the Oxford University Institute of Statistics*, March, 1951. (Joint paper with Mr. P. P. Streeten).

   14   *Bulletin of the Oxford University Institute of Statistics*, April, 1951. (Joint paper with Mr. P. P. Streeten).

   15   *Oxford Economic Papers.* June, 1949

   16   (*a*) *Times Literary Supplement*, 1953.
       (*b*) *Economic Journal*, June–September, 1944.

VI 17   *Oxford Economic Papers*, March, 1945. (This was written for a private conference organised by Nuffield College, Oxford, on ' International Aspects of Full Employment ', in September, 1943).

   18   *Bulletin of the Oxford University Institute of Statistics*, June, 1944. (Joint paper with Mr. E. F. Schumacher).

   19   *Bulletin of the Oxford University Institute of Statistics.* August, 1960. (Joint paper with Mr. P. P. Streeten; this paper benefited from discussion with Sir Donald MacDougall, who however obviously has no responsibility for any remaining errors, and from comments by Mr. M. Scott.)

INDEX